100 THINGS
THUNDER FANS
SHOULD KNOW & DO
BEFORE THEY DIE

Darnell Mayberry

TRIUMPH
BOOKS

No part of this publication may be reproduced, stored in a retrieval system, or transmitted in any form by any means, electronic, mechanical, photocopying, or otherwise, without the prior written permission of the publisher, Triumph Books LLC, 814 North Franklin Street, Chicago, Illinois 60610.

Library of Congress Cataloging-in-Publication Data available upon request.

This book is available in quantity at special discounts for your group or organization. For further information, contact:

Triumph Books LLC
814 North Franklin Street
Chicago, Illinois 60610
(312) 337-0747
www.triumphbooks.com

Printed in U.S.A.
ISBN: 978-1-62937-446-8
Design by Patricia Frey
Photos courtesy of AP Images unless otherwise indicated

To my precious Parker.
Daddy loves you very much.

Contents

Foreword

When I first heard about the trade, I was in shock and thought to myself, *Oh hell nah. I'm not going to OKC.* I called Danny Ainge, like, "What are you doing? Just hold off until the summertime at least." Danny was like, "Relax, Perk, you will love OKC and the organization." I started crying like a lil girl and went to KG, Ray, Paul, and Doc's hotel room like, "What's going on here?" Doc said, "Perk, it's hard for us to lose you, brother. But you are going to a great situation, and they want and need you. Trust me on this." So after I finished crying, we had one last card game in our hotel room with my brothers. And the next morning I flew out from Denver to OKC. And, boy, when I got off the plane I got greeted by so many great people telling me how I'm the missing piece of the puzzle and how happy they are that I'm here. I was, like, *Okay, let me see what this new beginning gonna be like.*

I was met by one of my favorite people, director of medical services Donnie Strack, and he took me straight to get my physical and a two-hour long MRI on both of my knees. Then I made my way to the old practice facility and while we were pulling up I'm like, "My God, Donnie, what the f—k is that smell?" He started laughing and was, like, "That's where they make dog food." In the back of my mind I'm thinking, *Damn, I have to smell that s—t every day?* But when I walked in that practice facility and saw all those young guys like KD, Russ, James, Serge, and Maynor punching in that clock after a back to back, I was like, *This might be where I need to be.*

Sam Presti was so stern back then and was like a major or some s—t. I was, like, *Oh, hold one mother f——g minute. I'm going to break him out of this s—t right here.* LOL. Then I met Troy Weaver, one of the most down-to-earth GMs ever, but he was about winning. Then I met my boy Coach Brooks and we clicked on all cylinders instantly. Oh yeah, please don't forget about Nick. Once I saw the structure and culture of the organization, it literally took me two days to get over the trade and I was all in. I'm like, *Damn, I got these young studs who listen to everything I'm telling them and they're about winning. This about to be some s—t right here.* And there started my OKC career.

It's so many memories. But one memory is how loyal the fans are to the Thunder and how they used to greet us at the airport, good or bad. And the food is great, too. LOL. One of the best series of my career is when we came back from being down 0–2 to the Spurs and beat them in the Western Conference finals. Besides the winning seasons, the most important thing I learned from the Thunder organization is STRUCTURE! The Thunder is a first-class organization across the board. They have one of the best practice facilities I've ever seen. Their medical and training staff is one of the best in sports. The equipment staff is great with Saint and Wilson running the thing. The PR with my boy Matt and John and Mike are great, too. They have *everything* a player needs and wants to be successful there. And also one of the best massage therapists I've ever had in Momma Val. The equipment and technology the Thunder have is light-years ahead of the NBA, in my opinion. I think about how I took so much of that for granted daily. Put it like this: on a scale of 1 to 10, the Thunder gets an 11 from me, and that's real talk.

I had a great 4½ years in OKC, on and off the court, and I still say to this day that OKC has some of the best fans in the world. The culture around that entire state is exceptional. It just feels like a big family—except for the dude with the big-ass mouth on the radio.

—Kendrick Perkins

1 Russell Westbrook

Prior to Game 5 of the Thunder-Mavs series in the opening round of the 2016 NBA Playoffs, Dallas owner Mark Cuban delivered some head-scratching comments about Russell Westbrook.

Cuban famously claimed the Thunder point guard wasn't a superstar.

Hours later, Westbrook closed out the series with a sensational 36-point, 12-rebound, nine-assist performance that sent Dallas home for the summer and made Cuban look silly. In the postgame press conference, a reporter asked Westbrook whether he was aware of Cuban's pregame comments and inquired about Westbrook's reaction to them. Before the reporter could finish the question, Kevin Durant, sitting to Westbrook's left atop the dais inside Chesapeake Energy Arena, extended his right arm in front of Westbrook's torso and preempted his teammate's answer.

"Hold up," Durant told Westbrook before responding for him. "He's a [sic] idiot. Don't listen to s—t. He's a [sic] idiot. All right? That's what *we* got to say about that. He's a [sic] idiot. Next question."

Cuban didn't just set fire to his credibility. The outspoken owner disparaged and disrespected one of the game's truly great players. More than that, he disregarded an inspirational rags-to-riches route rarely seen in NBA superstars. Cuban, a self-made man himself, failed to consider where Westbrook started and just how far he had come.

By the time Cuban delivered his comical claim, Westbrook already had helped captain the Thunder to the 2012 NBA Finals, scoring 43 points in Game 4 to become only the 10th player in NBA history to reach that mark and at only 23 years old, the second youngest to do so. He also had been named to five All-NBA teams, earned five All-Star Game selections, snagged two All-Star Game MVP Awards, recorded 37 triple doubles, notched one scoring title, and paced all players with a ridiculous record of durability.

Westbrook had done all that by 27.

"I'd take him," Mavs superstar Dirk Nowitzki said. "I'd definitely take him."

But when Westbrook arrived in Oklahoma City, he was far from a sure thing. Coming out of Leuzinger High School in Lawndale, California, a suburb of Los Angeles, Westbrook was overlooked by most major Division I teams. He entered high school standing 5'8" and weighing 140 pounds. He didn't start on the varsity until his junior year. He didn't receive his first recruiting letter until the summer before his senior year, when he shot up to 6'3" and could finally dunk. Most recruiting websites didn't have Westbrook ranked among their top 100 prospects. Rivals.com listed him as a three-star recruit.

Creighton, Kent State, and San Diego showed the most interest early on. They were mid-major programs looking to land a diamond in the rough. Miami, Wake Forest, and Arizona State also showed interest. They were high-majors yet middle-of-the-road programs hoping to get lucky after the true big boys had gobbled up the top talent. Westbrook held out. He bet on himself. He averaged 25.1 points, 8.7 rebounds, and 2.3 assists while leading Leuzinger to a 25–4 record as a senior. Still, the big boys were nowhere to be found.

"I coached against Russell in summer league," said Scott Pera, a former Southern California high school coach and Arizona State assistant. "He was fast. Very unpolished. I hate to use the word reckless because I don't want to use it in a negative light, but that's how he was. He was athletic, fast, tough, but at times completely

Russell Westbrook couldn't dunk until the summer before his senior year of high school, but he soon blossomed into the most athletic point guard in NBA history.
(AP Photo/Sue Ogrocki, File)

out of control. People [wondered] if all that could be reeled in and refined."

Years later, the world came to appreciate Westbrook's unbridled energy and his fondness for doing things his way. But Westbrook went against the grain from the start. He didn't play at a high school powerhouse, wasn't mentored by a prestigious prep coach, and didn't join an esteemed AAU team. Instead, he hung on to every morsel of tutelage he received from his father, Russell Westbrook Jr., a weekend warrior at inner city L.A. parks, and a select set of public school coaches. And it worked. A true basketball blue blood finally stepped up a month before Westbrook's graduation, and it sat in Westbrook's backyard. When it became clear Jordan Farmar would leave UCLA for the NBA, the Bruins had a late scholarship to offer. They handed it to Westbrook. After wearing No. 4 in high school, Westbrook had to select a new number because it was owned by Bruins standout Arron Afflalo. Westbrook chose No. 0. "You go with the zero when you've been through something and you are looking to get a new beginning," said Westbrook, whose best friend, Khelcey Barrs, collapsed and died during a pickup game when the two were high school sophomores. "It helps you get the swag back."

As a college freshman, Westbrook averaged only nine minutes. He backed up sophomore point guard Darren Collison, who had served as Farmar's backup the previous season. Westbrook didn't set his sights on the NBA until that summer, the window in which his UCLA coach, Ben Howland, said, "He really, really made huge strides." Westbrook worked out twice daily until the start of the season. He lifted weights. He went on long runs. He played pickup. "I didn't take a break," Westbrook said. It paid off. He cracked UCLA's starting lineup as a sophomore following the departure of Afflalo to the NBA. Still, Westbrook played in the shadow of Collison and a prized recruit named Kevin Love. The Bruins relied on Westbrook primarily for defense and energy. He averaged 12.7

points, 3.9 rebounds, 4.3 assists, 1.6 steals, and helped UCLA journey to a second consecutive Final Four. At season's end, Westbrook was named to the All-Pac-10 Third Team and was honored as the Pac-10 Defensive Player of the Year. "That was a turning point for me," Westbrook said.

Overlooked only two years earlier, Westbrook suddenly sky-rocketed up draft boards. He was raw, but his athleticism and length alone had turned him into a projected first-round pick. But no one knew what Westbrook would become. No one had a clue. DraftExpress, the most respected scouting site for basketball's top prospects outside the NBA, listed Westbrook's best-case scenario as Leandro Barbosa. But most projections pegged Westbrook as a top 10 pick.

On May 20, 2008, six weeks before they would relocate to Oklahoma City, the Seattle SuperSonics entered the NBA Draft Lottery with the second-best odds to win the top pick. But they fell to the fourth spot after Chicago, with the ninth-worst record, improbably landed the No. 1 selection. Miami, owners of the worst record from the previous season, dropped to No. 2. Minnesota remained at three. It was a disappointing outcome. The consensus was the draft featured two franchise-changing players, Michael Beasley out of Kansas State, and Derrick Rose out of Memphis. With the fourth pick, the Sonics were widely projected to select from a group of prospects that included Stanford center Brook Lopez, Indiana guard Eric Gordon, Arizona guard Jerryd Bayless, USC guard O.J. Mayo, and Westbrook's UCLA teammate Love. Westbrook wasn't on the radar. But the team had eyed him all along.

"We agonized over that draft," said then Sonics coach P.J. Carlesimo. "For us, essentially, it came down to Brook Lopez or Russell Westbrook.... We went back and forth, and we really liked both of them."

The team was in desperate need of a point guard and a center. Conventional basketball wisdom says quality big men are harder to come by than quality guards. So Carlesimo argued in favor of Lopez. He remembered General Manager Sam Presti circling back to Westbrook. "I remember Sam's words like it was yesterday," Carlesimo said. "He said, 'You know what scares me? I just think this kid can be so special that if we don't take him we're making a mistake.'"

After selecting Westbrook fourth overall, Presti received a heap of criticism. Many believed he blew it. Westbrook's selection was regarded as a reach. Lopez, Love, Bayless, and Gordon all remained on the board. But Presti praised Westbrook's athleticism and competitiveness. He complimented his work ethic and his ability to blend with the group. More than anything, Presti talked defense. Presti said, "He's got a real focus on the defensive end, and that's not an easy thing to find. He enjoys digging in and doing the little things that really contribute to winning."

"We felt that he was the best perimeter defender in the draft," Presti said. "The ability to contain penetration out front is something we think is important in today's NBA, and we feel like Russell's got the potential to be one of the best at that."

Westbrook was that in college. When Afflalo left Westwood, it was Westbrook who announced to the Bruins coaching staff he wanted to step in as the team's defensive ace. "I want to be Arron," he told his coaches. "I want to guard the best guy every week." Westbrook then went out and did it. He held Mayo, USC's freshman sensation, to a season-low four points and hampered him into a season-high 10 turnovers. He held Bayless, Arizona's stud scorer, to 13 points on 4-for-9 shooting. He hounded the nation's second-leading scorer, a wiry scoring prodigy named Stephen Curry, to 15 points on 6-for-19 shooting. The Bruins won each game by at least 10 points.

But a funny thing happened upon his NBA arrival. Westbrook didn't become a defender. He became a superstar. He averaged 15.3 points, 4.9 rebounds, and 5.3 assists as a rookie, becoming only the 10th rookie in NBA history to compile averages of at least 15 points, 4.5 rebounds, and five assists. By his third season, Westbrook was an All-Star who averaged 21.9 points, 4.6 rebounds, and 8.2 assists.

"I wish I could tell you that in June 2008 we could have forecasted that this guy was going to be a First-Team All-NBA, Hall of Fame–level player," Presti said. "The truth of the matter is we couldn't have done that.... We felt like this player was going to get the most out of whatever attributes that they had because of what was inside the jersey, and we didn't realize quite how deep the reservoir of potential was probably. But we felt like he was going to drain it of whatever was there because of how he is wired."

Westbrook had his share of flaws. He led the league in total turnovers in two of his first three seasons, shot a high volume at relatively low percentages, flashed his defensive tenacity only on occasion, and at times lost his cool and played out of control. But Good Russ far outweighed Bad Russ. His endless energy, competitive fire, and will to win were traits he seemed to inherit like a torch being passed from the game's all-time greats. He got it from Kobe Bryant, who received it from Michael Jordan, who inherited it from Isiah Thomas, who accepted it after it was shared by Magic Johnson and Larry Bird. And after years of picking him apart, much of the basketball world arrived at some variation of the same conclusion.

Let Westbrook be Westbrook.

2 Mr. Triple Double

They said he couldn't do it. They said it couldn't be done.

Other records were made to be broken. This one was deemed untouchable. This one was held by one man, who set it 55 years earlier, when the pace of the NBA game was far more conducive to stuffing a stat sheet.

Russell Westbrook didn't care what anyone said. He went out and did it.

In 2016–17, Westbrook joined Oscar Robertson as the only players in NBA history to average a triple double for an entire season.

In achieving a feat few thought they would ever witness, Westbrook made it look easy. He set the single-season record for most triple doubles with 42, one more than Robertson tallied in 1961–62. He became the first player to record five straight 30-point triple doubles, posted five 40-point triple doubles, and a record three 50-point triple doubles. His 57-point triple double at Orlando on March 29, 2017, marked the most points ever scored in a triple double.

Westbrook averaged a league-leading 31.6 points, 10.7 rebounds, and 10.4 assists. He posted those eye-popping numbers despite playing only 34.6 minutes a night, just the fourth highest of his career. He appeared in 81-of-82 games, sitting out Game 81 only because he got the night off for rest after the Thunder were locked into their playoff position. It was a season that immortalized the Thunder point guard, turning him into a living legend who would forever be part of NBA lore, a player people would tell their kids and grandkids they had the privilege to see play.

"It's an amazing accomplishment," Denver Nuggets coach Mike Malone said. "When you look at it from a historical perspective, the fact that it's never been done before, 42 triple doubles, and only the second guy to ever average that for a season, speaks to his desire, his passion, his toughness. To do that every single night for 82 games is remarkable. You tip your cap to him."

In a season in which Kevin Durant shifted the league's balance of power with his stunning decision to join Golden State, and LeBron James still loomed large as the game's undisputed best player, Westbrook stole the show. He was the story of the season, commanding the country's attention and turning the Thunder into must-see TV from late October through mid-April.

As his assault on the record books snaked through the NBA circuit, Westbrook transformed once hostile opposing fans who loved to hate him into spellbound spectators simply appreciative of witnessing history. He received raucous "M-V-P" chants at Brooklyn as he stood at the free throw line only 92 seconds into a game on March 14, 2017. He treated that night's crowd to a 25-point, 12-rebound, 19-assist performance. Fans at Orlando showered him with the same boisterous chants two weeks later. That was the night he erupted for 57 points, 13 rebounds, and 11 assists while captaining the largest comeback in Thunder history, a 21-point second-half deficit. With the Thunder trailing by 14 with 6:18 remaining, Westbrook detonated for 19 points, including a clutch game-tying three-pointer from 31' out with 7.1 seconds remaining to cap a 23–9 run and force overtime. The Thunder went on to win by eight.

His historic triple double quest later electrified crowds in Memphis, Phoenix, and Denver, his final three road games of the year. Against the Nuggets inside the Pepsi Center on April 9, 2017, Westbrook made his final case for why he deserved the league's Most Valuable Player Award. He produced his record third 50-point triple double while leading yet another come-from-behind win. After the Thunder trailed by 14 inside the final 5½ minutes, Westbrook scored the team's final 15 points, including a miraculous game-winning three from 36' as time expired. It was Westbrook's first game-winning buzzer beater, and it eliminated the Nuggets from playoff contention. That was also the night Westbrook passed Robertson with his 42nd triple double, a 50-point, 16-rebound, 10-assist effort that elicited a standing ovation from Nuggets fans.

"He's on the list of guys," said ESPN *SportsCenter* host Scott Van Pelt, "for when they play, it would take an act of God for them not to be on the show."

Westbrook was that dazzling, that dominant.

On June 26, 2017, he was named the league's Most Valuable Player, garnering 69 of 101 first-place votes.

"He's a Hall of Fame player," said Thunder coach Billy Donovan. "That's really what he is. He's a Hall of Fame player…. It's one of those things as a coach, you feel very, very blessed and fortunate to be able to work with someone like that every single day, just because he takes it so serious and he cares so much about the team and winning."

The basketball world waited with great anticipation to see what Westbrook would do in the absence of Durant; people wondered of he could average a triple double. Robertson, who averaged 30.8 points, 12.5 rebounds, and 11.4 assists in his historic season, was among the few to give Westbrook a vote of confidence. "Why do [people] think he wouldn't do it?" Robertson asked. "It's not impossible. I think he has all the tools to do it."

And when Westbrook did it, Robertson traveled to Oklahoma City to honor Westbrook during an on-court pregame ceremony at the Thunder's regular season finale. "I just felt I had to be here," Robertson told the crowd. "What he has done has been historic in nature. He's played with passion and pride. It's outstanding what he's done and the way he did it. You people should be really proud of him."

Oscar Robertson, left, traveled to Oklahoma City late in the 2016–17 season to honor Russell Westbrook during a pregame ceremony after Westbrook broke Robertson's record for triple doubles in a season. (AP Photo/Sue Ogrocki)

Westbrook averaged a triple double through his first four games, but most expected those numbers to dip as the season wore on. By early December, more and more were echoing Robertson's early thinking. After his average dipped below a triple double in Game No. 5—where it remained for only 14 games—Westbrook again secured a triple double average on November 28, in a road game at New York. It was the Thunder's 19th game of the season. Westbrook scored 27 points with 17 rebounds and 14 assists in a nine-point win. The performance pushed Westbrook's averages to

30.9 points, 10.3 rebounds, and 11.3 assists. He was turning skeptics into believers. "Westbrook can do it," LeBron said a week later. "He's capable of doing it, he's showing it. He's like the Energizer Bunny, man. He doesn't get tired. When you have that passion for the game as well, it's very doable."

Westbrook's averages never dipped below a triple double after that November night in New York.

He began making the extraordinary look ordinary. He achieved the feat so frequently fans came to expect him to post nightly triple doubles. They were more shocked when Westbrook didn't triple double than when he did. It was the standard he set. Home fans inside Chesapeake Energy Arena became consumed with the chase, audibly counting his every rebound and assist.

Westbrook posted seven straight triple doubles on two occasions in 2016–17, from November 25 through December 9 and from March 22 through April 4. They were the longest streaks for triple doubles since Michael Jordan had seven in a row in 1989 and came two shy of tying the NBA record of nine in a row set by Wilt Chamberlain in March 1968.

Westbrook rarely discussed his statistical dominance during the season. He grew irritated at questions about his historical chase after a mid-December road loss at Utah. After his first streak of seven straight triple doubles, it was his third straight game without one. "Honestly, man, people and this triple double thing is kind of getting on my nerves, really," Westbrook said. "People think if I don't get it, it's like a big thing. When I do get it, it's a thing. If y'all just let me play—if I get it, I get it. If I don't, I don't care. It is what it is. I really don't care. For the hundredth time, I don't care. All I care about is winning, honestly. All the numbers s--- don't mean nothing to me."

The next game, a home date with Phoenix, Westbrook exploded for 26 points, 11 rebounds, and a career-high 22 assists.

Facts and Figures

1: Number of triple doubles in NBA history in which a player made all of his field goal attempts and free throws. Westbrook went 6-of-6 on field goals and 6-of-6 from the line in an 18-point, 11-rebound, 14-assist triple double against Philadelphia on March 22.

4: Westbrook's ranking on the all-time list of triple doubles after the 2016–17 season. His 79 triple doubles trailed Oscar Robertson (181), Magic Johnson (138), and Jason Kidd (107).

7: Players in NBA history with more career triple doubles than Westbrook's 42 in 2016–17: Oscar Robertson, Magic Johnson, Jason Kidd, Wilt Chamberlain (78), Larry Bird (59), LeBron James (55), and Fat Lever (43).

14: Triple doubles Westbrook achieved in three quarters in 2016–17.

18: Teams that totaled fewer triple doubles from 1983–84 to 2016–17 than Westbrook did in 2016–17.

44: Years since a player averaged 30 points and 10 assists per game. Tiny Archibald did it in 1972–73. It had been 27 years since a player averaged 30 points and 10 rebounds. Westbrook became the first player listed at 6'3" or shorter to average 10 rebounds.

62: Double doubles by Westbrook in 2016–17. He totaled 85 in his previous two seasons combined. Westbrook had seven games in 2016–17 in which he finished either one rebound or one assist shy of a triple double.

247: Points scored by Westbrook, on 44.6 percent shooting, in the final five minutes of games within five points. The Thunder outscored teams by 85 points in Westbrook's 148 clutch-time minutes.

381: Fewer games played by Westbrook than Wilt Chamberlain to reach 78 career triple doubles.

4,472: Points produced by Westbrook baskets and assists in 2016–17. He accounted for 51.1 percent of the Thunder's points scored.

"I think people miss the point," said Thunder General Manager Sam Presti. "The thing I'm impressed with isn't the statistical accomplishments. What he's doing is more a feat of mental toughness and mental endurance."

Westbrook unexpectedly stepped into the perfect set of circumstances to capture history. It started with the significance of the stunning off-season departures of Durant and Serge Ibaka, which left Westbrook as the lone star standing from the franchise's glory days. Once a polarizing player even in Oklahoma City, Westbrook had transformed into a revered player who suddenly had unwavering support from his fan base and front office, both factions unabashedly offering him whatever backing necessary to ensure he too wouldn't bolt. Albeit not by design, Westbrook was also surrounded by a young team, which included three rookies and, at various stages of the season, eight other players with four years or fewer experience. Fourth-year players Steven Adams and Victor Oladipo both received lucrative contracts prior to the season, and Enes Kanter signed for top dollar two years prior. The team's next three best players were all well compensated and had no reason to try to prove their worth by posting gaudy numbers. A third fourth-year player, Andre Roberson, didn't agree to an extension to his rookie contract prior to the 2016–17 season, but Roberson was a defensive specialist who was limited offensively and selfless in his approach.

It all created justifiable reliance on Westbrook, leaving him the opportunity to chase history. He happily accepted. Westbrook shattered the NBA record for usage, or the percentage of a team's possessions that end with one player shooting a field goal, a free throw, or turning it over. He used 41.7 percent of the Thunder's possessions, eclipsing Kobe Bryant's 2005–06 mark of 38.7 percent. Westbrook led the league in shot attempts by nearly 400 attempts and finished with a career high in turnovers. He also manipulated the game in certain ways. He began lining up along the lane line during opponent free throws and having his big men box out so he could secure additional rebounds. Westbrook led all players in uncontested defensive rebounds and paced guards by more than 150, confirming what the eye test indicated—teammates often were getting out of his way so he could tack on rebounds to his nightly tally.

Of course, those things mattered only in understanding how Westbrook managed a triple double average. Westbrook proponents, however, rushed to his defense to prove he wasn't padding stats by arguing the team was better in transition when he grabbed defensive rebounds and, at 33–9 when he had a triple double and 14–26 when he didn't, the Thunder were a better regular season team thanks to his stuffing of the stat sheet. Most couldn't care less about comprehending Westbrook's magnificence. It had been 55 years since anyone had seen such dominance, and to some anything but marveling at the man making history seemed misguided. The how was trivial.

There was also the undeniable impact Westbrook's historic pursuit had on people, particularly Thunder fans in the Oklahoma community. Westbrook stabilized the Thunder franchise and lifted the collective spirit of sullen fans stung by Durant's decision. Westbrook and Westbrook alone replaced their pain with pleasure, their dejection with delight.

"Russ," said Thunder center Enes Kanter, "put an entire city on his back."

3 Kevin Durant

Adam Silver stepped to the lectern for the moment we all waited for.

"Good luck to all," the NBA Deputy Commissioner said. "The stakes are pretty high tonight."

It was the 2007 NBA Draft Lottery. The consensus top two picks were Ohio State center Greg Oden and Texas forward Kevin Durant, talents universally hailed as can't-miss franchise changers. The Seattle SuperSonics had the fifth best chance at the top pick, but the odds of landing it were only 8.8 percent. Then Silver revealed the No. 5 pick would go to the Boston Celtics, and suddenly there was hope. That meant the Sonics had jumped into the top three. After a commercial break, Dominique Wilkins, Lenny Wilkens, and Brandon Roy stood side-by-side as Silver announced the top three. Wilkins' Atlanta Hawks won the third selection, leaving the Sonics and Portland Trail Blazers as the big winners.

"The second pick," Silver said before pausing as he opened the oversized envelope featuring the team's logo, "in this year's draft," he paused again before finally ending the suspense with "will go to the Seattle SuperSonics."

It was the night that changed Oklahoma's sports landscape forever.

On June 28, 2007, the Sonics selected Durant with the No. 2 overall pick. Despite much debate, Oden was the consensus top selection. In taking Oden, the Blazers did what 62 percent of nearly 54,000 respondents to an NBA.com fan poll said they would do if they had the first pick. But that left Durant, a bony and baby-faced scoring savant born to get buckets. "A pretty good consolation prize if Portland does take Greg Oden. You expect them to do that," said ESPN basketball analyst Jay Bilas immediately after the lottery results. "I think that Seattle's going to get a player that is going to be a big, big-time scorer for a lot of years in the future."

Oklahomans rejoiced over the results because of the increasing likelihood Durant would soon be Oklahoma City bound. Even

Kevin Durant, left, fell into the Thunder's lap when he was drafted No. 2 overall by the Seattle SuperSonics after Portland selected Greg Oden first overall in 2007. (William Perlman/*The Star-Ledger* via *USA TODAY* Sports)

then, they had no idea how fortunate the Sonics were in getting the second selection rather than the first. Oden's body failed him from the start. Knee injuries cost him the entire 2007–08 season and limited him to 105 career games. Durant went on to assemble all that was expected of him and more.

As a rookie in Seattle, Durant averaged 20.3 points, 4.4 rebounds, and 2.4 assists. He scored 42 points with 13 rebounds and six assists in his season finale, capping a runaway victory for the 2007–08 Rookie of the Year Award. In 2009–10, Durant averaged a league-leading 30.1 points. It was the first of his four scoring crowns. He repeated as the league's scoring champion in the two successive seasons and again in 2013–14.

Durant also earned his first NBA All-Star appearance in 2010, selected by the Western Conference coaches as a reserve. In July 2010, Durant then signed a five-year contract extension with the Thunder. He drew universal praise for announcing the deal on Twitter, the day before LeBron James held "The Decision" on national television to announce he was "taking his talents to South Beach." Durant also exhibited his commitment to Oklahoma City by declining an option to get out of the contract after four years. That same summer, Durant led the USA World Championship Team to a 9–0 record and gold medal finish in Turkey. It was the USA's first World Championship since 1994. Durant was named MVP after averaging a team-best 22.8 points and 6.1 rebounds. His 38 points in a semifinal win over Lithuania set a USA World Championship record for most points scored in a single game.

In 2011–12, Durant helped the Thunder reach the NBA Finals. While going head-to-head with James, Durant averaged 30.6 points, six rebounds, 2.2 assists, and 1.4 steals, but Oklahoma City lost the series 4–1 to Miami. That summer, Durant captured his second gold medal and first Olympic gold. He averaged a team-high 19.5 points and 5.8 rebounds to key the USA's 8–0 record in London.

Durant joined the exclusive 50–40–90 club in the 2012–13 season, etching his name alongside the game's most efficient marksmen after he shot 50 percent from the floor, 40 percent from three-point range, and 90 percent from the foul line. He was only the sixth player in NBA history to achieve the feat, joining Larry Bird, Mark Price, Reggie Miller, Steve Nash, and Dirk Nowitzki.

Durant continued his dominance in 2013–14, when he earned NBA Most Valuable Player honors. He averaged a career-high 32 points, 7.4 rebounds, and a career-high 5.5 assists. While superstar teammate Russell Westbrook bounced in and out of the lineup and played only 46 games due to multiple knee surgeries, Durant carried the Thunder to a 59–23 record, the second best in basketball.

Durant had his 2014–15 season derailed due to a broken bone in his foot. He played only 27 games that season, and without him the Thunder missed the playoffs for the first time since 2009.

Durant played eight seasons in Oklahoma City, from 2008–09 to 2015–16. He appeared in 561 regular season games, averaged 28.4 points, 7.4 rebounds, 3.9 assists, 1.2 steals, and one blocked shot. He steered the Thunder to 91 playoff games, four Western Conference finals, and an NBA Finals.

He put Oklahoma City on the map, turned the Thunder into an internationally known brand, and supplied enough memories for a lifetime. His departure broke hearts in July 2016, but Durant will go down as the best player in Thunder history.

"He'll be one of those guys," said longtime teammate Nick Collison, "that you'll be able to tell people when you're done playing you got to play with."

4 July 4, 2016

"So many guys get criticized for making the decision that's best for them instead of what's best for everybody else. He's a guy that did that. You gotta respect that. I applauded him. I texted him and told him congratulations on the decision and told him I was happy for him."

—Kevin Durant on LeBron James' 2014 decision
to leave Miami and return to the Cleveland Cavaliers.

Kevin Durant couldn't have picked a worse day to stick a dagger in Oklahoma's heart.

When he announced his decision to join the Golden State Warriors on July 4, 2016, Durant's timing was as tone deaf as both his declaration and his desired destination.

On the day of the country's biggest community holiday, one Oklahomans revere and revel in as much as anyone, Durant didn't just rain on parades. He dropped an atomic bomb on them. In announcing his intentions, he did it in the hollowest way imaginable—through a written statement on The Players' Tribune website, the Derek Jeter–founded site for which Durant became deputy publisher nine months earlier.

The deputy publisher published at 10:39 AM central time. He told us in 351 words that reeked of being written by someone else. He labeled it "My Next Chapter," appearing at the top of the page, posing with his arms folded in a sleeveless white T-shirt as he stood between adjacent shrubs and stared into the distance. His sixth sentence, the last in the second paragraph, left you numb. "I have decided that I am going to join the Golden State Warriors," the statement read. Picnics became pointless. Cookouts lost their cheer. Firecrackers lost their fun. A day of celebration turned into a day of despair.

The face of the franchise was leaving.

And no one truly knew why. Only head-scratching generalities would be found in his carefully crafted prepared statement.

"This has been by far the most challenging few weeks in my professional life," Durant's statement read. "I understood cognitively that I was facing a crossroads in my evolution as a player and as a man, and that it came with exceptionally difficult choices. What I didn't truly understand, however, was the range of emotions I would feel during this process.

"The primary mandate I had for myself in making this decision was to have it based on the potential for my growth as a player—as that has always steered me in the right direction. But I am also at a point in my life where it is of equal importance to find an opportunity that encourages my evolution as a man: moving out of my comfort zone to a new city and community which offers the greatest potential for my contribution and personal growth."

The Fourth of July in Oklahoma would never be the same. The festive holiday would forever be remembered as the day Durant ditched the Thunder. Durant tried to soften the blow by sharing his sorrow, expressing how much he agonized over the decision, and how much it pained him to let down so many people. Didn't matter.

"I'm from Washington, D.C. originally, but Oklahoma City truly raised me," Durant continued. "It taught me so much about family as well as what it means to be a man. There are no words to express what the organization and the community mean to me, and what they will represent in my life and in my heart forever. The memories and friendships are something that go far beyond the game. Those invaluable relationships are what made this deliberation so challenging. It really pains me to know that I will disappoint so many people with this choice, but I believe I am doing what I feel is the right thing at this point in my life and my playing career.

"I will miss Oklahoma City, and the role I have had in building this remarkable team. I will forever cherish the relationships within the organization—the friends and teammates that I went to war with on the court for nine years, and all the fans and people of the community. They have always had my back unconditionally, and I cannot be more grateful for what they have meant to my family and to me."

Just like that, Durant was gone.

Here was the most celebrated Oklahoman since Will Rogers, a player who meant so much to and represented so much about his host city and state, walking away, giving up. It ran counter to everything everyone thought they knew about Durant, everything they had grown to love about him. Not so much as a person as a competitor. "If u can't beat um join um," NBA great Paul Pierce mockingly posted to his Twitter account one hour after Durant's announcement.

Only a month earlier, Durant and the Thunder blew a 3–1 series lead against the Warriors in the conference finals. Now Durant was joining them, with their reigning two-time MVP, their three All-Stars, their NBA record 73 wins, their Coach of the Year and, of course, their back-to-back Finals trips and championship-winning core. The insult to injury was the fresh memory of how Durant's poor play down the stretch of Game 6 of the 2016 Western Conference finals was largely to blame for the Thunder falling short of a title. It wasn't that the pieces around Durant weren't good enough. Durant wasn't good enough. Now he was running for the easy route.

After doing all they could to appease Durant, the Thunder were left high and dry, having journeyed only to the brink of The Promised Land, never crossing that threshold so many assumed they would plow through over and over again back when they were believed to be a future dynasty. Still, the organization went out of its way to take the high road.

"Kevin's contributions to our organization during his nine years were profound, on and off the court," said Thunder chairman Clay Bennett. "He helped the Thunder grow and succeed in immeasurable ways and impacted the community just the same. We thank him for his leadership, his play, and how he represented Oklahoma City and the entire state of Oklahoma."

Added General Manager Sam Presti: "Kevin made an indelible mark on the Thunder organization and the state of Oklahoma as a founding father of this franchise. We can't adequately articulate what he meant to the foundation of this franchise and our success. While clearly disappointing that he has chosen to move on, the core values that he helped establish only lead to us thanking him for the many tangible and intangible ways that he helped our program."

Fans, naturally, had trouble responding as kindly. Oklahoma City police officers were stationed outside of Durant's home in OKC's Deep Deuce neighborhood, ensuring no one vandalized his property. Heartbroken fans called Durant a traitor and a snake. It was the start of an ugly breakup that wouldn't find reconciliation anytime soon.

"I understand where they're coming from," Durant said. "It hurt me. I was hurt for a few days because I know I hurt so many people in Oklahoma City by changing teams. Of course, they're going to say what they have to say because everybody's emotional. I understand that. It's sports. It's a way to get away from the real world for a second. We provide that experience for them, and I understand how they feel. I can't say anything to make them feel any different, but [I'll] still just go out there and be who I am as a basketball player and a person and, like I said, life moves on."

Durant said he made a list of pros and cons on the night of July 3 and then slept on it. When he woke at 7:00 AM the next day, he said he felt comfortable in his decision. He was going to leave Oklahoma City to join Golden State. "That call to Oklahoma City was one of the hardest things I've ever had to do in my life," Durant said. "Tears were shed. But like I said, I trusted my guts, and I trusted my instincts. It's an unpopular decision, but I can live with it."

The backlash was swift and severe, and the prevailing sentiment was no matter what Durant accomplished with the ready-made Warriors, his legacy would forever be tarnished.

He was a ring-chaser and bandwagon-hopper, the first generational superstar in NBA history who couldn't beat 'em so he joined 'em.

5 August 4, 2016

Thunder fans were ready to trade Russell Westbrook.

They didn't want to. They simply felt the team had to.

When Kevin Durant skipped town, no one knew what would come next. Uncertainty led to anxiety. Anxiety led to fear. Fear led to panic. The Thunder, most figured, couldn't let their lone remaining star also walk without getting something in return. TNT and NBA.com reporter David Aldridge reported on the day Durant announced his decision that he was "told emphatically by a league source there's no chance Russell Westbrook will do a renegotiation/ extension of his contract." Not with only one year remaining on his deal. Not with the salary cap set to spike in 2017. "It just makes no sense financially," Aldridge reported. By the time a report surfaced a week later by *Bleacher Report*'s veteran NBA writer Howard Beck saying GMs at the NBA Summer League in Las Vegas thought Westbrook would get traded "sooner than later," resignation set in.

It was only a matter of time. Best hope for more Sam Presti magic.

Presti gave the people magic, all right.

On August 4, 2016, one month after Durant sent Oklahoma into deep despair, Westbrook restored state morale when he did what they said he wouldn't. He re-signed with the Thunder, committing to Oklahoma City through at least 2017–18 on a renegotiated three-year, $85.7 million contract. It essentially was a new contract, which increased Westbrook's 2016–17 salary from $17.8 million to $26.5 million. The deal included a player option for year three. It made a ton of sense financially. Westbrook raked in a $9 million raise for a season he already was under contract to play with the Thunder, and all he had to do was agree to one more guaranteed year beyond it. The timing was terrific, too, for Westbrook. He'd delay his right to become an unrestricted free agent by only one year, but when he hit the market he would have 10 years of service and be eligible for a significant raise.

The length of the deal and the benefits for Westbrook were beside the point. Westbrook was staying. With the stroke of a pen, he stabilized an organization and energized a state.

The Thunder set up a public press conference to announce the deal. They staged it inside an atrium at Chesapeake Energy Arena. On a sweltering Oklahoma summer day, hundreds of people congregated outside for hours to celebrate Westbrook. Between the throng of barricaded-facing fans was a narrow walkway where the Thunder rolled out blue carpet that led Westbrook to a small stage from which he would address the masses. "I love Oklahoma City, man," Westbrook said into a mic. "I wanted to tell you guys first."

Inside the arena were tributes to Westbrook. A short montage of Westbrook highlights looped on the videoboard hanging at center court. The video ended with the phrase, "The Roar Continues." Along the concourse, the team stationed action photos of Westbrook from each of his first eight seasons. Oklahoma City Mayor Mick Cornett even proclaimed August 4, 2016, Russell Westbrook Day.

Westbrook had become Mr. Thunder.

"There's nowhere else I would rather be than Oklahoma City," Westbrook said.

6 The Breakup

On the unforgettable holiday when Kevin Durant announced he was leaving the Oklahoma City Thunder for the Golden State Warriors, Russell Westbrook was having a picnic.

While Thunder fans mourned the end of the glory days and NBA fans mourned the end of whatever parity remained in this new world of superstars joining forces, Westbrook celebrated. Rather than give the people what they wanted—his reaction to Durant's stunning decision—Westbrook wished everyone a happy Fourth of July.

He posted a picture of decorative cupcakes, topped with sprinkles and red and blue stars and organized on a three-tiered stand. The caption read "HAPPY 4TH YALL…USUSUS." Everyone assumed Westbrook was going about his day unfazed by Durant's departure. Three months later, *Sports Illustrated* senior writer Lee Jenkins revealed in a preseason piece that Westbrook's photo could have been a message to Durant. He could have been calling him a cupcake. It was a term Kendrick Perkins adopted and used whenever he felt his Thunder teammates were playing or acting soft. Upon close examination, the photo contains eight cupcakes on the top tier, perhaps representing Westbrook and Durant's eight seasons together, and 35 cupcakes on the bottom two tiers, perhaps signifying Durant's jersey number. If it wasn't a veiled jab at Durant, it was an awfully big coincidence.

Westbrook never discussed the photo. Durant downplayed it, claiming he didn't consider it a shot at him. But it marked the opening salvo in a feud that quickly dissolved into a nasty public breakup.

The day after Durant's decision, *Bleacher Report*'s NBA senior writer Howard Beck reported that the Durant-Westbrook partnership "produced a simmering frustration that, in essence, paved the

Kevin Durant and Russell Westbrook formed one of the best duos in NBA history during their eight seasons as Thunder teammates. Durant's departure in 2016, however, led to a nasty public breakup. (AP Photo/Sue Ogrocki)

way for his exit." Citing an unnamed "person with insight into Durant's thought process," Beck wrote that Westbrook's playing style was a problem for Durant. "Ultimately, he got frustrated and felt that they had plateaued," the person is quoted as saying of Durant. "[Billy Donovan] came in, and [Durant] still had the same issues that he had with Russ under Scotty [Brooks]. The offense didn't change much. He still had to take a ton of contested shots every game; and that's when he had the ball at all." The person went on to say of Durant, "He's never going to have a game in Golden State where Steve Kerr has to say at halftime, 'You guys need to get Kevin the ball,' which happened in OKC."

Three days later, on July 7, Durant was introduced as a member of the Warriors. He told reporters he had spoken to Westbrook about his decision. But a month later, Westbrook refuted that claim. When asked how he learned Durant was leaving, Westbrook said, "Like y'all found out. On the news, on the cellphones, the social media. I talked to Kevin early on in the process, but nothing after. Just a text message from him, that's about it."

At the end of August 2016, Jordan Brand released a Westbrook commercial that took a not-so-subtle shot at Durant. The spot featured Westbrook, dressed in all black, dribbling alone on a blacktop, as if he was running a fast break from one foul line to the other. When he reached the opposite foul line, he jumped like he was about to attempt a dunk. But the blacktop had turned into an airplane runway. The commercial then ends with a voiceover saying, "Some run. Some make runways."

Durant then delivered peculiar comments at the start of training camp in October. Speaking at a ceremony at the Stanford Graduate School of Business, Durant trumpeted his new teammates. He called his move "an easy decision." He said he was grateful to "play with a bunch of players who are selfless and enjoy the game in its purest form." He praised the Warriors organization, calling their operation a perfect fit. "You hear 'family' a lot. That's just a word sometimes, but this is really a lifestyle here," Durant said.

Westbrook's response: "That's cute."

"My job is to worry about what's going on here," Westbrook added. "We're gonna worry about all the selfish guys we've got over here, apparently. We gonna figure that out."

In the same interview, Westbrook then declared he was done talking about Durant. That was October 13, 2016. Six days later, a *Rolling Stone* cover story on Durant paraphrased him as saying he and Westbrook were never more than work friends. The same article quoted Durant's mother relaying how Durant arrived at the conclusion the Thunder no longer had his back. "This summer he said, 'Mama, I can't do it anymore. They're not in this thing with me, we're not together like we were—I feel I need something different,'" Wanda Durant was quoted as saying. Durant was quoted as saying, "Where other teams went out and got that veteran guy, we kept getting younger."

The next day, *Sports Illustrated* released its cover story on Westbrook.

Durant and his camp were digging a deeper hole—with Westbrook, with the Thunder, with Oklahomans, and with Thunder fans throughout the country. Instead of taking the high road after he broke so many hearts, he was directly and indirectly pointing the finger at Westbrook and the Thunder. Instead of owning his failure to win a championship, he was pinning the blame on everyone else. Westbrook, meanwhile, shrewdly began capitalizing on the breakup by marketing shoes. The Jordan Brand released Westbrook's wildly popular "Do What I Want" commercial on the day of the Thunder's season opener.

The Thunder and Warriors met four times in the 2016–17 regular season. Westbrook arrived to the first meeting on November 3, 2016, the Thunder's fifth contest of the season, wearing a bright orange photographer's vest that read "Official Photographer." Many assumed it was a shot at Durant's affinity for photography. Westbrook denied it had anything to do with Durant, whose 39 points in that night's 122–96 Warriors win tied the NBA record for the most by a player facing his former team for the first time. Westbrook and Durant never acknowledged each other during the game. In the second meeting, a 121–100 Warriors win on January 18, 2017, they exchanged their first words in more than six months. It appeared to be not-so-friendly trash talk after a sequence late in the third quarter. Westbrook mostly avoided it, choosing to not make eye contact with Durant as he said his piece.

The third meeting was the most hostile. It was the first in Oklahoma City, Durant's debut inside Chesapeake Energy Arena as a visitor. It was February 11, 2017, a Saturday night primetime game on ABC. Durant was booed from the moment he took the court for warmups. He was booed when he was introduced in the starting lineup. He was booed every time he touched the ball. The crowd, having picked up on Jenkins' cupcake revelation, flooded the arena with cupcake signs, cupcake T-shirts, and cupcake chants. There was even a 9-year-old girl covered in a really creative yellow cupcake costume. Durant and the Warriors tried to make light of the treatment, with Durant saying of the boos, "I actually thought it would be a little louder," and Draymond Green and Stephen Curry emerging from the Warriors' locker room for their postgame interviews wearing cupcake shirts.

The emotions of the evening boiled over when a timeout was called with 4:25 remaining in the third quarter. Durant and Westbrook turned to the other and yelled back and forth as they walked to their respective benches. After seven months of subtle shots, spiteful words, and Durant's unsuccessful attempts to downplay the feud as media-created "fake drama," that one scene shined a light on their severed relationship. Westbrook repeated

"I'm coming," declaring to Durant his intentions of captaining a Thunder comeback from down 18. Durant simply shrugged and said, "You're losing." Minutes later, Durant and Andre Roberson stood nose to nose and had to be separated after Roberson fouled Durant on a drive. Both received technical fouls.

But the game went the way all the other matchups did. Golden State again thumped the Thunder by double digits, this time winning 130–114. Eight days later, Durant and Westbrook were teammates again as Western Conference All-Stars. They spent much of the weekend in New Orleans deflecting questions about their fractured relationship and dodging each other. Their friendliest moment came midway through the first quarter, when they hooked up on a give-and-go that resulted in an alley-oop pass from Durant and a two-handed dunk by Westbrook. Their All-Star teammates circled around Durant and Westbrook during an ensuing timeout and showered them with exaggerated cheers.

A sprained knee kept Durant out of the fourth Thunder-Warriors showdown in 2016–17. He traveled to Oklahoma City and sat on the bench as the Warriors won 111–95 without him on March 20.

Once again, Durant and Westbrook didn't speak.

7 Now I Do What I Want

At 12:45 PM on August 19, 2016, Russell Westbrook posted a 10-second Twitter video of himself dancing shirtless while driving. Before you ask, yes, he was buckled in and his eyes focused mostly on the road. But blaring over the speakers was a tune titled "Do What I Want," a catchy ditty by an up-and-coming Philadelphia rapper named Lil Uzi Vert.

> *"Boy I started on the bottom, made my way to the top.*
> *Boy I'm gon' keep winning, no I cannot stop.*
> *'Member I had a little [I did], turned that s——t to a lot.*
> *Always been 100, put that on my block.*
> *Used to want a 4-door, now I want that drop, yeah.*
> *Now I do what I want, now I do what I want.*
> *Now I do what I want, now I do what I want."*

In the full-length, two-minute, 55-second version of the song, that final stanza, "Now I do what I want," is repeated 32 times. It's a braggadocios line about the musician's rise to fame and fortune and his ability to do whatever he pleases with his newfound wealth. In his 10-second Twitter video, Westbrook giddily bobs his head and waves his hand as the repetitive catchphrase is heard six times. When he tweeted the video, Westbrook explained simply, "Friday's Mood," accompanied by his customary hashtag #whynot.

And people absolutely ate it up. The video garnered more than 930,000 views. The post received more than 25,000 retweets and more than 33,000 likes.

It was the right song for the right player at the right time.

A month and a half earlier, Kevin Durant ditched Westbrook and the Thunder to join the Golden State Warriors. Westbrook had hardly been heard from since. But two weeks before posting the video, Westbrook signed a contract extension to remain in Oklahoma City as the Thunder's lone star. And the connotation was clear. Westbrook was now free from playing second fiddle to Durant. Free to do what he wanted.

Of course, the video didn't go unnoticed by Westbrook's biggest sponsor. Two months after it posted—the day before the Thunder tipped off the 2016–17 regular season—the Jordan Brand released a one-minute commercial featuring Westbrook and others vigorously dancing to the same song. The "Now I do what I want" refrain is heard 18 times before the ad ends, promoting the Jordan Westbrook 0.2 canvas shoe.

Again, fans loved everything about it. The spot received more than 1.5 million views on the Jordan Brand's official Twitter account. The post was retweeted more than 30,000 times and liked by more than 41,000 users. And just like that, Westbrook transformed into a cult figure. After years of absorbing criticism while Durant stood as the golden boy, it was now Westbrook who could do no wrong, who the fans adored while spewing their venom at Durant.

Sure enough, the "Now I do what I want" catchphrase carried over onto the court, where Westbrook played without consequence or criticism. With Durant in the Bay Area, Westbrook handled the ball as much as he wanted (leading the league in usage), fired as many shots as he wanted (leading the league in attempts), hoisted as many three-pointers as he wanted (jacking a career high), turned the ball over more than he ever had, and chased as many triple doubles as he could. All the while, his flaws were excused, if not altogether ignored. He stayed and Durant didn't. And in the eyes of Thunder fans and the Thunder organization, that's all that mattered.

Russell Westbrook could now do what he wanted.

8 James Harden

Just before the 2009 NBA Draft, an unexpected email landed in the inbox of Thunder General Manager Sam Presti. It was from a college sophomore from Arizona State who was seeking employment.

His name was James Harden. He wanted to play for the Thunder, and through that email he stated his case to be selected with that year's No. 3 overall pick.

"He made it clear that he understood the ethos of the organization," Presti said. "He understood the dynamic of our team, that it wasn't going to be a typical situation for someone drafted that high. Instead of being worried about it, he was motivated by it."

The note left an impression on Presti, and it played a part in the GM making Harden the first draft selection in Thunder history on June 25, 2009. "He wanted to be a part of building and sustaining a winning tradition," Presti said.

Harden averaged 20.1 points, 5.6 rebounds, and 4.2 assists in his sophomore season at Arizona State. He earned Pac-10 Player of the Year honors and was named a consensus All-American. But he was joining a Thunder roster that fielded Kevin Durant, Russell Westbrook, and Jeff Green. Harden would have to blend with the group. But that's one of the things Presti and the Thunder liked most about Harden. He was a connector, someone who wasn't interested in launching a lot of shots but rather keeping his teammates involved and making them better with ball movement. "That's why I think Sam Presti and those guys chose me," Harden said after being drafted, "because I'm a pass-first guy. They have great scorers over there, so with my ability to pass first and score second…it helps that organization a lot."

In his rookie season, Harden averaged 9.9 points, 3.2 rebounds, 1.8 assists, and 1.1 steals in just 22.9 minutes per game. While he was busy blending on an eventual 50-win team, Harden watched fellow rookie guards Tyreke Evans, Stephen Curry, and Brandon Jennings receive much more publicity as they racked up significantly more playing time on less talented teams. Harden placed behind all three in voting for the All-Rookie Teams, finishing on the All-Rookie Second Team. It was much of the same in Harden's second season. Though he grew more confident and showed flashes of being on the cusp of a breakout season, Harden continued to play sparingly. He averaged just 26.7 minutes in 2010–11. His role in the first half of the season once again led to him being overshadowed. Originally, Harden wasn't selected for the 2011 Rookie Challenge, the All-Star Weekend showcase that pits first-year players against second-year players. He ultimately received an invitation after being named a replacement for an injured Evans, the reigning rookie of the year.

It wasn't until Green was traded to Boston in the deal that brought Kendrick Perkins to Oklahoma City that Harden received more opportunities to flourish. His minutes began to rise and so did his production. He averaged 15.7 points on 46.1 percent shooting in 26 games following the trade and began establishing himself as a reliable playmaker and steady scorer off the bench. After a disappointing debut postseason in 2010, Harden used the Thunder's run to the 2011 Western Conference finals as a personal showcase. He averaged 13 points, 5.4 rebounds, 3.6 assists, and 1.2 steals while shooting 47.5 percent in 31.6 minutes, all in a reserve role. His signature performance came in Game 5 against Dallas in the West finals. Although the Thunder lost the game and the series that night, Harden scored 23 points on 7-of-11 shooting while dishing six assists, pulling down five rebounds, and turning it over only twice. He marched to the free throw line a game-high

10 times, making eight. The Mavs had no answer for Harden as he orchestrated one high-ball screen after another to perfection.

"The things that he was able to do and how easy it looked for him," said Thabo Sefolosha, "you were like, 'He's going to be special.'"

Entering his third season facing heightened expectations, Harden exceeded them all. He averaged 16.8 points, 4.1 rebounds, 3.7 assists, and shot 49.1 percent. He scored at least 20 points 15 times in the shortened 66-game season and punctuated his break-out season with a career-high 40 points in a road win at Phoenix on April 18, 2012. Harden's stellar season earned him Sixth Man of the Year honors. He ran away with the award, garnering 115 out of 119 first-place votes from a panel of sportswriters and broadcasters throughout the United States and Canada. He was the second youngest player to win the award. "In our eyes, James has won an award for far more than simply being a productive player," said Presti. "The Sixth Man of the Year Award is not only an award for on-court production that enables team success, but above all else it acknowledges sacrifice and commitment to the greater good of the team."

Harden went on to assemble his second consecutive extraordinary postseason. He averaged 17.6 points through the Western Conference finals, playing an integral role in helping the Thunder to the 2012 NBA finals.

But everything he accomplished became a distant memory after Harden's performance in the Finals and what would come next in his career.

9 The Harden Trade

"It's easy to say we were supposed to be together for the rest of our careers. But it didn't play out like that. I think all three of us will have memorable careers. And it'll be a journey we'll always remember, something that's different and unique, playing with two different guys who are doing incredible things in the league right now. But when you look back, think about the fun times instead of what could've been."

—Kevin Durant

This chapter isn't for you.

You know who you are. You are the expert on the James Harden trade, the fan with all the answers. You have your mind made up about what should and should not have happened. There's no talking to you and certainly no convincing you otherwise.

You remember the night of October 27, 2012, like it was yesterday. You remember where you were, who you were with, and what you were doing. You remember the news coming across your smartphone. You remember the rest of your night being ruined.

You never need to be reminded of the particulars. You know them all too well. Harden, Cole Aldrich, Daequan Cook, and Lazar Hayward to Houston. Kevin Martin, Jeremy Lamb, a 2013 first-round draft pick that turned into Steven Adams, a 2013 second-rounder that turned into Alex Abrines, and a 2014 first-rounder that turned into Mitch McGary to OKC. You feel the Thunder got fleeced.

In your mind, the Thunder should have done whatever it took to keep Harden in town. With him, the team was a perennial championship contender. The way you see it, you can't break up championship-caliber cores. Not over money. Definitely not when the return is rentals and draft picks.

You heard Harden talk sacrifice and float the word "dynasty" at the end of his last season with the Thunder. You figured he must have wanted to stay. You knew he had earned more and could get more elsewhere, more minutes, more shots, more money, more fame. But you believed something special was brewing in OKC. You believed Harden wanted to be a part of it. You never envisioned the Thunder wouldn't see to it. You did envision Harden teaming with Russell Westbrook and Kevin Durant, the founders of "Thunder U," for the next seven to 10 years and capturing multiple championships.

When it didn't happen, you devoured every detail you could find about the deal. You learned the Thunder offered Harden an extension to his rookie contract in the neighborhood of $54 million over four years. You learned he demanded a max deal, something closer to $60 million. You learned the Thunder, after nearly five months of negotiating, finally gave Harden one hour to take the deal or be traded. You grew irate when Harden was traded.

You blame management. You blame ownership. To you, the Thunder irresponsibly signed Serge Ibaka to a four-year, $49 million deal that summer before coming to terms with Harden. You are convinced the team chose its shot-blocking stud over its playmaking phenom. Worse, you will never understand why the Thunder didn't just amnesty Kendrick Perkins for crying out loud.

You watched Harden head to Houston. You couldn't believe your eyes as you watched his introductory news conference, Harden posing for pictures wearing a Rockets hat and holding up a Rockets jersey. You couldn't believe he was really gone. You learned four days after the trade that Harden inked a five-year, $80 million contract extension with the Rockets. You knew the Thunder couldn't offer the same deal since their designated five-year extension had been given to Westbrook a year earlier. You also knew the

Thunder had incentive to make the trade prior to the October 31 deadline for rookie extensions to entice the Rockets to part with as many assets as possible so they could lock Harden up to the more lucrative deal.

But to you, collective bargaining agreement matters were moot. The arrival of a new CBA in 2011 following the 161-day lockout meant nothing. You don't view basketball as a business. You don't think owners should ever look at the bottom line. You know the new CBA brought about widespread changes designed to break up super teams. You know it carried more punitive penalties for teams that annually blew past the luxury tax. You know it gave Durant a retroactive raise that fell into the Thunder's lap. You just concluded the Thunder were cheap.

You hoot and holler about how the Thunder should have signed Harden and figured it out later! You point to the timing. How the Thunder didn't have to trade Harden when they did. How they owned his restricted free agency rights and could have matched any offer he received the following summer. You know another team could have offered a toxic contract, perhaps a front-loaded deal that could have sabotaged the Thunder's salary structure and sent them deep into the luxury tax year after year. You don't care. Figure it out later, you say. Your counter to the Thunder operating not out of fear but restraint in the face of the newly implemented repeater tax is, "If the owners want to make a profit, they should sell the team." In your mind, the Thunder's long-established plan of trying to ensure Durant and Westbrook had a quality team around them not just at 23, 24, and 25 but also in their primes at 27, 28, and 29 was a flawed premise. You say the Thunder should have gone for it. They should have been in win-now mode. You argue that championship windows don't come around often and, when they do, don't last long.

You swear it could have worked, three ball-dominant players, all at their best while playing out on the perimeter. You never question what the chemistry would have been like, whether they would have been content. You never had concerns about future depth, what kind of battalion stood behind the stars. To you, the nucleus of Westbrook, Harden, Durant, and Ibaka alone made OKC championship material. And the Thunder threw it away the moment Sam Presti pulled the trigger on the trade.

You don't care that the Thunder were a better team in 2012–13 than they were in Harden's final season. You don't care that they won an Oklahoma City–era record 60 games that season, winning by a league-best 9.2 points per game and producing the highest-rated offense and defense of any Thunder season to that point. All you know is they didn't win a title without Harden and never even got back to the NBA Finals. You belittle the significance of the Thunder's string of injuries—Westbrook in 2013, Ibaka in 2014, Durant in 2015—on keeping OKC from returning to the championship round. For you, they were just confirmation the Thunder shouldn't have made the trade.

And when Durant ditched Oklahoma City in 2016, you promptly mounted your high horse, pounded your chest and screamed "See, I told you so!" You tied Durant's decision to a deal done nearly four years prior.

Or maybe I've got it wrong. Maybe you're not that fan. Maybe you disagreed with the trade then and still do now.

But you understand why it happened.

10 Serge Ibaka

Serge Ibaka was an afterthought.

On the night of the 2008 NBA Draft, no one knew who he was. Not the fans in Seattle. Not the people in Oklahoma City rooting for the Sonics to soon relocate.

So when NBA Commissioner David Stern called Ibaka's name with the 24th overall pick, reaction fell somewhere between disappointment and indifference. That all changed when everyone learned what the franchise had found.

Ibaka was a 6'10", 220-pound power forward, an athletic marvel with a spectacularly chiseled frame. Still just 18 when he was drafted, Ibaka was the youngest prospect in the 2008 class. He became the first NBA player from the Republic of Congo and the first international selected by team General Manager Sam Presti.

Ibaka entered the NBA with an amazing backstory. He was the third youngest of 18 children. His mother, a former basketball player on the national team of the Democratic Republic of Congo, died when he was 8. His father played professional basketball in Africa and was a member of the Republic of Congo national team. When Ibaka was a child, his father served a yearlong prison stint after being apprehended simply for working in the neighboring country of the Democratic Republic of Congo during a tense time of political strife. Ultimately, Ibaka chose to wear jersey No. 9 as a tribute to his father's old jersey number. While his father was imprisoned, Ibaka lived with his grandmother, who survived civil unrest in their native country in the 1990s while living in a house with no electricity and no running water. Ibaka learned basketball playing on outdoor courts, wearing shoes lined with cardboard inserts to cover holes in the soles. "I have come a long way," Ibaka said during his rookie season.

Ibaka never dreamed of playing in the NBA, only hoping to play professionally outside of his native country. His big break came when he was named Most Valuable Player at the 2006 U18 African Championships in Durban, South Africa, where he led all players in scoring and rebounding. At 17, Ibaka moved to Europe, leaving his family to fulfill his dream of playing professionally. First, he competed briefly in France. Then he jumped to Spain, where he immersed himself into the culture and without formal lessons became fluent in Spanish in only three months. He burst onto the radar of NBA scouts after being invited to the adidas Nations camp in New Orleans in the summer of 2007. There, Ibaka floored front-office executives with his athleticism. During vertical leap testing, Ibaka sprung higher than the maximum point on the measurement's pegs. Camp officials raised the bar. Ibaka again hit the apparatus' high point.

"All of the information that we were able to gather about his focus, his work ethic, and just his story, coming from where he came from, intrigued us that this would be a guy that would fit the kind of profile that we wanted to add to our team," Presti said.

After remaining in Spain for a year following his selection, Ibaka made the jump to the NBA for the 2009–10 season. When he arrived in Oklahoma City, he spoke only minimal English. But the team arranged for an English teacher from his native country to meet him at the practice facility for regular lessons. The two would sit in a media workroom roughly the size of a walk-in closet and hammer away after reporters had left for the day. By 20, Ibaka had lived on three continents, learned three languages, and adapted to the NBA game. It soon became obvious Ibaka was not just driven but also a quick study. Soon, he put his knack for rapid development on display on the court.

In his preseason debut, a road game against Memphis on October 7, 2009, Ibaka registered four points with two rebounds in only four minutes. He made both of his field-goal attempts. Three nights later, Thunder coach Scott Brooks unleashed Ibaka by playing him 26 minutes off the bench at New Orleans. He scored 12 points on 6-for-10 shooting with nine rebounds and two blocked shots. The mystery man wasn't so raw after all. "You don't have to run a play for him and he ends up with 12 points," said Kevin Ollie, a reserve guard on that year's team. "It's a great find by the organization. I tip my cap to them. I think he'll be a great surprise for a lot of people. But he won't be a surprise for long because a lot of people are witnessing what he can do once he gets minutes out on the court."

By the 14th game of the regular season, Ibaka was a rotation player. Filling in for injured forward Nick Collison in a road game against the Los Angeles Lakers on November 22, 2009, Ibaka scored 11 points with a game-high 13 rebounds and five blocked shots in 32 minutes. He was the Thunder's lone bright spot in a 101–85 loss. In only his seventh game, Ibaka achieved his first double double.

Midway through his second year, the 2010–11 season, Ibaka became the team's starting power forward and defensive anchor following Jeff Green's trade to Boston. Ibaka's insertion into the first string, coupled with the arrival of center Kendrick Perkins, changed the course of the franchise. Ibaka became the league's most feared shot blocker, leading the NBA in total blocked shots for four consecutive seasons starting with that 2010–11 campaign. He averaged a league-best 3.7 blocked shots in the 2011–12 season and earned All-Defensive First Team honors, the first in a string of three straight seasons he was named a first-teamer. Starting with the 2011–12 season, he finished in the top five of Defensive Player of the Year Award voting in three straight seasons, including a runner-up finish in 2011–12.

After focusing solely on rebounding, blocking shots, and running the floor in his first couple of seasons, Ibaka's offensive game soon evolved to the point he became virtually automatic with his mid-range jumper and, eventually, a near 40-percent three-point shooter. As he blossomed, Ibaka did so *avec classe*, the French phrase he grew fond of using to boast that everything he did was "with class." The words rang true, as Ibaka was a model citizen and teammate. You never heard of him running into trouble off the court, and despite being relegated to the third and, at times, the fourth and even fifth offensive option, he almost never complained about his role.

"I think he's a special player and a special person, the way he handles himself, the class that he exudes," said San Antonio coach Gregg Popovich during the 2014 West finals between the Thunder and Spurs. "I think he's the best defensive player in the league, but I think he's been overlooked to some degree in that regard. But he also does what he does at the offensive end. I think he's one of the most gifted players in our league because he's a dual player. He does it at both ends of the court. But he's also a fine man, so that's a pretty great combination."

The Ibaka era ended when the Thunder traded him to Orlando during the 2016 draft, swapping him for Victor Oladipo, Ersan Ilyasova, and the draft rights to No. 11 overall selection Domantas Sabonis.

But the one-time afterthought departed as one of the most beloved players in Thunder history.

"I have a lot of appreciation for those fans because I remember the first year when I got there nobody knew me, who I am, who I was," Ibaka said of Thunder fans. "But they gave me a lot of trust."

Serge Ibaka wasn't given anything. He earned everything.

11 The Serge Ibaka Trade

Serge Ibaka believed he'd be back. At least that's the story he told reporters following the Thunder's heartbreaking elimination from the 2016 playoffs.

"I'm going to wear the Thunder jersey next year," Ibaka insisted. "So there's nothing to talk about right now because it's not important."

That was June 1. Three weeks later, Ibaka was traded. It happened June 23, draft night. The Thunder sent their sensational shot-blocking and sudden three-point-shooting big man to Orlando in a deal no one saw coming. Ibaka was said to be sound asleep in Paris when the trade went down. And just like that, a remarkable seven-year run that started so humbly, blossomed so wonderfully, yet ultimately fell just short of the crown achievement, was over.

In exchange for Ibaka, the Thunder received Victor Oladipo, Ersan Ilyasova, and the rights to No. 11 overall pick Domantas Sabonis, the son of legendary Lithuanian center Arvydas Sabonis. Snap reaction across the national media viewed the deal as largely favorable for Oklahoma City. Some even said the Thunder fleeced the Magic. SI.com graded the deal an A for the Thunder and a C- for the Magic. ESPN.com graded it a B+ for the Thunder and a C for the Magic. CBSSports.com graded it an A for the Thunder and a B for the Magic. The haul helped soften the heartbreak of seeing yet another fan favorite traded away. "The combination of players that we're getting back we feel really fit our team," said Thunder GM Sam Presti. "And we always have to do what is best for our team."

The truth is more should have seen the move coming. After enjoying steady statistical improvement over his first five seasons, either in his points, rebounds, assists, or blocked shots averages, Ibaka's production regressed in each of his final two seasons in OKC. His 12.6-point average in 2015–16 was his lowest since his third year, when he posted 9.1 points per game. His 6.8 rebounds and 1.9 blocked shots in his final Thunder season were his lowest since his rookie campaign. Ibaka noticeably struggled with consistency, as well. He registered 29 double doubles in 81 games during the 2013–14 season but had just 26 combined double doubles in 142 regular season contests from 2014–16. His field-goal percentage also plummeted from a career-best 57 percent in 2012–13 to 47 percent in those final two seasons. And the jaw-dropping athleticism and explosiveness that turned him into a feared shot-blocker and fabulous finisher were seldom seen.

Some fans grew frustrated with Ibaka's inexplicable drop off. Others dismissed it due to his evolution as a better all-around player. He became one of the Thunder's most reliable three-point marksmen, one who ranked third on the team in both makes (77) and percentage (.376) in 2014–15. In his first five seasons, Ibaka hit just 45 three-pointers, but in his final two in OKC he made 137. His expanded range came at a time when the league was gravitating to small-ball lineups that played fast and let shots fly freely from afar. Ibaka's evolution, depending on your perspective, was either necessary to spread defenses and allow Russell Westbrook and Kevin Durant more room to operate, or a curse because he fell in love with floating on the perimeter and seemingly lost his passion for controlling the paint. But Ibaka developed his skills on both ends. No longer was he solely a rim protector. He transformed into a perimeter defender, a 6'10" terror who could close out on shooters and slide his feet to contain guards.

Despite his declining statistical production, Ibaka was believed to be boosting his value. But for all his evolution—and his new-found versatility was enormous when the Thunder went small with him at center—Ibaka's biggest strength defensively remained shot blocking. It's what moved an emotional Durant during his 2014 MVP acceptance speech to tell Ibaka, "You clean up so many of our mistakes, man, and we appreciate that." Only now Ibaka's biggest skill was being negated in true small-ball lineups, when he would get sucked away from the basket. By 2015–16, the days of Ibaka anchoring the Thunder's defense as an irreplaceable interior force were gone. The notion that he was a mandatory presence had become a myth, fueled by past performance rather than present day production. OKC's defense was regressing with him. Meanwhile, his lack of post skills and overall offensive versatility prevented Ibaka from taking full advantage of teams playing small and defending him with guards.

Couple all that with Ibaka nearing the end of his contract, which was set to expire after 2016–17, and his growing desire for a larger role, it seemed the writing was on the wall. Sprinkle in the emergence of center Steven Adams and guard Andre Roberson as dirty-work defenders, and Ibaka became virtually expendable, perhaps even a mandatory casualty given he was the biggest trade chip the Thunder had to improve the roster. It never seemed likely the Thunder would lavish Ibaka with a new contract that could have far exceeded his $12.25 million annual salary—not in the same summer that Westbrook, Adams, and Roberson all could hit free agency as well.

There was also the matter of whether Ibaka truly wanted to remain in Oklahoma City. Following a win at Toronto on March 28, 2016, Ibaka sounded off for the first time about his role in the team's offense. "I'm gonna tell you the truth. It's hard sometimes when you play hard, you play your [butt off]," he said. "You play so hard on defense, then you come to offense and you're going to be out there in the corner for four, five, six, sometimes eight minutes and you don't touch the ball. We human, man. It's hard."

Three days after the deal, *The Vertical* reported Ibaka never demanded a trade and the Thunder's decision had nothing to do with finances and everything to do with the organization's belief it wouldn't be able to re-sign Ibaka. The report quoted Ibaka's agent, Andy Miller, as saying promises to his client weren't kept. "There was an expectation of a larger role," Miller was quoted as saying. "It was overpromised and under-delivered. Everyone should be held to the same level of accountability across the board."

Ibaka spent less than one full season in Orlando. In February 2017, the Magic traded him to Toronto for Terrence Ross and a first-round pick. Four months later, the Thunder flipped Oladipo and Sabonis to Indiana for Paul George. But Ibaka's seven seasons with the Thunder produced three NBA All-Defensive First Team awards, four consecutive years as the league leader in total blocked shots, a runner-up finish for Defensive Player of the Year, a trip to the NBA Finals, and three other postseasons that ended in the Western Conference finals.

It was a good run.

"He was a really good player for us who really helped us become an elite team and make some deep runs," Nick Collison said. "He deserves a lot of credit for the success we had."

12 The 2012 NBA Finals— Game 1

All eyes were on Kevin Durant and LeBron James.

By the time they met in the 2012 NBA Finals, they were the game's undisputed two best players. Some had even scooched Durant ahead of James. Durant's 24 first-place votes for the 2011–12 MVP Award marked the closest he came to James in any of his three runner-up finishes. As the 2012 postseason commenced, Durant was the reigning three-time scoring champion who carried a reputation as a clutch performer and was now striking fear into opponents with a well-rounded game. James was coming off a remarkable regular season but entered the championship series still covered with the stench of his 2011 Finals stinker against Dallas. The world couldn't wait to see what would happen, how it would play out.

In a seven-game series between the game's biggest stars on the biggest stage, Round 1 went to Durant. He dazzled the Chesapeake Energy Arena crowd and delivered the Thunder a tone-setting 105–94 win over Miami in Game 1. It was June 12, 2012, a Tuesday night. Durant scored a game-high 36 points, the second most by a player in his Finals debut since the ABA-NBA merger in 1976. Allen Iverson held the record with 48 points in 2001. As he had been throughout that postseason, Durant was marvelous when it mattered most. He scored 17 points in the decisive fourth quarter, helping the Thunder outscore the Heat 31–21 in the period. It was the eighth time that season that Durant pumped in at least 15 fourth-quarter points. This time, his heroics lifted the Thunder from a 13-point, second-quarter deficit and a seven-point hole at the half.

Durant added eight rebounds, four assists, and a blocked shot. He made 12-of-20 shots and turned the ball over just twice. Second to none on the scale of significance was how Durant took the challenge of defending James for the first three quarters. Over that span, the Heat's star and back-to-back MVP scored 23 points on 18 shots. James, meanwhile, was assigned to Kendrick Perkins. James' final stat line: 30 points, 11-for-24 shooting, nine rebounds, and four assists. His fourth-quarter defense: absent. "KD got a couple looks that we don't like…. We need to make adjustments with that. We will make adjustments," James said confidently after the game.

Durant downplayed his defensive impact. "You can't really stop a guy like that," he said of James. "Just got to play hard and contest.… It's a tough match-up, but I've got to play with some fire and we'll see what happens."

Russell Westbrook flirted with a triple double in his Finals debut, assisting Durant with 27 points, eight rebounds, and a game-high 11 assists against only two turnovers. He scored six in the final 12 minutes and dished four assists in the final frame, three of them leading to seven of Durant's 17 fourth-quarter points. In the end, the Thunder looked confident and in control. Durant looked like he could outduel James. Westbrook looked like he'd have his way. Heat guard Dwyane Wade looked old. Miami big man Chris Bosh looked ordinary.

To Thunder fans, this series looked like it could be over.

The 2012 NBA Finals— Game 2

The play preceded the NBA's push for greater awareness and accountability, but even an admission in one of the league's Last Two Minute Reports wouldn't have revealed anything we didn't already know.

Kevin Durant was fouled.

With the game on the line and homecourt advantage hanging in the balance, LeBron James got away with egregious and excessive contact on the night's most critical play. It ended up costing the Thunder a 100–96 decision against Miami in Game 2 of the 2012 NBA Finals and, for all we know, potentially a championship. What we do know is the referee should have blown his whistle. There is video proof.

Trailing by two with 12.3 seconds remaining after a furious rally from 13 down in the final frame, the Thunder had the ball

With a core of Russell Westbrook, James Harden, Kevin Durant, and Serge Ibaka in 2012, the Thunder looked to be a dynasty in the making. But after losing to Miami in five games in the NBA Finals, that foursome never took the court together again. (Derick E. Hingle/*USA TODAY* Sports)

and a chance to tie or take the lead. Derek Fisher inbounded to Durant from the left sideline. Durant caught the pass, turned, took one dribble along the baseline, and went up for a shot from the short corner. James stuck his hands in, first grabbing Durant by the bicep to prevent a blow-by, then hooking Durant under his shooting arm just before he gathered. When he finally let go, James raked his left arm across Durant's body, sliding his arm down his chest to his waist and finally across his right thigh as Durant elevated. "That's illegal contact," ABC color commentator Jeff Van Gundy said during the network's instant replay. "That's a foul. At that angle, there's no question that's a foul."

The baseline official stood just feet from the play. No call.

Durant's off-balance pull-up from his desired spot on the left block bounced off the rim. Russell Westbrook soared in and got a paw on it, but the ball fluttered into James' hands. Westbrook immediately wrapped up James and sent him to the free throw line, where he made both shots amid a chorus of boos for the game's final margin. Westbrook missed a hurried three-pointer, and that was that. The series was tied at one game apiece and shifting to Miami for the next three contests. Those Finals never returned to OKC.

"I was open and I missed the shot," Durant said after the game.

Asked if there was contact Durant said, "I was just worrying about the shot. I really couldn't tell you. I've got to watch the film, I guess." When pressed further Durant said, "I missed the shot, man."

It was Durant taking responsibility and not relying on excuses. It was the Thunder way. "That would have been a nice opportunity for us to make that or get to the free-throw line and send it into overtime," Thunder coach Scott Brooks said. "But, unfortunately, we didn't get the play and we moved on."

Said James: "I figured they were going to go to him. He got a small step on me. I just wanted to try to keep a body on him, make him take a tough shot. He's made tough shots all year, all series, and that one he just missed."

It went down as a defining moment, both in the series and the Thunder's history. Go up 2–0 and the Thunder would have held serve at home and headed to Miami with all the confidence of a team two wins away from a title. They also would have been guaranteed a Game 6 back in OKC, with a potential Game 7 also being played inside Chesapeake Energy Arena. Instead, when the series shifted, all the pressure was put squarely on the Thunder to secure a victory inside American Airlines Arena, where the Heat had won 36-of-43 in the regular season and playoffs. That victory never came. Two years later, the NBA altered the NBA Finals sequence from the 2–3–2 format to 2–2–1–1–1.

"In my opinion, I think it was [a foul], but I'm not the referee," Thunder center Kendrick Perkins said. "He must have seen something different. But it shouldn't have come down to that possession. We should have put ourselves in a position that it didn't come down to the last shot."

Another early offensive drought forced the Thunder to dig out of a deep hole. Oklahoma City trailed 18–2 in the first seven-plus minutes. Over that span, the Thunder missed 11-of-12 shots and turned over the ball four times. Miami extended its lead to as many as 17 before the Thunder shaved it to 12 at the end of the opening quarter. In Game 1, the Thunder trailed by 11 late in the first period. "I liked the way we came back and fought and made it a one-possession game at the end," Brooks said. "But when you get down 17, too many things have to happen well for you and perfect for you."

Games 3 and 4 in Miami were each decided by six points. Westbrook famously erupted for 43 points in Game 4. But the Thunder were unable to produce the pivotal plays needed late to close out either contest. The Heat then clinched the championship with a commanding victory in Game 5.

But the toughest pill to swallow from the 2012 Finals was the final seconds of Game 2. Who knows how things might have played out had the referee blown his whistle?

14 The Photo

The party began with 3:01 remaining inside the arena by South Beach.

LeBron James, Dwyane Wade, and Chris Bosh, wearing their home white uniforms, had just exited for good. Their work was done. Miami owned a 22-point lead. Music blared. The Heat were on their way to a date with destiny. So they celebrated, congratulating each other at one end of the court with heartfelt hugs and high-fives inside the final minutes of Game 5. Pat Riley stood with the rest of the American Airlines Arena crowd and applauded in approval.

That's when it happened, an impromptu moment—caught by the broadcast and captured in screenshots—that will live forever in Thunder lore.

As James giddily jumped up and down, pumping his arms in anticipation of winning his first NBA championship, the future of the league convened in the corner in front of the bench at the opposite baseline.

Russell Westbrook, James Harden, and Kevin Durant stood shoulder to shoulder in their customary road blues.

Together, they watched.

Harden was in the middle. Westbrook was on the left. Durant, with a white towel hanging from his head, was on the right. Harden threw his arms around both. There, they absorbed the final 148 seconds of their 2011–12 season.

You could feel the anguish on their faces, see the sorrow in their eyes. They were 22 and 23 years old. And they were devastated. They were about to be eliminated in the NBA Finals and go home with a feeling no player wants to experience. But there, in that moment, they knew they'd be back.

Everyone did.

"I told them embrace it," Harden remembered communicating to Westbrook and Durant as the trio stood there, dazed and confused. "Just look back at this as a learning experience. I'm telling them that, 'We're going to be back here next year. And we're going to win, and it's going to feel a lot better.' They were like, 'I got you.' And we agreed."

James, meanwhile, couldn't stop jumping up and down.

After previously coming up empty in two trips to the NBA Finals, James finally had cemented his legacy as an all-time great with a Finals MVP–clinching 26-point, 11-rebound, 13-assist masterpiece in the Heat's 121–106 mugging. His dominance and subsequent coronation defined the series. Still, the world couldn't stop wondering what type of storm was brewing in Oklahoma City. Soon, LeBron would again have to see the boys in blue. Or so everyone thought.

"When I think of Game 5," Bill Simmons wrote, "I will remember LeBron's brilliance first, then Mike Miller having that crazy sports-movie montage of threes…. And then I'll think of the Oklahoma City kids huddled in the corner at the end, waiting their turn, knowing that's how the NBA works. We'll see if LeBron ever lets them on the ride."

Harden never played another regular season game with the Thunder. He was traded to Houston just before the start of the 2012–13 regular season. Durant signed with Golden State as a free agent in the summer of 2016.

The Oklahoma City kids never returned to the NBA Finals.

That photo now illustrates one of the NBA's all-time "What ifs?" The trio of Westbrook, Harden, and Durant never reached their prime years together. Westbrook and Durant splintered just as they entered theirs.

"That's something that will never happen again," Harden said of that collection of young talent. "Especially when you draft three times in a row and you get three superstars."

Ask 10 Thunder fans what they think when they see the photo and you might get 10 different responses. When asked during the 2016–17 season what comes to his mind when he sees the photo, Harden's answer could have doubled as an explanation why it makes so many fans feel so many different ways.

"It's over," he said.

15 The 2016 West Finals— Game 6

They were five minutes away.

Five minutes from flipping the script on the never-ending narrative surrounding the James Harden trade. Five minutes from shedding their cheap label. Five minutes from overcoming unfortunate and untimely injuries, one after another after another, that derailed three once-promising seasons. Five minutes from validation that a first-year coach from the college ranks could do it.

After four years of setbacks and scrutiny, the Thunder, finally, were five minutes away from returning to the game's most elusive stage, the NBA Finals.

All they had to do was finish off the Golden State Warriors in Game 6 of the 2016 Western Conference finals.

It was May 28, a Saturday night. The Thunder were at home, in control of the game and the series. Oklahoma City had stunned both the 73-win Warriors and the basketball world by stealing the opening game and surging to a 3–1 series lead. After losing Game 5 at Golden State, Game 6 was the Thunder's best chance at getting another crack at the Larry O'Brien Trophy, a shot they desperately desired since coming up short against Miami in the 2012 Finals. The Thunder didn't want to bank on clinching in a road Game 7. And for much of Game 6, it appeared they wouldn't have to.

In front of a raucous home crowd ready to celebrate, the Thunder led for 42 of the game's first 45 minutes. Their lead swelled to as many as 13 in the second quarter. They entered the fourth quarter ahead by eight. When Kevin Durant drilled a 14' fadeaway jumper with 5:09 remaining, OKC's lead stood at seven.

Then came those fateful and franchise-changing final five minutes, a gut-wrenching finish Thunder fans will never forget.

After Durant's bucket, the Warriors closed the game on a 19–5 run. Over that span, the Thunder had 13 possessions, including offensive rebounds. They went 1-for-5 with six turn-overs and made 3-of-4 free throws. The Thunder's only field goal down the stretch came on a putback layup by Andre Roberson. The Thunder turned the ball over on their final four possessions, on five of their final six and six of their final 10. "We got a little stagnant coming down the stretch," said first-year Thunder coach Billy Donovan, who was silencing all critics by excelling at the helm after jumping from the University of Florida to the NBA. "I just didn't feel like we ran our offense with the pace and the tempo that we needed to run it."

Most shocking was that it was the Thunder's stars, Durant and Russell Westbrook, who captained the collapse. They combined for all six of the Thunder's fourth-quarter turnovers, each of them coming during that momentum-swinging stretch. Westbrook had four in the final 1:40. He was stripped by Warriors guard Andre Iguodala as he attempted a turnaround baseline jumper. He lost the ball off his foot and out of bounds on a fast break. He was stripped by Iguodala again as he looked to start a fast break. He had his inbounds pass picked off by Stephen Curry. His miscues led to seven quick Warriors points. Durant had a pass out of a double team stolen by Iguodala with 2:55 remaining, a giveaway Curry converted into a quick three-pointer that tied the game at 99–99. Durant then had the ball stolen from him by Harrison Barnes after an inbounds pass on the Thunder's final possession.

In the final minute of a closeout game in the Western Conference finals, the Thunder never even got up a shot attempt.

Not that Durant and Westbrook were very effective when they were shooting. Durant shot an extremely uncharacteristic 10-of-31 for the game. He went 1-for-7 in the fourth quarter. Westbrook was 10-for-27 that night. He was 2-for-7 in the fourth quarter.

Meanwhile, their Warriors counterparts couldn't seem to miss as the game wore on. Klay Thompson put on a shooting display for the ages and scored 19 of his game-high 41 points in the fourth quarter. He went 11-for-18 from three-point range, setting an NBA record for three-pointers made in a playoff game. His final bomb came after one of Westbrook's turnovers and gave the Warriors a 104–101 lead they never relinquished. Curry shook off a scoreless first quarter and pumped in 22 of his 31 points in the second half. His high-arcing, running bank shot over Serge Ibaka after another of Westbrook's turnovers put the Warriors ahead by five with 14.3 seconds to play. Curry then capped it by intercepting Westbrook's inbounds pass.

In that five-minute window, every bad habit and head-scratching moment the Thunder had exhibited over the previous seven seasons manifested itself: their over-reliance on their two stars, their tendency to resort to hero ball, their lack of trust, their questionable decision-making, their infuriating shot selection, their inability to consistently execute late-game inbounds plays, their high turnover rate, their leaky defense. It was an unbelievable display, a comedy of errors rarely seen in the magnitude of that type of moment. And it cost the Thunder their last real chance at a championship.

Two nights later, the Warriors finished the job, taking a 96–88 win in Game 7 inside Oracle Arena. Golden State became only the 10th team in NBA history to overcome a 3–1 deficit and win a postseason series.

"We survived by the skin of our teeth," Warriors coach Steve Kerr said. "They had us on our heels constantly in this series. They deserved to be there just as much as we do, really."

Five unforgettable minutes made the difference.

16 M-V-P

It started with a quote.

Sports Illustrated senior writer Lee Jenkins procured it from the mouth of the man himself. The magazine then plastered the words onto its esteemed cover.

"I've been second my whole life," Kevin Durant was quoted as saying in an April 2013 issue. "I was the second-best player in high school. I was the second pick in the draft. I've been second in the MVP voting three times. I came in second in the finals. I'm tired of being second…. I'm done with it."

Two weeks after his quote made national news, Durant officially finished second in the NBA's Most Valuable Player Award voting for the third time. And for the third time in four seasons, he lost out to LeBron James, who in that 2012–13 season came one vote shy of becoming the first player to win the league's highest regular season honor unanimously. The lone other first-place vote? It went to New York's Carmelo Anthony.

With that as the backdrop, Durant assembled a season for the ages the following year. While co-star Russell Westbrook was saddled for 36 games due to multiple knee surgeries, Durant set the league on fire. He carried the Thunder, putting up one eye-popping performance after another before finally capturing his first MVP Award. His averages in 2013–14: a career- and league-best 32 points, 7.4 rebounds, a career-high 5.5 assists, 1.3 steals, and 0.7 blocked shots. His percentages: 50.3 percent from the field, 39.1 percent from three-point range, and 87.3 percent from the foul line.

Durant strung together 12 straight games of 30 points or more, dropped 12 40-point games, and exploded for two 50-point games, including a career-high 54 pointer in a home game against Golden State on January 17, 2014. He registered three triple doubles, 27 double doubles, and topped 25 points in 41 consecutive games during a scorching-hot stretch from early January to early April. Most importantly, the Thunder won. Oklahoma City finished second in the West at 59–23, three games behind San Antonio. Durant played 81 games, and the Thunder went 58–23 in those contests. In games without Westbrook by his side, Durant captained the Thunder to a 24–11 record.

After three second-place finishes, the NBA crowned Durant as its Most Valuable Player on May 6, 2014. He totaled 1,232 points, including 119 first-place votes from a panel of 124 sportswriters and broadcasters throughout the U.S. and Canada as well as an NBA.com MVP fan vote. This time, it was James who finished a distant second.

Durant's long-awaited coronation turned into a community celebration. It was held at the Thunder's first practice facility, a nod to where Durant's rise with the Thunder emanated. State dignitaries such as Oklahoma Governor Mary Fallin and Oklahoma City Mayor Mick Cornett had front-row seats. Select season ticket holders were on hand to see history. Kids from a local Boys & Girls Club served as special guests. And that was just inside the building. About 1,000 more fans watched the proceedings outside the warehouse-style facility, where the parking lot transformed into a block party with music, games, and all the Thunder's customary game-night entertainment.

Durant then delivered a beautiful MVP speech that was heartfelt and honest, tearful and thorough, surprising and sensational. It was 25½ minutes, 3,000 words, and by the time he closed his remarks with "the end," one of the greatest acceptance speeches of all time.

He began by thanking God. He traced his steps to his Prince George's County, Maryland, roots, when he moved from house to house as a child and had modest dreams of becoming a rec league coach. He made mention of both the people who helped him reach that MVP dais and the people who doubted him along the way. He said both groups pushed him and motivated him. He then singled out each of his teammates. He started with the veterans: Derek Fisher, Nick Collison, Kendrick Perkins, Thabo Sefolosha, Caron Butler, Serge Ibaka, and Hasheem Thabeet. He told the world quick stories about each. He thanked them individually. He became an emotional wreck before he could get through Butler. "I don't know why I'm crying so much, man," he said, after his voice cracked and he sniffled uncontrollably. He then moved to his "young guys"—Jeremy Lamb, Perry Jones, Steven Adams, Reggie Jackson, and Grant Jerrett. He did the same for them. He told them all he loved them.

"I know you guys think I forgot Russ," Durant then said, drawing laughter from the waiting-and-wondering audience. "But I could speak all night about Russell; an emotional guy who will run through a wall for me. I don't take it for granted. It's days when I want to just tackle you and tell you to snap out of it sometimes. But I know it's days you want to do the same thing with me. I love you, man. I love you."

Durant then thanked the Thunder organization. Chairman Clay Bennett. General Manager Sam Presti. Assistant General Manager Troy Weaver. The basketball operations staff. The coaching staff. Coach Scott Brooks. The fans.

He thanked family and friends. His brothers, Tony and Rayvonne. His father, Wayne. His grandmother, Barbara. And, finally, his mother, Wanda.

His final 48 words to his mother marked the speech's defining moment.

"We wasn't supposed to be here. You made us believe," his voice quivered. "You kept us off the street. You put clothes on our backs, food on the table. When you didn't eat, you made sure we ate. You went to sleep hungry. You sacrificed for us.

"You the real MVP."

17 The Iron Man

Before he was a scoring champion and a two-time All-Star Game MVP, before he was a walking triple double and an All-NBA First Teamer, before he was a fashion icon and a globally recognized brand ambassador, Russell Westbrook was unbreakable.

Through his first five NBA seasons, Westbrook never missed a game. He appeared in 394 consecutive regular season contests from the start of the 2008–09 season through the end of the 2012–13 season.

Of all the phenomenal feats the Thunder's prodigious point guard amassed, his one-time streak of sensational durability ranks right alongside his most amazing. During that five-year window, Westbrook was the NBA's leading iron man, pacing all players for consecutive games played.

A.C. Green is the NBA's all-time leader with 1,192 straight appearances, a streak that spanned 15 seasons from 1986 to 2001. Cal Ripken Jr. remains the standard-bearer for consecutive games streaks, playing 2,632 straight games over 17 years with the Baltimore Orioles.

But Westbrook's commitment to taking the court every night was remarkable in its own right. No player in Westbrook's era played with more ferociousness and fearlessness. He was a one-man wrecking crew, willingly and dutifully laying his body on the line each night to help his team win. He seemed indestructible as he continued suiting up game after game despite unleashing a uniquely unbridled playing style that only made him susceptible to bumps and bruises, aches and pains.

Including postseasons, Westbrook appeared in 439 straight games. He also never missed a game in high school or college.

"I try to come in every day and try to take care of my body to where I can get an opportunity to come out every night and play at a high level," Westbrook said. "It's tough sometimes. But that's the nature of the game. And I take pride in coming in and trying to take care of myself and being ready to play."

Westbrook's streak disappointingly ended on October 30, 2013. He missed that night's season opener while recovering from the second of two off-season knee surgeries to repair a torn meniscus. It was a fluke injury he sustained when Patrick Beverley dove into him as he attempted to call a timeout during Game 2 of the Thunder-Rockets series in the opening round of the 2013 playoffs.

There were close calls and several scares before that. He suffered a nasty left ankle sprain in a game at Orlando on March 1, 2012. He trudged out of the Amway Center that night with a severe limp, leaving onlookers believing there would be no way he'd be able to go two nights later at Atlanta. Two nights later, Westbrook laced up his sneakers against the Hawks. Wearing a protective sleeve on his ankle, he dropped 25 points with four assists in 38 uncomfortable minutes. On New Year's Eve 2012, Westbrook took an inadvertent elbow from Phoenix forward Luis Scola just before halftime. The blow drew blood above Westbrook's right eye, forcing him to the locker room where he required stitches to close the gash. Westbrook returned midway through the third period. He missed only six minutes, 49 seconds of game time.

"It's about his toughness and about how he was raised," said former Thunder coach Scott Brooks, who often marveled at how Westbrook also rarely missed practices. "His family has done a great job of instilling in him that he's not entitled to anything. He knows he has to earn it."

In the 2012–13 regular season finale against Milwaukee, the 60-win Thunder had nothing left to play for. They had already wrapped up the Western Conference's top seed. But Brooks played coy about whether he would play his starters. A reporter playfully asked Westbrook if there would be a fist fight if Brooks asked him to sit out the finale.

"No, no, no. There won't be a fistfight," Westbrook said with a smile, "but he won't ask me that."

Brooks rested Kevin Durant, Kendrick Perkins, Kevin Martin, and Nick Collison that night. Westbrook started and played seven minutes. It was the last game of his regular season streak.

Westbrook's superstition grew along with his streak. He became careful to not jinx his good fortune and bordered on paranoia even discussing his durability. At a practice late in the 2011–12 season, the day before a Sunday afternoon showdown with Derrick Rose and the Chicago Bulls, Westbrook was asked the key to his ability to stay healthy. He paused for nearly five seconds.

"Uhh," he said, before another nearly five-second pause. "Just coming in and working out and trying to stay fit, I guess. I don't know."

Westbrook then fessed up. "I'd rather not talk about it, to tell you the truth," he said. "The last time I did, I twisted my ankle the next game."

Westbrook's durability was so amazing he even recovered from surgery ahead of schedule. When a loose stitch from the initial procedure on his torn meniscus caused swelling and required a second operation, Westbrook was supposed to be sidelined the first four to six weeks of the 2013–14 regular season. He missed just two games. He made his return on November 3, 2013, scoring 21 points with seven assists in a seven-point win against the Suns.

Typically the first player announced in pregame introductions at home games, Westbrook was saved for last that night. Durant, who was always last, volunteered his customary spot. The Chesapeake Energy Arena crowd ate it up, welcoming back Westbrook with a thunderous ovation.

"It's a blessing, man," Westbrook said. "You can't take things like that for granted. Just [having] the opportunity to get your name called and the opportunity to play the game of basketball is great."

But Westbrook's iron man days were done. Attempting to protect his long-term health, the Thunder held out Westbrook from a home game against Utah on November 24, 2013. It was the first time in his life he didn't play a game when he was physically able to perform. Following a third surgery to the same knee on December 27, 2013, due to increased swelling, Westbrook missed 27 consecutive games. When he returned, the team then held him out of six additional games that were parts of back-to-back sets.

"It's tough," Westbrook said. "But I realized once I got hurt that's what it was going to take from the get go, just being patient and listening to the training staff and listening to the doctors as well."

Through it all, Westbrook's competitive spirit never wavered. He overcame three surgeries on the same knee in one calendar year and returned more ferocious than ever. He went on to accomplish so much that shaped his legacy and etched his name among the game's all-time greats. But for all his achievements, only one truly defined him. It was something not even his harshest critics could take away from him.

Russell Westbrook was a gladiator.

18 Patrick Beverley

Patrick Beverley was a bit player nobody knew. At least not the bulk of Thunder fans.

That all changed on April 24, 2013. That was the night Beverley became the most hated basketball player in Oklahoma history.

It was Game 2 of the opening round of the playoffs, a Wednesday night inside Chesapeake Energy Arena. The Thunder were hosting Houston in a 1–8 matchup most figured would be a breeze for the West's top seed. Oklahoma City ran the Rockets out of the building in Game 1, cruising to a 29-point victory. But even in that blowout, a rookie point guard making his playoff debut had commanded the Thunder's attention.

Beverley came off the bench and scored 11 points with four rebounds, four assists, and two steals in 28 minutes. He provided some pesky defense—stripping Thunder point guards twice—and thoroughly outplayed Jeremy Lin, the Rockets point guard starting ahead of him. A 2009 second-round pick who bounced around in Europe, from Ukraine to Greece to Russia, Beverley latched on with the Rockets in early January 2013 after signing for the league minimum. He entered the series with 41 career NBA games under his belt. "I think it's apparent that he only knows one way to play the game," said Thunder guard Derek Fisher after Game 1. "That's to go hard, to play hard, to play with aggression and confidence. He impacted the game [Sunday] night."

Three nights later, Beverley changed the course of the series, the postseason, and Thunder history.

It all started when Rockets forward Greg Smith grabbed one of Houston's 19 offensive rebounds and converted an uncontested putback dunk. It gave the Rockets a 42–41 lead with 5:42 remaining in the second quarter. Thunder coach Scott Brooks had seen enough. As Russell Westbrook advanced the ball past halfcourt, everyone knew a timeout was coming. Beverley, however, dove at Westbrook in an attempt to steal the ball along the sideline near the Thunder's bench. Beverley's left hip crashed into Westbrook's right knee. Westbrook fell to the floor but popped right up and hopped on his left leg toward the scorer's table. He pounded the blue padding with his palm in frustration, sending a cloud of rosin powder into the air. He turned and glared at Beverley. Then he hopped some more. He doubled over and clutched his knee in clear pain.

But the Iron Man remained in the game. No one knew what Beverley had just done. There was no indication he had just busted up Westbrook's knee. Westbrook simply shook it off and finished the game in sensational fashion, scoring 20 points with three assists and four steals following the collision. The Thunder won 105–102. "I was basically playing on one leg, kind of just hobbling around," Westbrook later said. "I was in pain."

The diagnosis didn't come down until two days later. Westbrook would miss the remainder of the postseason with a torn lateral meniscus. The vitriol was swift and severe. Thunder fans called Beverley every name in the book. They labeled his play cheap, dirty, and unnecessary. A Thunder ball boy was investigated by police for sending Beverley death threats via Twitter. "I just hope it wasn't a dirty play," Westbrook said.

No longer was Beverley an obscure rookie. Now he was a household name. But all the attention was negative. Not just in Oklahoma. Nationally. "I knew my actions and my intent," Beverley explained. "My intent was for no one to get hurt. I keep saying this. It's an unfortunate situation."

Not even Westbrook knew the severity of his injury. He remembered being in pain after the game and the next morning, but he still conducted a postgame interview following Game 2, which suggested he was fine. "It's fun," Westbrook said of his battle with Beverley. "During this time of the year, as a team we got one goal and we can't let nobody get in the way. That's how I feel, and that's how I want my team to respond as well."

Westbrook never made it to Game 3. On the morning of that night's contest, he underwent surgery at the Stedman Clinic in Vail, Colorado. Hours later, a No. 0 jersey hung in its usual stall inside the visitor's locker room at Toyota Center before the game. Westbrook was gone but not forgotten. On the Thunder's first possession of that Game 3, only 29 seconds in, center Kendrick Perkins tried to flatten Beverley with a not-so-subtle illegal screen as Beverley pressured replacement Reggie Jackson the length of the court. The message had been sent. The damage, however, had been done.

Without Westbrook, the Thunder survived the Rockets in a six-game series. OKC then fell in five games to Memphis in the semifinals. Just like that, a 60-win season that seemed destined for a return trip to the NBA Finals was over.

And Patrick Beverley will forever be to blame.

19 Clay Bennett

Let's just tell it like it is. Your opinion of Clay Bennett probably depends on your location.

If you're in the 206 area code, you probably hate him.

If you're in the 405 area code, you probably love him.

It's really that simple. And it's totally understandable.

Bennett is the chairman of the Oklahoma City Thunder. He's not the sole owner. He represents a group of Oklahoma City businessmen collectively known as the Professional Basketball Club, LLC. This group purchased the Seattle SuperSonics in July 2006 for $350 million. Bennett became the group's lead man and managing partner. The sale was approved by NBA owners in October 2006.

For two years, from the team's purchase date in July 2006 until the Sonics relocated to OKC in July 2008, Bennett took almost all of the bullets. Not just from Seattle but also from the rest of the country. The immediate assumption was Bennett and his band of businessmen was a bunch of robber barons, purchasing The Emerald City's first major league love with the sole intent of stealing it away. But you can't steal what you paid for.

Still, a nasty breakup between the Bennett-led Sonics, the team's rabid fans, and the Seattle government ensued. It was fueled by revelations that the ownership group did intend to relocate the franchise to Oklahoma City. Their intentions initially were exposed by Aubrey McClendon, the late minor partner of the Thunder who was the CEO and chairman of Chesapeake Energy and a close friend of Bennett. McClendon in August 2007 was quoted in *The Journal Record,* an Oklahoma City business newspaper, saying, "We didn't buy the team to keep it in Seattle, we hoped to come here." The NBA fined McClendon $250,000 for his comments. In a subsequent court case in which Seattle city leaders sought to enforce the team's lease with KeyArena, incriminating emails revealed the group's desire to move the team to OKC as soon as possible. The conversation, which took place in April 2007, consisted of Bennett, McClendon, and then partner Tom Ward.

Clay Bennett is the chairman of the Professional Basketball Club LLC, the ownership group of the Thunder. (AP Photo)

Ward: Is there any way to move here for next season or are we doomed to have another lame duck season in Seattle?

Bennett: I am a man possessed! Will do everything we can. Thanks for hanging with me boys, the game is getting started!

Ward: That's the spirit!! I am willing to help any way I can to watch ball here next year.

McClendon: Me too, thanks Clay!

The exchange flew in the face of Bennett's stated promise to make a "good-faith effort" to keep the Sonics in Seattle. But the evidence did little else than confirm for many that Bennett's failed attempts in securing a renovated or new arena in Seattle were all a charade. A settlement was reached on July 2, 2008, that allowed the Sonics to ditch the final two years on their KeyArena lease and relocate immediately under certain conditions. When he stood before a gathering of Oklahoma City media members a day later, Bennett started his news conference announcing the franchise relocation with three words.

"We made it," he said.

"Congratulations," Bennett added. "The NBA will be in Oklahoma City next season playing their games."

No matter how it happened, Bennett instantly was a hero in Oklahoma. He delivered a major league franchise to Oklahomans who previously could only dream of having one they could call their own. On the opening night of the 2008–09 season, the Thunder's inaugural regular season game, Bennett was saluted by his home state accordingly. The Thunder hosted Milwaukee. NBA Commissioner David Stern was in town to welcome Oklahoma to the big leagues alongside Oklahoma City Mayor Mick Cornett during a ceremony just before tip-off. When Cornett recognized Bennett, he received prolonged applause that eventually lured him to the edge of the court. Bennett waved to the crowd and tapped his heart twice.

He had made it.

"There are many in this community that give much, and there are many that don't want any credit," Cornett said. "But I don't think there's very many people that give more or want to be remembered for it less than Clay Bennett."

20 Big League City

Ron Norick needed answers. Really, he had but one question.

Why?

The Oklahoma City mayor in 1991 wooed United Airlines and wooed it hard when the air carrier sought a home to erect its planned $1 billion state-of-the-art maintenance facility. Norick spearheaded the city's efforts over a highly competitive 21-month bidding war that began with pitches from 90 cities. He lobbied for a rare sales tax and ultimately saw the passage of his proposal to subsidize the company's plant with a sweetheart deal in the range of $200 million. The airline instead chose Indianapolis. Oklahoma City lost an opportunity United claimed would eventually create 7,000 jobs and pour $700 million into the local economy. Norick and other city officials took the loss hard. Admittedly, they were despondent, depressed even.

The disappointment came on the heels of Oklahoma City previously losing a bid for a Boeing facility and only a year earlier coming up short in its attempt to lure an American Airlines plant. A disturbing pattern had developed of Oklahoma City finishing as an also-ran. Norick needed to know why. Why did United bypass OKC? The answer he received was equally deflating. United couldn't fathom forcing its employees to live in Oklahoma City. Indianapolis, Norick was told, had a better quality of life.

It was a kick in the teeth but one Oklahoma City civic leaders needed. After a decade of economic turmoil brought about by the oil bust of the early 1980s, Oklahoma City sunk to a sleepy town with stunted growth. Its citizens and its corporations were fleeing for greener pastures in neighboring states. Something needed to be done. Action needed to be taken.

Led by Norick, the Greater Chamber of Commerce and the city council, Oklahoma City introduced a unique and ambitious initiative, a set of major projects that would revitalize downtown and improve the city's quality of life and national image through new and upgraded cultural, sports, recreation, and convention facilities. They called it Metropolitan Area Maps, or MAPS for short. "When it became clear that United and other industries thought Oklahoma City just didn't have the quality of life they wanted, we had a vision," Norick said. "We dreamed that we could come together as a city and build the vital infrastructure that we needed."

To do it, Norick needed Oklahoma City residents to approve a one-cent, five-year sales tax that would fund the projects. He deemed the vote an "up" or "down" for the city's future. Needing a simple majority vote, the measure narrowly passed with just under 54 percent on December 14, 1993. Norick happily announced to a crowd that night, "Oklahoma City, welcome to the big leagues."

The tax-funded initiative generated more than $350 million in total revenue. It pumped life into nine projects, which included downtown trolleys, the construction of the 13,000-seat Chickasaw Bricktown Ballpark, the Bricktown Canal, Chesapeake Energy Arena, and an immaculate four-story downtown library, aptly named after Norick. MAPS also revitalized the Cox Convention Center, the Civic Center Music Hall, a stretch of the North Canadian River, later renamed the Oklahoma River, and the State Fairgrounds. Each project was carried out without the city accruing debt.

After the success of MAPS, city leaders relied on the same formula to continue efforts to push Oklahoma City forward. They introduced a second one-cent sales tax they called MAPS for Kids to provide resources for Oklahoma City's struggling public schools. The project was approved by 61 percent of voters in November 2001. The tax would last seven years. It generated more than $500 million, along with a $180 million Oklahoma City Public Schools bond issue used for facility improvements and technology and transportation projects. The program constructed or renovated 70 public school buildings in Oklahoma City, while providing funding for hundreds of other metro area school projects.

Just as the MAPS for Kids tax was nearing its end, Oklahoma City was turning into an NBA hotbed. The displaced New Orleans Hornets proved during their two-year stay from 2005–07 that Oklahoma City could support a professional basketball franchise. Prior to the Hornets' second season in town, an Oklahoma City–based ownership group purchased the Seattle SuperSonics in July 2006. Suddenly, the city's major-league dreams were gaining serious steam. Back in the mid-1990s, Norick pursued a National Hockey League franchise only to see Oklahoma City again fall short. But his vision for someday luring a major league sports franchise was the impetus for including a downtown arena in the original MAPS.

In November 2007, the Sonics filed an application with the NBA to relocate to Oklahoma City. The downtown arena built by MAPS was only five years old, and with the exception of the Central Hockey League's Oklahoma City Blazers' home dates, it sat empty on most winter nights. But it was a bare bones building built on the cheap—an initial cost of $90 million that was less than half of even the most inexpensive NBA arenas constructed at that time. Inside the arena was cold concrete that wrapped around a dark and dull 100-Level concourse. Amenities were few and far between.

Lavish facilities were nowhere to be found. The Ford Center, which it was named at the time, just wasn't fan friendly.

Oklahoma City leaders wanted to change that reality and send the NBA a message. The league's board of governors would vote on the Sonics' relocation application in April 2008, and with a long history of rejection city leaders now obsessed over gaining approval. If there was any chance the Sonics would relocate to Oklahoma City—and no one wanted to leave it to chance—the state's leaders were going to roll out the red carpet and provide first-rate accommodations.

Government officials thought to extend the MAPS for Kids tax, which was set to expire at midnight on December 31, 2008. But if Oklahoma City residents voted to extend it through June 2010, the Ford Center would receive a much-needed makeover. The tax would generate a projected $121 million, $20 million of which would be used for the construction of a standalone training facility for the Sonics. Improvements at the arena would include a new grand entrance, decorative floors and walls, new bathrooms and concession areas, new restaurants, suites, and revamped locker rooms among other bells and whistles. The renovations were deemed necessary to bring the Ford Center up to NBA standards, and passing the tax, Oklahoma City Mayor Mick Cornett claimed, was vital to the city's hopes of luring the Sonics. He also asserted the renovations would help OKC attract major concerts, Big 12 Conference and NCAA tournaments, and other events. "No one is forcing us to do this," Cornett said. "This is a choice. We can choose to be an NBA city, or we can choose not to be. We're not going to get a franchise if we don't pass it."

In January 2008, Cornett and the Greater Oklahoma City Chamber of Commerce put on a full-court press to persuade voters to pass the measure. They spearheaded a nearly two-month-long campaign. They dubbed it "Citizens for a Big League City." The campaign quickly became known simply as "Big League City." It cost $843,007, of which $385,000 was funded by the Professional Basketball Club, LLC, the Oklahoma City-based owners of the Sonics.

On March 4, 2008, residents overwhelmingly supported the proposal, with 62 percent of voters casting ballots in favor of the project. Cornett said the city's momentum was on the line with the vote and proudly expressed excitement that residents agreed. "We really are creating a city where people want to be, and this is a golden age in Oklahoma City," Cornett said after declaring victory to thunderous applause at a watch party inside a Bricktown restaurant. "I think someday we will look back and people will realize it."

Three weeks after the vote passed to renovate the Ford Center, the Sonics, led by chairman Clay Bennett, hosted the NBA's relocation committee in Oklahoma City. Three of the committee's seven members made the trip—Lewis Katz of the New Jersey Nets, Herb Simon of the Indiana Pacers, and Jeanie Buss, filling in for her father and Lakers owner Jerry Buss. They were joined by NBA Commissioner David Stern, NBA Deputy Commissioner and Chief Operating Officer Adam Silver, President of League and Basketball Operations Joel Litvin, and several other senior executives on the one-day visit.

On the same day the city council approved a 15-year lease between the Sonics and the Ford Center, the NBA brass received a comprehensive tour of the arena, viewed a thorough presentation of its planned improvements, heard ideas and concepts for the construction of the off-site practice facility, and met with city and state business and civic leaders at The Skirvin Hotel. They were floored by the unified front of a who's who of Oklahoma leaders, including Cornett, Tulsa Mayor Kathy Taylor, Governor Brad Henry, Oklahoma State House Speaker Chris Beng, former Governor Frank Keating, leading businessmen, and Sonics part owners Aubrey McClendon, Tom Ward, Jeffrey Records, Everett

Dobson, and Bob Howard, Oklahoma State University President Burns Hargis, University of Oklahoma football coach Bob Stoops, University of Oklahoma Athletic Director Joe Castiglione, and Oklahoma State University Athletic Director Mike Holder.

"There's just something about being in the room with all of the people who are in charge," said Stern, who echoed Cornett's claim when he confirmed Oklahoma City would have "no chance" of landing an NBA team if voters didn't approve tax funding for renovating the Ford Center. "I think in its totality, the way it was presented, it had a great influence on the committee members. It was very impressive, and one understands why it's more than Oklahoma City. It's Oklahoma."

On April 18, 2008, NBA owners approved the Sonics relocation to Oklahoma City by a 28–2 vote. The lone dissenters were Dallas Mavericks owner Mark Cuban, and Portland Trail Blazers owner Paul Allen, a Seattle native who also owned the NFL's Seattle Seahawks.

On July 2, 2008, the contentious court case between the Sonics and city of Seattle ended in a settlement. That day, Bennett announced the franchise would move to Oklahoma City in time to play the 2008–09 season.

Oklahoma City, finally, had become a big league city.

21 Sam Presti

Sam Presti sat to Clay Bennett's left and delivered a short opening statement at his introductory press conference as the team's general manager. When he finished, he welcomed questions.

"With that," Presti said, "I will open it up, and we can start talking about my birthday."

It was June 7, 2007. He was 29 years old.

Presti became the youngest general manager in the NBA by five years when he took over the Seattle Supersonics. He was a surprising selection, yet a rising star everyone endorsed. "When I interviewed Sam, initially I, of course, had the age in the front of my mind," said Bennett, the team chairman. "When I sat down with him, I never thought about it again. At the end, I thought it was an asset."

Along with the players he would go on to meticulously pick, Presti became the lifeblood of the Thunder. From business to basketball to benevolence, most all franchise matters have Presti's fingerprints on them. "Sam is as thorough a general manager as I've ever been around," said former Thunder coach Scott Brooks.

A native of Concord, Massachusetts, Presti stood out early and quickly found and functioned on the fast track. He studied communications, politics, and law at Emerson College, where he became the school's first Rhodes Scholar finalist. At Emerson, he was also a four-year basketball letterman, a team captain in his junior and senior seasons who once took a school-record six charges in a game. He earned All-Academic honors two times and was twice selected to the Great Northeast Athletic Conference All-Tournament team. While working a basketball camp in Aspen, Colorado, Presti met San Antonio Spurs General Manager R.C. Buford. The meeting of the minds resulted in Buford offering Presti an internship. Presti signed on in 2000. After one season, he was named the Spurs' basketball special assistant. A year later, he was promoted to assistant director of scouting. A year after that, he was named the team's director of player personnel. In September 2005, he became assistant general manager.

Presti's claim to fame with the Spurs came when, at 24, he convinced the front office brass to take a second look at an underwhelming teenage point guard from France named Tony Parker. They ultimately drafted the kid and watched him turn into an offensive maestro who helped usher in four championships. The Spurs later credited Presti for leading the design and implementation of their respected and replicated scouting database. "We knew it was a matter of time before a team came calling," said Spurs coach Gregg Popovich.

When the Sonics did, Presti arrived with all types of labels. Boy Wonder. Whiz Kid. Scouting Guru. Salary Cap Wizard. Genius. "He got the job because of who he is, how he does things," Bennett said. "He is thoughtful. He is methodical. He is measured."

Presti quickly proved his worth. He selected Kevin Durant, Russell Westbrook, and James Harden in consecutive drafts, cementing his status as one of the league's sharpest drafters. As he gradually built his roster, the Thunder improved their winning percentage in each of the team's first five seasons. They won five out of six Northwest Division titles from 2011–16. Over that same span, they journeyed to the conference finals in four of six years. In 2012, they came three wins shy of an NBA championship.

Despite the Thunder's success, Presti has never won the NBA's Executive of the Year Award. Under Presti's guidance, the Thunder's progression was organic. He built from within and looked to hit singles and doubles rather than triples and home runs. He employed prudence and patience but grew aggressive and unapologetic when opportunity arose. He quickly became one of the league's most active and audacious executives in the trade market. He traded Ray Allen for rentals, cap space, and a fifth overall draft pick that became Jeff Green. He traded Rashard Lewis in his prime for cap space and a trade exception. He traded Green, a fan favorite in Oklahoma City, for Kendrick Perkins. He traded Harden for rentals and draft picks, one of which became Steven Adams. He traded Serge Ibaka for Victor Oladipo and Domantas Sabonis. He traded Oladipo and Sabonis for Paul George. "Sam is not afraid to pull the trigger," said P.J. Carlesimo, the former coach of the Sonics/Thunder. "There are some GMs in this league who are not going to make a move until they know whether it's popular or unpopular. If he believes something is the right thing to do he's going to do it."

Critics of Presti point to the team never winning a championship in the Durant era, him pulling the trigger on the controversial Harden trade, not landing marquee free agents, and losing Durant to Golden State.

But Presti's impact extends far beyond on-court implications. Spend any time around Presti, any time at all listening to his press conferences or, better yet, paying attention to his actions, and it would soon become clear he is full of pride for his adopted home. The way he went about his business and approached his responsibilities, you knew he cared deeply not just about the Thunder organization, but also for his community and his role in it.

Presti serves on the board of the Oklahoma City National Memorial, as chairman of the Oklahoma Standard campaign and heads the Forward Thinking Leadership Development, a mentoring program for high school sophomores and juniors at three inner-city Oklahoma City high schools. His outreach efforts extended nationally and internationally, as well. He played a prominent role in Shooting Touch, a Boston-based organization that uses basketball to educate and empower at-risk youth in urban Boston and Rwanda, and in Peace Players International, which uses the game to help improve divided communities worldwide. In 2016, the Oklahoma Center for Community and Justice awarded Presti as its Humanitarian of the Year.

"I very much support his approach to building this organization on the basketball operations side," said Bennett. "But I'm most impressed with the man as an individual—his personal character, his loyalty, his sincerity in his relationships, his aspirations to always learn. His desire to always find ways to do things better is inspiring."

Sam Presti always was more than the Thunder general manager. He was an Oklahoma ambassador.

22 Scott Brooks

The Scott Brooks era began much like the P.J. Carlesimo era ended.

After receiving the reins on an interim basis following Carlesimo's dismissal, Brooks went 1–12 in his first 13 games. It was an identical record to what Carlesimo had compiled in his tenure with the Thunder during the 2008–09 season. Carlesimo was 20–62 in 2007–08 in Seattle.

There was one difference.

Improvement was evident under Brooks. The Thunder immediately became more competitive despite the mounting losses. They stood toe to toe with playoff teams and improved their margin of defeat from a ghastly 13.3 points per game under Carlesimo to 8.2 points per game in Brooks' first 13 contests.

Brooks promptly adopted a more forward-thinking approach predicated on shortening his bench, leaning on his most talented players, and putting everyone in better positions to succeed. He slid Kevin Durant from shooting guard to small forward and moved

Jeff Green from small forward to power forward. It brought about a smaller, more versatile, and more athletic lineup that used exuberance to compensate for what it lacked in experience.

Durant's minutes in Brooks' first 13 games shot up to 39.7 per game, 4.4 more per night than when he played in Carlesimo's 13 games. Brooks also kick started the Russell Westbrook era, inserting the rookie point guard as the starter only five games into his coaching tenure.

Scott Brooks, right, is largely responsible for creating the Thunder's winning culture. He compiled a 316–160 record in his final six seasons in Oklahoma City. (AP Photo/Jeff Roberson)

"He's a quick study," Brooks said of a rookie Westbrook. "He wants to be good, and he's improving every night."

Players quickly responded to Brooks. He brought credibility from his 10-year NBA playing career, which included a championship as a member of the 1994 Houston Rockets. He displayed a consistently positive demeanor, which helped stabilize and encourage an increasingly frustrated roster. He connected by replacing Carlesimo's sideline shouting with steadfast support.

Brooks was also as unassuming a coach as you will ever find at the pro level. If he had a big ego you'd never know it. Brooks was selfless and self-deprecating, gracious and grateful. He deflected credit when it was due and would have stepped down before speaking a bad word about his players publicly. Raised by a tough-as-nails single mother, Brooks, the youngest of seven, attributed his humility to his upbringing. From a personality standpoint, the new Thunder coach couldn't have been a better fit.

"Not taking anything away from P.J., he wanted the best out of us. But Scott did a great job of giving us a little bit of room for error," Durant said after Brooks' debut at New Orleans on November 22, 2008.

Starting with a New Year's Eve victory, the Thunder finished the 2008–09 season by going 20–30. The significance of that mark is made clear when you remember OKC began that season with a 3–29 record. Brooks' impact could not be denied. On the morning of the final day of the regular season, the Thunder rewarded Brooks by lifting the interim tag and inking him to a three-year contract that immediately paid dividends.

Led by Brooks, the Thunder soon established a winning culture. In his final six seasons in OKC, Brooks compiled a 316–160 record. He steered the Thunder to a league-best 27-game improvement in 2009–10 and won Coach of the Year that season. He led the Thunder to the Western Conference finals in 2011, the NBA Finals in 2012, a 60-win season in 2013, and another

Western Conference finals berth in 2014. He also helped develop Durant into a scoring champion and league MVP, James Harden into a Sixth Man of the Year, Serge Ibaka into a three-time All-Defensive First Team selection, and Westbrook into the most electric point guard the game has ever seen.

"Those are things that I can never ever, ever take for granted," Brooks said. "It wasn't because of me. It was because we had great players who continued to work together and build themselves and compete against themselves in practices and have that competitive spirit at 7:00 PM every night."

23 Bye-bye, Scott Brooks

Unfulfilled postseason runs and an unbelievably unfortunate run of injuries marred the Scott Brooks era and left the basketball world to wonder what could have been.

By repeatedly falling short of a championship, the Thunder opened the door for observers near the end of Brooks' tenure to question whether he had taken the team as far as he could. As the years went by, critics began picking apart Brooks' coaching acumen, blaming him for the Thunder's basic offense, a rigid, almost robotic substitution pattern, an overreliance on veterans who were past their primes, being slow to make in-game adjustments, and for lackluster late-game play-calling.

Like most coaches tasked with guiding great talent, Brooks' impact was devalued and he became an easy target. But two post-season gaffes came to define Brooks as much as all the winning. The first came during the 2012 Finals.

Against a Miami Heat squad that was ushering in a new brand of small ball, Brooks stubbornly stuck with his customary starting lineup that featured two big men, Serge Ibaka at power forward and Kendrick Perkins at center. Both became victims of problematic matchups, Perkins being charged with keeping up with the increasingly perimeter-oriented Chris Bosh and Ibaka being pulled away from his natural post as rim protector to defend a deadly spot-up shooter in Shane Battier.

It was an obvious disadvantage, a chess match everyone could see Heat coach Erik Spoelstra was winning. After only two games, Sebastian Pruiti, a respected blogger who pioneered in-depth film studies on play-calling, asked, "When is Scott Brooks going to get tired of falling behind early because Kendrick Perkins is in?"

A week later the Thunder were watching the Heat hoist the Larry O'Brien trophy. After taking a 1–0 lead, Oklahoma City lost four straight. The Thunder's most used lineup was their starting five: Russell Westbrook, Thabo Sefolosha, Kevin Durant, Ibaka, and Perkins. They were outscored by 22 points, the most among all lineups. The Heat's most used lineup was their starting five: Mario Chalmers, Dwyane Wade, LeBron James, Battier, and Bosh. They outscored the Thunder by 17 points, tied for the second highest among all lineups. Miami shot 43 percent from three-point range in the series.

Brooks never made the adjustment.

Pruiti was hired by the Thunder three months later as a video analyst.

The next postseason saw Brooks make the same mistake, only this time the Thunder narrowly avoided elimination. In a first-round series with Houston, the top-seeded Thunder were the heavy favorite. But much like Miami, the Rockets baffled Brooks and the Thunder with a small-ball lineup that utilized only one big man and spaced the floor with shooters.

After starting two big men in Game 1, Houston coach Kevin McHale promptly pinpointed the edge and downsized his first five the rest of the way. By the second half of Game 3, the Rockets most-used starting lineup—Patrick Beverley, James Harden, Chandler Parsons, Francisco Garcia, and Omer Asik—began to pulverize its counterparts, an emergency unit of Sefolosha, Durant, Ibaka, Perkins, and Reggie Jackson, who stepped in for the injured Westbrook. Predictably, the Thunder again struggled to defend the perimeter and watched Houston grow confident enough to turn a 3–0 series deficit into a hard-fought six-game series. Over the final 14 quarters, the Rockets shot 42 percent from beyond the three-point line.

Even though Brooks was dealt some hard injury luck—Westbrook's knee in 2013, Ibaka's calf in 2014, Durant's foot in 2015—the memory of such noticeable strategic slip-ups became hard to erase. More significantly, they forced the Thunder to answer the question everyone had been asking: was Brooks the right man to get Oklahoma City over the hump? The answer came on April 22, 2015, the day the Thunder fired Brooks with one season remaining on his contract.

The decision stunned most given Brooks had just turned in perhaps his finest coaching job yet. He kept the Thunder afloat despite a tumultuous season in which players missed a combined 220 games due to injury/illness. Durant missed 55 games, Ibaka 18, and Westbrook 15. Still, the Thunder missed the playoffs only on a lost tiebreaker to New Orleans, which finished with an identical 45–37 record.

It was the first time the Thunder had missed the playoffs since 2009, but Thunder General Manager Sam Presti made it clear the decision to part ways was not based on the result of Brooks' final season. In doing so, Presti confirmed the front office felt Brooks had indeed taken the team as far as he could.

"It is very important to state that this decision is not a reflection of this past season, but rather an assessment of what we feel is necessary at this point in time in order to continually evolve, progress, and sustain," Presti said. "We determined that, in order to stimulate progress and put ourselves in the best position next season and as we looked to the future, a transition of this kind was necessary for the program."

24 Hello, Billy Donovan

One week after the Thunder fired coach Scott Brooks following the 2014–15 season, the team announced Billy Donovan as its new lead man.

To some, it was a questionable hire. Donovan was a college coach with no NBA experience. Add to that, Kevin Durant was entering the final year of his contract, and here was the Thunder handing the keys to a man who was accustomed to coaching 19-year-olds.

But this wasn't Leonard Hamilton going from the Miami Hurricanes to the Washington Wizards, or Reggie Theus from New Mexico State to the Sacramento Kings, or Tim Floyd from Iowa State to the Chicago Bulls. This was Billy Donovan, a two-time national championship–winning coach at the University of Florida, a man who, in addition to his impeccable resume, had a long track record of leading NBA talent.

In 19 seasons guiding the Gators, Donovan led the program to seven Elite Eights, four Final Fours, and back-to-back titles in 2006 and 2007. In Gainesville, he oversaw the development of more than a dozen future pros, including Al Horford, Joakim

Noah, Corey Brewer, Chandler Parsons, Bradley Beal, David Lee, and Mike Miller among others. Still a month shy of his 50th birthday at the time of his hire, Donovan had amassed 502 career college victories. Bobby Knight was the only other coach with at least 500 victories before his 50th birthday. Mike Krzyzewski and Jim Calhoun were the only coaches with more national titles than Donovan in 20 years preceding his hire.

And then there was this—Donovan had 21 years of head coaching experience, including his two-year stint at Marshall.

After 19 seasons and two national championships at the University of Florida, Billy Donovan, right, jumped to the NBA as head coach of the Thunder prior to the 2015–16 season. (AP Photo/Darren Abate)

Brooks, the same age as Donovan, had only seven, all coming with the Thunder.

"You can't just downplay what he's done in the college ranks and just automatically say he's not going to be great in the pros," Durant said.

In his near 40-minute introduction to the Oklahoma City media, Donovan answered every question about the challenges he would face jumping from college to the pros. He did so thoughtfully and thoroughly, confidently and candidly. When he spoke, Donovan exuded self-assurance. He was even self-deprecating, delivering the perfect punchline to a question about his lack of professional coaching experience.

"I've been an NBA coach before. It was only for a day," he said, referencing the Orlando Magic coaching job he accepted in 2007 before backing out a day later to return to Florida.

Donovan didn't come into the job claiming to have all the answers. He actually displayed the complete opposite approach, likening his transition to "starting from scratch." But he covered his blind spots by surrounding himself with experienced NBA coaches. He hired Maurice Cheeks and Monty Williams as assistants, both of whom had been head coaches in recent years. Cheeks was an assistant under Brooks from 2009 to 2013 and was returning to OKC after serving as head coach in Detroit in 2013–14. Williams had just been fired after five seasons as the head coach of the New Orleans Hornets/Pelicans. Donovan was also well connected and could tap into the minds of many—Rick Pitino, his mentor and former coach at Providence and with the New York Knicks. Jeff Van Gundy, a former assistant during his days at Providence. Lon Kruger, the man he succeeded at Florida who was 30 minutes south coaching the University of Oklahoma's men's basketball team.

"One of the things with me is I'm going to work extremely hard," Donovan said. "I'm curious to learn and grow. I think there's unbelievable people that are going to be around me. I'm excited about learning and growing. That's really, really important to me. And I hope I can put people inside the organization, and even the players, in a position where they can learn and grow as well."

Much of the reason the Thunder identified and selected Donovan was because the team had begun stagnating, if not regressing. Presti and the front office wanted a new voice with new philosophies, a coach who could clean up the Thunder's bad habits and continue moving the franchise forward.

"We wanted to identify a person with the traits associated with high achieving leaders in their respective fields; a continuous learning mentality, the ability to adapt, evolve, and innovate, intrinsically motivated, humility, and great tactical competence," Presti said.

It was those final three words that jumped out—great tactical competence. Many felt Donovan had it. Many grew to learn Brooks did not. Donovan believed in a simple philosophy but one the Thunder had long struggled to embrace.

Player movement. Ball movement. Extra pass.

"And creating multiple actions on different sides of the floor," Donovan added. "Keeping the floor moving, keeping it spaced, and the ball continuing to move."

Progress would soon be evident. In the Thunder's first season under Donovan the team went 55–27 and enjoyed its highest offensive rating to that point, 113.1 points per 100 possessions. Oklahoma City ranked third in field goal percentage and 10th in assists per game, the first time the franchise had cracked the top 10 in assists. Under Brooks, the Thunder ranked in the top 20 only once, finishing 13th in 2013–14. OKC also ranked first in rebounding and fifth in defensive field goal percentage.

The team's development was never more apparent than in the 2016 playoffs. It was Donovan's shining moment. The Thunder averaged 20.5 assists, their highest of any postseason, raced to

108.5 points per 100 possessions, and outscored opponents by 5.3 points per game, also a franchise best mark. Along the way, Donovan turned Andre Roberson into an offensive threat, Serge Ibaka into a three-point shooting terror and defensive menace in small-ball lineups, Dion Waiters into a surprisingly savvy two-way player, and Enes Kanter and Steven Adams into a lethal 1-2 punch.

"I thought Billy did an excellent job through the year," Presti said. "He was intentional. He was curious. He was supremely disciplined.... I thought he had an excellent first year."

25 What Is a Jones Fracture?

The first major problem in a potentially promising 2014–15 Thunder season arrived remarkably early. It was an unforeseen hurdle, a force so far out of left field you never could have fathomed it would derail the team's championship hopes.

It was the preseason.

Rookie forward Mitch McGary, in his debut with the Thunder after being selected 21st overall, fractured the second metatarsal in his left foot in the exhibition opener at Denver. A day later, the Thunder announced the skilled big man out of Michigan would miss five to seven weeks, joining many of his sick-and-sidelined teammates who had dropped like flies. Three days later, the Thunder's real problems began.

On October 12, 2014, the Thunder announced Kevin Durant had been diagnosed with a Jones fracture, a broken bone at the base of his right small toe, the fifth metatarsal. The league's reigning Most Valuable Player would require surgery and six to eight weeks of recovery.

Many had never heard of a Jones fracture. Thunder General Manager Sam Presti explained it was a stress injury, meaning it occurred over time as opposed to one specific incident. That still didn't diminish the disbelief and certainly not the disappointment. Durant had played in each of the team's first two exhibition games and showed no signs of discomfort. He scored 11 points in 12 minutes against the Nuggets and followed that with 12 points in 18 minutes two nights later at Dallas. Following a team practice in Oklahoma City the day after the Mavs game, Durant went to the Thunder's medical staff reporting pain in his foot. He immediately received an MRI, which revealed the fracture. It was the first time Durant had expressed pain or discomfort in his foot. "We're very fortunate that Kevin notified us yesterday, and we're catching it on the front end before this became a little bit more of an acute issue," Presti told the media a day later.

Four days later, on Thursday, October 16, 2014, Durant underwent surgery at the OrthoCarolina Foot and Ankle Clinic in Charlotte, North Carolina. The operation was performed by Dr. Robert Anderson. He inserted a screw in Durant's foot to facilitate healing. Estimates based on the initial announced recovery time projected Durant to miss the first 15-20 games of the regular season. When he addressed the media on the Tuesday following surgery, rolling into his news conference on a knee scooter with his propped-up right lower leg snugly wrapped in a cast, Durant vowed to give his recovery however long it needed. "I'm not going to rush it at all," he said. "That's one thing I'm not going to do."

Durant had enjoyed exceptional health throughout his first seven NBA seasons, appearing in 542 of a possible 558 regular season games. He was every bit as dependable as he was durable, averaging 38.2 minutes for his career in the regular season and 42.3 minutes in 73 postseason games. But those mounting minutes, coupled with his time with Team USA and his penchant for playing summer pick-up ball, might have contributed to the injury. Durant

The Foot

Wondering why Kevin Durant's famous foot injury from the 2014–15 season is referred to as a Jones fracture? It's named after the late orthopedic surgeon, Robert Jones, who first identified the injury by self-diagnosis in 1902. Jones said he sustained the ailment as a result of dancing, a fact that has led some to refer to it as the Dancer's fracture.

had logged 20,717 minutes since entering the NBA in 2007, more than any player over that span. LeBron James ranked second to that point at 20,215. Only three other players had reached 19,000 total minutes over those seven seasons.

Prior to his foot injury, Durant's longest continuous absence was a seven-game stretch during the 2008–09 season, his second year. When asked what's the most serious injury he had endured previously Durant said a "couple sprained ankles." His fractured foot, however, forced him to miss the season's first 17 games. The Thunder went 5–12 without him in that stretch.

Durant made his season debut on December 2, 2014, in a road game against New Orleans. While on a 30-minute restriction, Durant scored 27 points on 9-for-18 shooting in an eight-point loss. "I'm just glad I'm out there playing, man," Durant said after the game. "Once you're away from the game so much you just appreciate every second you're on the floor. That's how I felt tonight."

The feeling was fleeting.

Nine games into his return, Durant rolled his right ankle on December 18 at Golden State. He stepped on the foot of Warriors center Marreese Speights while driving to the basket just before halftime. It was the same foot Durant had surgically repaired two months earlier. Speights slid in to take a charge. Durant got the worst of it. Durant exited the game and did not return. He'd just poured in a season-high 30 points in only 19 first-half minutes, setting a new mark for the most he had ever scored in a half. "I felt like I was starting to hit my stride and feel better," Durant later said. The team listed Durant's injury as a mild ankle sprain, and Durant said it wasn't serious. But he missed the next six games, including a showcase Christmas game at San Antonio, and his extended absence sparked fear the injury was more than the team was letting on. "It's not like I might have surgery or my foot is messed up," Durant said.

After going 3–3 while he nursed the sprain, the Thunder welcomed back Durant on New Year's Eve against Phoenix. He erupted for 44 points, 10 rebounds, and seven assists. He made 13-of-23 shots in 40 minutes to lead the Thunder to a three-point win. He looked like his old self. And in a 12-game stretch starting with that victory over the Suns, Durant averaged 27.9 points, eight rebounds, 4.5 assists, and 1.1 blocked shots in 36.9 minutes. But a sprained left big toe then cost him 4-of-5 games from January 26 to February 4.

Injury History

Prior to his injury-plagued 2014–15 season, Kevin Durant missed only 16 of a possible 558 regular season games (or 631 if you include the postseason). Here is a quick look at Durant's prior injury history:

2013–14: Missed one game with a strained shoulder.

2012–13: Sat the last regular season game to rest for the playoffs.

2010–11: Missed two games with a sprained left ankle and two games with a sprained left knee.

2008–09: Missed one game with a sprained left ankle and seven games with a sprained right ankle.

2007–08: Missed one game with a sprained finger and one game with the flu.

When he returned from that setback, he played five games and appeared in obvious discomfort. Whenever he wasn't on the court, he wore a bulky, black protective boot to alleviate pressure from both his toe and what the team insisted was "general soreness" stemming from surgery. His production didn't hint at a problem. He averaged 30.5 points in his first four games back from a bum toe. But Durant didn't look healthy. In that fourth game, a home date with Memphis that was the final contest before All-Star Weekend, Durant limped around the court, wincing and grimacing as he attempted to play through discomfort. After the game, Durant spent nearly an hour getting treatment before leaving the arena in a pair of black Nike slippers. He couldn't even put on a pair of shoes. Something clearly wasn't right. But the Thunder insisted he wasn't at risk of further injury, and Durant was determined to travel to New York to partake in All-Star festivities. "He is sore," Thunder coach Scott Brooks said. "But that's part of the process."

Durant played 10 minutes in the 2015 All-Star Game, a career low. The owner of the highest scoring average in NBA All-Star Game history finished with just three points. In his first game out of the break, Durant played 37 minutes, scoring just 12 points on 4-for-14 shooting. It was his last game of the season.

On Sunday, February 22, 2015, Durant underwent a second surgery to his right foot to alleviate increasing soreness. This time, the initial screw inserted into Durant's foot was replaced with a different type of screw. The first screw, which had a head, was said to be pushing against another bone, causing his soreness. The new screw did not have a head. Publicly, Thunder officials remained encouraged, saying Durant would be re-evaluated in one week. "The good news is the fracture itself is healing excellently, and from what the doctors conveyed to us we continue to feel very good about the prognosis moving forward," Presti relayed.

One month later, Durant again began experiencing foot soreness. Durant had increased his on-court activity and even participated in portions of team practices. Further consultations with multiple doctors, however, found continued inflammation. It was determined Durant's Jones fracture was now showing signs of regression. On March 31, 2015, Durant underwent a third surgery, this time a bone graft. The operation was performed by Dr. Martin O'Malley at the Hospital for Special Surgery in New York. Durant would need four to six months just to return to basketball-related activities. His 2014–15 season was done.

Durant appeared in only 27 games that season, averaging 25.4 points, 6.6 rebounds, and 4.1 assists in 33.8 minutes. The Thunder went 18–9 with him in the lineup and 27–28 without him. "You don't replace Kevin Durant," Presti said. Oklahoma City missed the playoffs for the first time since 2009 after finishing with an identical 45–37 record as New Orleans. The Pelicans won the tie-breaker with a 3–1 head-to-head record over the Thunder.

It was the last of three straight years of injury-related gut punches to the Thunder's postseason chances. A franchise that had enjoyed exceptional health for four consecutive seasons suddenly had become snake bitten ever since Russell Westbrook went down in the first round of the 2013 playoffs.

An organization that once seemed destined for a dynasty after journeying to the 2012 NBA Finals, Oklahoma City never made it back.

Following his final surgery, Durant posted a picture of himself resting in his hospital bed. The accompanying message, a 129-word note of positive reassurance to his fans, effectively summed up both his and the Thunder's year in only the first sentence.

"Not what I envisioned coming into this season," Durant wrote.

26 Welcome to the 50-40-90 Club

Kevin Durant didn't deny or downplay his aspirations. He knew all about the illustrious 50-40-90 club, and he wanted in.

Etching his name among the list of the game's all-time elite shooters had been a goal Durant carried since his second season. It wasn't until his sixth season, the 2012–13 campaign, that Durant finally gained admittance.

A footnote in the season that saw the Thunder defiantly post a banner 60 wins after the preseason trade of James Harden was Durant becoming only the sixth player in NBA history to shoot at least 50 percent from the field, 40 percent from three-point range, and 90 percent from the foul line. The others were Larry Bird, Mark Price, Reggie Miller, Steve Nash, and Dirk Nowitzki. Bird accomplished the feat twice. Nash pulled it off four times. Stephen Curry would later become the seventh name on the list following the 2015–16 season. Durant, though, was the youngest to join the club when he did so at just 24.

Durant averaged 28.1 points, 7.9 rebounds, 4.6 assists, 1.4 steals, and 1.3 blocked shots while playing 81 games in that season. His final shooting numbers were 51 percent from the floor, 41.6 percent from long distance, and 90.5 percent from the foul line.

"To be his size, to be that athletic, to be able to shoot that well, the guy is off the charts," said Mark Jackson, the former point guard turned color commentator and coach. "And he's efficient. I think those numbers speak volumes about how efficient he is as a basketball player. This game has not seen anybody like Kevin Durant in its history."

Durant was spectacularly steady during what was then the most efficient season of his career. He scored at least 20 points 71 times and shot at least 45 percent on 62 occasions. He made all of his free throws in 33 contests, and that included a 21-for-21 night in a 52-point eruption at Dallas in mid-January.

"He could easily score 35 to 37 a night on 40-40-90," said Kevin Martin, the stopgap sharpshooter OKC received from Houston in the Harden trade. "But that's just not him. He's in it for the team and that's why he's such a special player."

Durant tailored his game to ensure he'd secure such lofty shooting splits. After hovering around 20 shots per game the previous three seasons, he hoisted only 17.7 in 2012–13, the fewest since his 17.1 average as a rookie. His three-pointers also plummeted from more than five per game the previous two seasons to a 4.1 average. Late that season Durant divulged that maintaining a 40-percent three-point clip was his most difficult category.

"Because you can easily have a bad three-point shooting week or a month," Durant explained. "I remember I went 0-for-6 against Denver and all of them looked good. So it's not one of those things where you lose your confidence, but all your shots look good and you still want to continue to shoot them over again because the ones you missed looked like they were on line. So it's kind of difficult. It messes with your head a little bit."

As a counter, Durant shored up his shot selection. He deliberately traded in certain long-distance heaves for more high-percentage drives to the basket. He averaged 4.6 assists that season, then a career best, and his improved playmaking skills soon served as a healthy alternative to settling for a contested shot. Still, Durant's 17.7 average attempts ranks as the fourth highest total among 50-40-90 seasons, trailing Bird's 22 attempts per game and Bird and Curry's 20.2 shots per game. Nowitzki, who took 17.2 shots per game in 2006–07, is the only other player in the club who has averaged more than 13.5 shots.

"That's truly historic," said Nash of Durant.

Durant had spent the previous two seasons grooming to take his place among the game's greatest shooters. He bulked up and adapted to physical play, which allowed him to become a better finisher in the paint and at the rim. He embraced coach Scott Brooks' oft-questioned decision to deploy him at all five positions, giving him the chance to play closer to the rim and grow comfortable creating with the ball in his hands. He even hired an analytics specialist whose sole job was to dissect how he could be more efficient. The end result was Durant seeing the game differently, thinking it differently.

"Let's say you've got 40 apples on your tree. I could eat about 30 of them, but I've begun limiting myself to 15 or 16," Durant explained in an April 2013 *Sports Illustrated* cover story. "Let's take the wide-open three and the post-up at the nail. Those are good apples. Let's throw out the pull-up three in transition and the step-back fadeaway. Those are rotten apples. The three at the top of the circle, that's an in-between apple. We only want the very best on the tree."

Asked where he ranks his 50-40-90 club status, Durant didn't hesitate.

"Right up there with the First Team All-NBA," he said.

27 Sixth Man of the Year

James Harden went into the season wanting to win the award. He made no secret about his desire.

"That's definitely one of my goals," he admitted.

If he was going to come off the bench again, he wanted to be the best bench player he could be. That meant being the best bench player in the NBA.

Harden had averaged 15.8 points on 46.5 percent shooting after the All-Star break in 2010–11. In the 2011 Western Conference finals against Dallas he was virtually unstoppable, serving as the ideal buffer between Russell Westbrook and Kevin Durant and showing he was ready to bloom in his third season. Going into the 2011–12 season, most felt Harden had earned a promotion into the starting lineup. But with the 2011 lockout being lifted only 17 days before the start of the regular season, no one was sure what coach Scott Brooks would do with his lineup.

"If that's his role this year, he should be in that race," Thunder reserve center Nazr Mohammed said. "There's no reason why he shouldn't be Sixth Man of the Year."

Prior to the season, 11-of-30 ESPN writers and analysts predicted Harden would win the award. Lamar Odom and Jason Terry tied for second in their predictions with four votes each.

"He's got a chance to fight for it," Odom said of Harden. "He's one of the best bench players in the league. He's definitely a game-changer.... He's got a lot of game."

Harden spent the entire season showing the world.

Harden averaged 16.8 points, 4.1 rebounds, and 3.7 assists—all career-highs to that point—and helped lead the Thunder to a 47–19 record and their second consecutive Northwest Division title. He ran away with the award, receiving 584 of a possible 595 points, including 115 first-place votes from a panel of 119 sportswriters and broadcasters throughout the U.S. and Canada. At 22, Harden became the second youngest Sixth Man in league history, only months older than Ben Gordon when he won it in 2005. Philadelphia guard Lou Williams finished second in the voting, with Terry coming in third.

"In our eyes, James has won an award for far more than simply being a productive player," Thunder General Manager Sam Presti said. "The Sixth Man of the Year Award is not only an award for on-court production that enables team success, but above all else it acknowledges sacrifice and commitment to the greater good of the team. It's special and fitting to have James recognized for this award because it really does symbolize so many of the attributes that we want the Thunder to be known for many years to come."

Brooks remembered meeting James for lunch in the summer of 2011. The conversation the two had that day marked the moment he believed Harden was committed to coming off the bench.

"I just asked him, 'What are your goals going into the summer?' thinking that he would tell me, 'I want to start,'" Brooks said. "All he said was, 'Coach, I want to do whatever it takes for the team to get better.' And right then and there I knew that he had bought in to the job that we needed him to do."

Harden didn't always have that mindset.

"Being drafted with the third overall pick, most guys would come in and think that they're going to be a starter on any team," Harden said. "At first, as a rookie, I didn't get it. I just thought I was going to go in there and score and just do all the things that every other player thought."

But Harden quickly learned to accept the role and excel at it despite sacrificing minutes and scoring opportunities. He had a gift for fitting with any group Brooks threw on the floor and consistently coming into the game ready to make an immediate impact.

By the 2011–12 season, Harden also had developed unflappable confidence.

"A lot of guys convince themselves that they can't be as effective coming off the bench," said Dallas coach Rick Carlisle, who coached four former Sixth Man of the Year winners in Odom and Terry with the Mavericks, Corliss Williamson with the Pistons, and Darrell Armstrong with the Pacers.

At 22 years old, James Harden became the second youngest player in league history to win the Sixth Man of the Year Award when he took home the honor for the 2011–12 season. (AP Photo/Sue Ogrocki)

Harden went the other way. On a team with Westbrook, Durant, Jeff Green, and Serge Ibaka, touches were sparse. He had to do more with less. So he found his niche in the second unit. But it wasn't until the 2011 trading deadline, when the Thunder sent Green and Nenad Krstic to Boston for Kendrick Perkins, that Harden fully seized control of the second string.

"I had to make sure every single game I was focused on doing my role at its best," Harden said.

Harden shot 50 percent or better in 34 of his 62 games that season. He scored at least 20 points 15 times, shooting an incredible 63.2 percent when he topped the 20-point mark. Even after going on to become an MVP candidate in Houston, his 49.1 percent field goal shooting and .660 true shooting percentage from that 2011–12 season remained career best marks through his first eight seasons.

"He had that command of the second unit," Durant said. "He knew that was his group. I would sit down on the bench and play 21 minutes sometimes because they'd take the game over and we'd win by 20 or 30. It was just a joy to see. Then he had 40 coming off the bench one night and I was like, 'Yeah, this guy's different.'"

That 40-point night came in a win at Phoenix on April 18, 2012. Harden scorched the Suns by sinking 12-of-17 shots, 11-of-11 free throws, and 5-of-8 three-pointers. He added seven rebounds, three assists, and four steals in 36 minutes.

"Playing with the second unit, he's our KD," Mohammed said.

For how much longer soon became the question. Harden was emerging not just as a bona fide starter but a star. By then, the world could see it.

"If we're winning championships, I have no problem," Harden said. "That's all that matters—championships."

28 A Star Is Born

Kevin Durant was god-awful.

There's really no other way to put it.

In the same season that he captained his team to a 27-win improvement, earned his first All-Star selection, and captured his first scoring title, Durant made his highly anticipated postseason debut. It came against the defending champion Los Angeles Lakers in a 1–8 matchup to open the 2010 playoffs. But with bulldog Ron Artest blanketing him throughout the series, Durant was dreadful. He finished Game 1 with 24 points on 7-for-24 shooting, the first of four games in which he shot less than 40 percent.

Meanwhile, the Thunder had a Tasmanian devil who couldn't be stopped in second-year point guard Russell Westbrook. In that same Game 1, Westbrook scored 23 points with four rebounds, eight assists, and only one turnover. He made 10-of-16 shots in 38 minutes. The Thunder lost by eight that night, but it was clear what needed to happen.

The Thunder was going to have to let Westbrook be Westbrook. That meant no more taking a backseat in the offense. No more playing a supporting role. No more deferring to Durant.

"Here's the startling truth about Game 1: For maybe the first time in the Thunder's two-year history, Kevin Durant wasn't Option A," *The Oklahoman* columnist Berry Tramel wrote.

This was Russell Westbrook's coming out party.

He was 21 years old. He should have been a senior in college. Instead, he was shredding the defending champs.

A 12-minute stretch spanning the second and third quarters of Game 1 showed just how special Westbrook could be. With the Thunder offense stuck in neutral, Westbrook scored every field goal for the Thunder, netting 17 of his team's 18 points in that span to single-handedly keep the Lakers from turning the contest into a laugher. He unleashed a beautiful blend of hard drives to the basket and an array of rhythmic jump shots that kept the Lakers off balance.

Over the next five games, Westbrook drove the Lakers crazy with more of the same. In the process, he became the Thunder's lone consistent source of offense. More than that, he was the best player in the series.

"He's the guy on that team who runs the show," Lakers reserve guard Jordan Farmar said during the series. "Kevin Durant's the scorer, but everything runs through Russ."

The matchup was tailor-made for Westbrook. Starting at point guard across from him was Derek Fisher, then a 35-year-old who was still tough and tenacious but had no chance of slowing Westbrook. Everyone knew at the start of the series that Westbrook held a huge advantage and would likely have his way.

By the end of Game 4, Westbrook was averaging 21.8 points on 55.2 percent shooting, and the Thunder had stormed back to tie the series 2–2. That's when Kobe Bryant, through his actions, paid Westbrook the ultimate compliment. Then a nine-time All-Defensive Team selection, Bryant switched onto Westbrook defensively for Game 5. If nothing else, the wrinkle threw off Westbrook's rhythm. He scored just 15 points on only 4-for-13 shooting. Once-open driving lanes dried up with Bryant attached to him. Layups turned into jumpers. Rhythmic mid-range shots became three-pointers. The comfort Westbrook enjoyed from Games 1 through 4 was gone. He committed eight turnovers in Game 5. The Lakers won by 24 to take a 3–2 lead.

"He's been playing sensational," Bryant said of Westbrook after the game. "If we're going to be eliminated, then I don't want to go into the summer thinking I could have done something about it. So I accept the challenge."

The adjustment helped change the complexion of the series, but it cemented Westbrook's status as a rising star. But in typical Westbrook fashion, he didn't concern himself with the significance of Bryant's switch.

"It's not like he's the best defender in the world," Westbrook said prior to Game 6. "I don't think he's, like, the best defender in the NBA to where I'm like, 'Okay, Kobe's guarding me now,' and I tighten up."

The statement was a sneak peek into the mental toughness that transformed Westbrook from an overlooked high school prospect into one of the most competitive players the NBA has ever seen.

In Game 6, Westbrook then poured in 21 points, albeit on 7-for-20 shooting, and added five rebounds, nine assists, and three steals against zero turnovers in 42 minutes. The Lakers won and advanced on a last-second tip-in by Pau Gasol.

But the basketball world never looked at Westbrook the same. He had arrived. He joined Bryant and LeBron James as the only players that postseason to average at least 20 points, six rebounds, and five assists. His final numbers: 20.5 points, six rebounds, six assists, 1.7 steals, and only 2.3 turnovers. He shot 47.3 percent—41.7 percent from three-point range, and 84.2 percent from the foul line—while playing 35.3 minutes per game. With his blazing speed, sneaky steals, high-soaring dunks, and unbridled passion, Westbrook commanded the attention of the casual fan and soon blossomed into one of the biggest matchup problems in all of basketball.

"To be able to play well in the playoffs is the ultimate confidence booster for anybody," Nick Collison said. "It's such a better feeling to go home in the summer knowing you've played well and you played well for your team in the playoffs. I think that'll be huge for him."

29 The New Orleans/ Oklahoma City Hornets

George Shinn was a showman.

More than that, the former New Orleans Hornets owner was a salesman. And there was one sales pitch Shinn was particularly fond of.

"I can't guarantee that we're going to win," Shinn would say. "But I can guarantee you're going to have a good time."

For two seasons, Shinn made good on that promise.

From September 2005 through April 2007, Oklahoma City was home to the displaced New Orleans Hornets, uprooted in the wake of destruction brought about by Hurricane Katrina. Through an agreement with the NBA, the team was officially called the New Orleans/Oklahoma City Hornets. Most times, the team referred to itself simply as "your hometown Hornets." Their stay was a smashing success, and it was that unique two-year trial run that paved the way for the Thunder.

"The energy was incredible," said Desmond Mason, a former Oklahoma State star who played on those Hornets teams and later the Thunder in their inaugural season. "All you heard about was the Hornets, everywhere you went, and how proud people were. And how excited they were for the team to be here."

The Hornets played 36 of their 41 2005–06 home games inside what was then known as the Ford Center. They played another 35 home games in OKC in 2006–07. The remaining 11 home games over their two displaced seasons were split between New Orleans (nine), Baton Rouge, and Norman. The Hornets went 43–28 in Oklahoma City and sold out 30-of-71 games played in OKC. In their first season in town, the Hornets averaged 18,717 fans in games played inside the Ford Center. That attendance would have ranked the Hornets ninth among the league's 30 teams in 2005–06. In New Orleans the season before, the team drew a league-worst 14,221 fans per game.

It was a remarkable show of support by a community that had only 40 days from the announcement of the temporary move to opening night. It was unprecedented for a team that finished a dismal 18–64 the previous season and arrived with a roster void of a single household name. But when fans showed up largely because of civic pride, they had no idea they would walk away hooked on the NBA.

Meanwhile, the league office was watching what Oklahoma City was doing. A city that only a few months earlier was nowhere near the NBA's radar suddenly was providing overwhelming evidence that it could support a major league franchise. Approximately 11,500 season tickets had been purchased. The business community buoyed the franchise with lucrative sponsorships. Five corporations paid $1.5 million apiece to become the team's "pioneer partners." Less than a month into OKC's inaugural Hornets season, then NBA Commissioner David Stern proclaimed, "In my view, they've moved to the top of the list if an NBA team were ready to move."

The success sparked heightened expectations. Once Oklahomans got a taste of the Hornets, they had trouble letting go. They had welcomed the franchise like a homeowner opening his home to a guest. They soon eyed the Hornets like a hound that spotted steak. Fans thought of the team as theirs. Many wanted the Hornets to stay. With the city of New Orleans on the long, hard road to recovery, and the reality of the Hornets receiving poor support in their three seasons prior to Hurricane Katrina, the prevailing belief was the franchise was better off in Oklahoma City. It became a delicate dance for OKC's cautious civic leaders and the team's colorful owner. Words were dissected. Announcements picked apart. Decisions despised. Everything was scrutinized, from the official team name, to the "OKC" patches just above the right pec, to how long the Hornets would stay in Oklahoma City, to whether they ever would go back to New Orleans, to any complimentary statement about the other state.

And rightfully so.

New Orleans, in the months that followed the costliest and third-deadliest hurricane in U.S. history, needed hope. The Hornets returning and committing to a rebuilding community represented exactly that. Oklahomans, on the other hand, had never had a major league franchise, and most natives thought they never would see the day they did. The Hornets turned them optimistic.

On winter nights, Oklahomans became exposed to entertainment unlike anything they had ever seen. Elements that now are staples in the Thunder's game-night presentation were presented by the Hornets. The list is long, and Thunder fans have come to love most everything on it: a pregame invocation, standing until the home team scores its first basket, tributes to Loud City, the Kiss Cam, the Dance Cam, pulsating music one second, a familiar jingle when a player scores the next, the "MidFirst Bank Show Me the Money" contest, halfcourt shots, bat spin relays, trampoline dunk artists, makeshift Mardi Gras parties, Rob Nice, Hugo the Hornet, and OKC's first dance team darlings, the Honeybees.

"The one thing that we could control, the one thing we could make sure of, is that everybody who paid for a ticket and came into that game left knowing that they had a great time whether or not the team won," Michael Thompson said.

Thompson played a big part. The fabulous former Hornets public address announcer, who no one could ever demand he "stick to his day job" as the team's director of corporate communications, created the revered call-and-response line, "Whose ball is it? Hornets ball." The Thunder still use the call. Thompson first used it on November 1, 2005, opening night. The Hornets hosted Sacramento.

"I remember we trapped somebody and turned them over. And I can remember Byron Scott jumping up off the bench clapping. And that was the first time I did it," Thompson said. "I said, 'Whose ball is it?' And it wasn't the entire crowd. But there were enough people that kind of said 'Hornets ball.' And we looked at each other and we said, 'That actually worked.'"

Not much went wrong for the Hornets in Oklahoma City. It was a two-year love affair everyone knew from the start was temporary. Still, that didn't stop most Oklahomans from growing strong feelings. "You have to think about it in a short-term way, so that you don't end up crushed when the day comes the team is gone," advised Clay Bennett, the local business and community leader who helped orchestrate the Hornets' temporary stay.

But, Bennett added, "I would be surprised if we go through this and somehow don't have a team," he said.

30 Air Congo

Kevin Durant recovered a loose ball just beyond the free throw line with only two seconds showing on the shot clock. When he snatched the ball out of the air, he quickly gathered his feet and fired a 15' jumper that hit back iron and ricocheted high in front of the rim. Three Toronto Raptors stood in the paint waiting to collect the rebound. One Thunder player went up and got it.

It was Serge Ibaka, who flew in past Amir Johnson and skied for a powerful two-handed putback dunk.

"How about Serge Ibaka? That is nasty!" the Raptors broadcaster exclaimed.

Ibaka swung on the rim for a second, and as his feet hit the floor his arms were spread wide, exposing his massive 7'3" wingspan. As he trotted back on defense, Ibaka left both limbs extended.

That was the debut of "Air Congo," Ibaka's patented post-highlight celebration. It made its way onto the court and into the hearts of Thunder fans on March 19, 2010, an eventual 115–89 road rout of the Raptors, during Ibaka's rookie season.

"When you dunk, you fly," Ibaka explained when asked about Air Congo, a name that was a nod to his native country.

Ibaka flashed the signature celebration after sick putback slams and dazzling alley-oop dunks. He also uncorked Air Congo after big-time blocked shots. Three nights after unveiling the celebration, Ibaka unleashed it for the first time in front of his home fans when he blocked a shot by San Antonio's Tim Duncan with 8.8 seconds remaining, a play that nearly helped the Thunder rally to victory.

Air Congo soon doubled as one of many popular nicknames for Ibaka, joining "Dr. Nasty," "I-Blocka," and "Chewbaka" among others. Ibaka's Air Congo routine was also the first of several fun celebrations he flaunted during his tenure with the Thunder. He began wagging an index finger after swatting shots, but ultimately he retired that move out of respect for the man who popularized the finger wag. "Dikembe Mutombo told me the next time I do it I have to give him a check," Ibaka once joked. Ibaka found a fantastic replacement at the start of the 2015–16 season, when he began celebrating blocked shots by throwing a thumbs-up sign before quickly turning his thumb down. He instantly had a crowd-pleasing celebration he could call his own, with no more playful threats from his friend Mutombo. "I got mine now," Ibaka said proudly.

As the years went on, however, Air Congo was seen less and less. It took 22 games for Air Congo to take flight in the 2011–12 season. But it finally took off in a seven-point home win over Memphis on February 3. Ibaka flashed it again the next night at

San Antonio after a monster alley-oop dunk. Asked before a game against New Orleans in January 2012 why he doesn't flash Air Congo anymore, Ibaka responded, "I'm getting old."

By the 2012–13 season, Ibaka's fourth, Air Congo had become a seldom seen celebration. "Only after nasty dunks," he said. By then, though, Ibaka had substituted style for substance. He had a career best 15 double doubles in his fourth season, blossoming into a well-rounded offensive player who suddenly was stepping out and hitting three-pointers with consistency. He also led the league in blocked shots for the third consecutive season.

"Every game, he's learning something new," said Thunder guard Thabo Sefolosha. "He's playing with more and more confidence."

Ibaka's celebrations always added a fun element to Thunder fans' experience. But he was always careful to not allow them to overshadow his commitment to improving and doing everything in his power to help his team win.

"I work hard. I try to do the best I can," Ibaka said. "I'm getting better and better. I don't want just to be like people used to know Serge Ibaka four years ago.... So I'm trying to get better at everything."

31 Air Congo Gets Grounded

This time, there wasn't a scapegoat. This time, the franchise's post-season hardship simply was hard luck.

For the second consecutive year, the Thunder suffered a significant injury in the playoffs when Serge Ibaka sustained a left calf strain in the team's series-clinching Game 6 road win over the Los

Angeles Clippers in the 2014 semifinals. The injury sidelined Ibaka for the first two games of the Western Conference finals against San Antonio, altering the course of OKC's playoff run and perhaps once again preventing the franchise from journeying back to the NBA Finals.

A year earlier, Russell Westbrook was lost for the 2013 postseason after the infamous Patrick Beverley play in Game 2 of the opening round against Houston. Unlike that unforgettable moment, Ibaka's injury happened in the normal course of play. He exited the game with 7:24 remaining in the third quarter, limped to the locker room, and did not return. Team officials weren't even sure how the injury happened. Game replays later revealed the moment the team's fortunes changed—a routine possession one minute prior to Ibaka's exit when he challenged a Chris Paul layup and landed awkwardly. The next day, a Friday, the Thunder announced Ibaka would miss the remainder of the postseason.

The news came as a shock. Until then, Ibaka had missed only four games due to injury in his five-year career: two as the result of a chest contusion and one apiece due to flu-like symptoms and lower back soreness. He was more durable than most everyone. "We all know him," said Thunder GM Sam Presti. "The last thing he wants to do is miss any time on the floor. But this is one that needed to be looked at pretty closely." The diagnosis was a Grade 2 calf strain. The region of the calf Ibaka injured is called the plantaris, or the upper portion of the calf, just behind the knee. Typical recovery was said to be four to six weeks. "The recovery process is lengthy because the re-injury rate is so extraordinarily high," Presti added.

Before going down, Ibaka was enjoying a career year. He averaged regular season career highs of 15.1 points and 8.8 rebounds, while leading the league in total blocked shots for the fourth consecutive season. He was also in the midst of his best postseason, with per-game averages of 12.2 points, 7.3 rebounds, and 2.23

blocked shots, while shooting 61.6 percent from the field. An interesting subplot in that series-clinching Game 6 against the Clippers, however, was how a 20-year-old rookie center named Steven Adams stepped in for Ibaka and helped the Thunder advance. Adams played a career-high 40 minutes, including the game's final 21, and registered his first playoff double double with 10 points and a career best 11 rebounds. Adams' defense also neutralized Clippers center DeAndre Jordan. Looking back, it might have been the first time the Thunder pondered Adams' potential as the replacement to Ibaka as the team's defensive anchor.

But there was no replacing Ibaka's impact against the Spurs. OKC swept San Antonio in the regular season's four-game series, and Ibaka averaged 14 points, 11.5 rebounds, and four blocked shots. In the regular season, the Spurs scored 108.2 points per 100 possessions. Against the Thunder, the Spurs scored only 93 points per 100 possessions when Ibaka was on the court. The Thunder, though, announced that Saturday, the day before traveling to Texas, Ibaka wouldn't accompany the team. San Antonio responded with skepticism. "I don't really believe it," Spurs guard Tony Parker said on the eve of Monday night's Game 1. "I'll believe when I see tomorrow he is not on the court."

The Thunder appeared to leave a glimmer of hope that Ibaka might return. The team announced Ibaka "is expected to miss the remainder of the 2014 postseason." Presti, though, tried to quash speculation. "It's never easy to put timetables on recoveries. We've seen that before," he said. "But we are also putting a timetable out there that extends past where the season would end. So it would be unlikely he would return if we were fortunate enough to make it past this next series, which we know is going to be a challenge for us." The team did its best to turn the page. "We have a mentality here, 'Next man up,'" Thunder coach Scott Brooks said. "We have enough to win." Added center Kendrick Perkins, "Obviously we're gonna miss Serge, but one thing about us, we like being counted out. Then after Game 1, we like hearing what y'all say next."

Game 1 came. The Thunder got slaughtered. And everyone agreed. OKC sorely missed Serge.

With Ibaka back in OKC, the Spurs routed the Thunder 122–105 inside AT&T Center. Media and fans were ready to hand Ibaka next season's Defensive Player of the Year Award at halftime, when the Thunder yielded 67 points, 40 of which were scored inside the paint. When it was over, the Spurs netted 66 largely uncontested paint points. Tim Duncan, at 38, scored 21 of his team-high 27 points in the first half, finishing 9-for-12.

The thumping only amplified the Ibaka comeback chatter, which prompted Brooks to declare after the game, "Contrary to what San Antonio was thinking, he's not coming back. He's not coming through those doors." The next day, Yahoo! Sports reported Ibaka was "defiant and determined" to get back as quick as possible, even hoping to do stationary shooting by the end of the week. But on the morning of Game 2, Ibaka posted a message to fans on his personal website, thanking them for their support and reiterating the company line that he would be unable to play in the conference finals. He made no mention of a possible return.

That night, the Thunder got pummeled even worse, losing 112–77. The Spurs' 52-point margin of victory in the first two games was the largest scoring differential in history through two games of a conference final.

But with three days off before the series shifted to Oklahoma City, the Thunder delivered a surprise announcement when they upgraded Ibaka to "day-to-day" more than 48 hours prior to Game 3. Presti explained excessive swelling in Ibaka's calf had subsided to a "substantial and unexpected" degree. "We're a little surprised by it," Presti said. "But, you know, he does a lot of things at a level that are not normal." Spurs coach Gregg Popovich wasn't surprised. "I know Sammy," Popovich said. "We knew he'd be back."

Ibaka returned for Game 3 and changed the complexion of the series. He was announced second-to-last in pregame introductions, receiving an ear-splitting roar that topped the ovation for league Most Valuable Player Kevin Durant. Ibaka then swished his first jumper, a patented pick-and-pop feed from Westbrook for the game's first points. He made another jumper off an assist from Westbrook. And then another off a dish from Reggie Jackson. Ibaka scored six of the Thunder's first 10 points and 15 on the night, pumping life into what had been a listless Thunder offense down in San Antonio. Defensively, he registered two of his four blocked shots in the first three minutes, one on Spurs center Tiago Splitter and the other on Duncan. The Thunder had just six blocked shots in the first two games combined. After shooting 57.5 percent and 50 percent, respectively, in the first two games, San Antonio was held to 39.6 percent shooting. The Thunder won 106–97.

"Words can't describe it," said Thunder forward Caron Butler. "It was a great moment. In my career, I've been a part of a lot of great moments in basketball history and that was a special one right there."

The Thunder tied the series at two games apiece with a 105–92 victory in Game 4. Ibaka had nine points, eight rebounds, and three blocked shots in 35 minutes. But the Spurs again throttled the Thunder with a 117–89 win in Game 5 before clinching the series in Oklahoma City with an overtime victory in Game 6.

Most observers thought the series would have played out differently had Ibaka been available from the beginning. Ibaka later labeled his comeback a miracle, revealing he played through extreme pain and nearly underwent surgery. "But I felt being on the court, my presence was going to help my teammates," he said. "I wanted to just do whatever it takes to give my teammates confidence."

Ibaka inspired his team and his town with storybook courageousness. It just wasn't enough to thrust the Thunder back to the championship round. And for a franchise that ultimately faced more than its share of heartbreak, Ibaka's fluke calf injury will live forever as one of its all-time what-if scenarios.

32 The Name Game

Clay Bennett filed for relocation from Seattle to Oklahoma City on November 2, 2007. David Stern deemed the move "an inevitability" on February 16, 2008. Oklahoma City voters approved $121 million in improvements to the city's downtown arena on March 4, 2008. NBA owners approved the franchise's relocation application on April 18, 2008.

Through it all, and an additional three months on top of that, no one had a clue what Oklahoma City's new NBA team would be called.

Some, including Oklahoma City Mayor Mick Cornett, wanted Bennett and the rest of the team's ownership group to retain the name SuperSonics. Others wanted them to leave it in Seattle and start anew. But coming up with a can't-miss name wasn't so simple. All the easy choices were gone, having long been gobbled up by the 100-plus other professional franchises throughout the U.S. and Canada.

In late April 2008, *The Oklahoman* launched an online "Name Game" contest, a three-week tournament bracket in which fans could vote for their favorite names for Oklahoma City's potential NBA team. It was a 64-name field. More than 1,000 people registered. In all, the paper received 208 reader-submitted suggestions, from Alligators to Zingers. The final four names were Barons, Outlaws, Thunder, and Thunderbirds. The final two were

Thunder and Outlaws. The paper listed the pros and cons of the final team names as well as potential names for the dance teams, the signature songs, possible promotions, and mascots. On May 18, 2008, the paper revealed that Thunder won, receiving 159 votes to the Outlaws' 103.

Two months later, Mark Rodgers, then the sports director at the ABC affiliate and a local radio personality, reported Thunder would be the team name. The team and the league office both declined comment on the report. Of the interest in the name, a team spokesman said only, "We love the excitement and the discussion." But the report checked out. Corporation Service Company, the registrar of record for the NBA whose mission was to prevent cybersquatters from profiting from a brand, registered okcthunderbasketball.com and okcthunderbasketball.net on July 10. Less than two weeks later, the NBA filed for trademark rights to six names—Barons, Bison, Energy, Marshalls, Thunder, and Wind.

More evidence the team would be named Thunder leaked on the morning of August 6, 2008, a Wednesday. NBA.com listed the "Oklahoma City Thunder schedule" as part of the leaguewide schedule release. Clicking any of the team's 82 games sent users to NBA.com/thunder, a URL format in line with each of the league's other teams. By that afternoon, the URL no longer functioned and instead generated an error message that read, "We apologize for the inconvenience, but the page you are looking for might have been removed, had its name changed, or is temporarily unavailable." Three weeks later, multiple team websites offered tickets for games against the Thunder. Later, a photo of a basketball wrapped in plastic emerged online. It had a Thunder logo. Another URL popped up in early September with links to merchandise for the Oklahoma City Thunder, featuring everything from polo shirts to luggage.

Finally, on September 3, 2008, during a public press conference held in the atrium of a downtown office complex known by locals as Leadership Square, Bennett unveiled the team name and logo. With a gigantic blue banner hanging behind him, and the familiar intro to AC/DC's "Thunderstruck" blaring from speakers around him, Bennett officially announced the name and unveiled the logo.

"We just felt it connected," Bennett said. "We liked the name. We felt it reflected the identity we hope to establish for the team and thought the word connected to Oklahoma in an effective way; a word of power and strength and clarity. It was a favorite early on. Thunder was the leader for a long time."

Bennett then made a vow to Thunder fans.

"We will build this brand into one of the great brands in the league," he said.

33 Stand Until the Thunder's First Basket

If you consider yourself a die-hard Thunder fan, you absolutely must do two things when attending a game in Oklahoma City: be in your seat before tip-off, and stand until the home team scores its first basket.

In the NBA, those two staples are traditions unlike any other. They've set Thunder fans apart from the rest of the league and established Oklahoma City's fan base as among the very best in basketball. Thunder fans have proudly participated in the custom since the team's first contest on October 29, 2008, against the Milwaukee Bucks.

Standing until the home team scores its first basket is a tradition that started when the New Orleans Hornets played in Oklahoma City for two seasons. But like so many other elements in the Hornet's game-night presentation, it transitioned seamlessly to the Thunder. Now it's a source of pride among fans and a site to behold for visitors.

"I love that they stand. I'm surprised the league office hasn't fined them, because you can't do that if you're a player," ESPN analyst Jeff Van Gundy once joked. "I'm waiting for the league office to fine the Thunder people. Every fan is going to get a $5 fine."

Said play-by-play man Marv Albert: "It's kind of a college atmosphere with the crowd so enthusiastic. I love the fact that they stand until the [home team] hits their first field goal. They have such passion for basketball."

Players have repeatedly said the passion Thunder fans exhibit goes a long way in pushing the team over the top. It's a particularly important advantage in the NBA, where players can go through stretches over the course of a grueling 82-game season where they simply don't have much energy.

"There's some games that you're going to be down, you're going to be hurt, you don't feel like playing, you're tired," former Thunder forward Jeff Green said. "But fans always have a big part in whatever we do."

Still Standing

Standing until the Thunder scores their first basket sometimes backfires. Game 1 of the 2013 Western Conference semifinals against Memphis was one memorable example. With the Thunder still scoreless at the first timeout with 8:18 remaining in the opening period, fans weren't sure what to do. Ultimately, they sat during the stoppage. But to their credit, they stood again at the end of the timeout. Fortunately, forward Serge Ibaka made a pair of free throws 13 seconds after play resumed to allow Thunder fans to sit back and relax. Yes, free throws count as made baskets in the standing-until-the-first-score tradition.

"A good fan base is just keeping the players energized, keeping the building energized," former Thunder guard Kevin Ollie added. "It's not like you're sitting back waiting for something to happen great from the team. You actually urge them on to go out there and do their best."

Legendary coach Phil Jackson didn't seem to understand that logic. During the Thunder's inaugural 2008–09 season, Jackson delivered what sounded like a slight to Oklahoma City's rabid NBA fans. "They haven't quite figured out the NBA game, the length of it," the then-Lakers coach said. "They get all fired up in the beginning, and it's a marathon. It's 48 minutes of basketball. It's not like college, where you can come out and get a 10-point lead or 15-point lead and you can win the game."

After the game, Jackson did an about face. "Their crowd energizes that team," he said. "It makes it much more difficult to win. All teams will have a hard time when they come here."

Former Thunder coach Scott Brooks raved about the team's fans in that first season. They set the bar in 2008–09, and Brooks, inaccurately, believed it'd be the best they'd get. "This may sound corny, but I don't think they can improve," he said. "What they did last year—sticking with us when we were on the bad start—our players appreciate that. I don't know if they can get much better, but if they can, I'll love to see it."

Over the years, Thunder fans continued to show steadfast support by showing up early, standing until the home team's first basket, cheering loudly and proudly, almost never booing, sporting team-issued shirts during playoff games and staying late into games. They are all small but significant ways fans did whatever they could to uplift the players.

"The lack of negativity that we have to deal with here from outside that a lot of cities do helps us, too, especially in our growth and with young players—all players, but particularly in the last three or four years," Nick Collison said. "If you're also dealing with constant negativity from the city or you don't feel that loyalty that everyone is on board it's more difficult. It's not impossible. People deal with it all the time. But I think it is an advantage for us that we've kind of had that unwavering support."

34 Gasol, Folks

The Thunder weren't even supposed to be here.

Yet here they were, battling the big, bad Los Angeles Lakers, standing toe to toe with the defending champions, threatening to force an improbable Game 7.

One year earlier, the Thunder had won just 23 games, the third fewest in all of basketball. Yet here they were, a fearless 50-win bunch now taking on the top-seeded and star-studded Lakers in a win-or-go-home Game 6 in the opening round of the 2010 playoffs.

It was April 30. The setting was the Ford Center, which packed in 18,342 fans who formed a sea of blue by proudly sporting T-shirts that read "Let's Go Thunder." Together, they giddily greeted their team prior to its most pivotal game to date.

The Lakers were stacked, led then by reigning NBA Finals MVP Kobe Bryant, Pau Gasol, Andrew Bynum, Lamar Odom, and the artist formerly known as Ron Artest. Those five averaged 28.4 years. The Thunder's best five players—Kevin Durant, Russell Westbrook, James Harden, Jeff Green, and Serge Ibaka—averaged just 21 years. On the sidelines were coaches Phil Jackson, already a 10-time champion as a coach, and Scott Brooks, who had never coached a playoff game.

It was pups against seasoned pros.

Los Angeles won the regular season series 3–1, and nobody outside the most delusional of Thunder fans gave Oklahoma City a chance to actually win the series.

It didn't help that the Thunder stumbled into the showdown with L.A. After being in position in mid-March to potentially host a first-round series against a more favorable matchup, the Thunder went 9–8 over the final 17 games, including four losses in their final six. Publicly, the team tried to save face by defiantly claiming its late-season swoon was no big deal, that they actually didn't mind playing the defending champs.

"Our guys are not going to give in just because they're the Lakers and they're good," said Brooks. "We feel like we can beat anybody."

The series began as most expected it would. In Game 1, the Thunder never led and got beat up inside by Bynum and Gasol, who combined for 32 points, 25 rebounds, four assists, and seven blocked shots in the Lakers' 87–79 win.

In Game 2, the Thunder couldn't close. They held a two-point lead inside the final 2½ minutes but went 1-for-3 and committed three turnovers down the stretch. Green missed a potential game-tying three-pointer with 1.9 seconds remaining. Green, Westbrook, and Durant combined for 17 points on 3-for-11 shooting in the fourth quarter, while Bryant scored 15 in the decisive frame, including eight straight during one stretch. The Thunder lost 95–92, but after two competitive contests, and with the series shifting to OKC, they suddenly believed they could beat L.A.

Powered by Durant's best game of the series—he scored 12 of his game-high 29 points in the fourth quarter while adding 19 rebounds, four assists, and one huge fourth quarter-block on Bryant, who went 2-for-10 with four points in the final period—the Thunder hung on for a 101–96 victory in Game 3. It was the first playoff win in Thunder history. After going scoreless in the first two games, Harden came alive with 18 points, five rebounds, three assists, two steals, and some inspired defense on Bryant.

Games 4 and 5 were blowouts, with the Thunder taking a 21-point victory to even the series at two games apiece before the Lakers thumped them back with a 24-point drubbing inside Staples Center.

Which set up the pivotal Game 6.

It was the Thunder's first taste of an elimination game, and it was a grind throughout. There were nine ties, 15 lead changes, and neither team went ahead by double digits.

Bryant, still considered the game's ultimate closer, scored 16 of the Lakers' 23 third-quarter points and made 6-of-8 shots, including all three of his three-point attempts. While Bryant was sizzling, sitting on 30 points through three quarters, Durant and Westbrook had a combined 32 points on 7-for-29 shooting. But the Thunder trailed by only three entering the final period.

A three-point play by Westbrook gave the Thunder a one-point lead with 3:04 remaining. A driving layup by Durant pushed the margin to three, OKC's largest lead of the night with just 2½ minutes to play. Bryant responded with an 18' jumper to cut it to one. The Thunder then missed their next four shots, the fourth being a 12-footer by Westbrook with 19.9 seconds showing on the game clock. It set up Bryant with one final chance to be the hero.

Jackson declined to use his final timeout, leaving Bryant with Westbrook isolated at the top of the three-point line.

Eight…Seven…Six….

Bryant drove right, pounding three hard dribbles until he got to the spot he desired just beyond the right low block. He stopped, rocked back, and fired a 13' contested fadeaway from the short corner. It missed long by mere inches, hitting left rim and bouncing back to the right side of the backboard, where Gasol had snuck past Ibaka and between Nick Collison. Gasol tipped in the miss with five-tenths of a second remaining.

After a timeout, Westbrook missed a would-be game-winning three-pointer from the right corner as the final buzzer sounded, sparking a collective sigh from the blue-clad Ford Center crowd.

Gasol had averaged 19.8 points on 56.1 percent shooting in the first five games. In Game 6, he finished with just nine points on 4-for-11 shooting. But he snared a game-high 18 rebounds, including the biggest one of the game and the series.

The headline on the cover of the sports page of *The Oklahoman* the next morning screamed, GASOL, FOLKS.

But the Thunder, against all odds, had announced their presence. They were the team of the future and everyone knew it the moment that final buzzer sounded.

As Bryant passed Durant in the Ford Center hallway after the game, he paid homage to the young and hungry crew that had just given his Lakers all they could handle.

"Y'all some bad motherf——s," Bryant said. "I'm glad we're done with you."

Durant, who had huddled his teammates on the court only 90 seconds after their most deflating defeat and told them, "Next season starts now," didn't disagree.

"It's all a process," Durant said. "It's all about going through ups and downs, and tonight was one of the downs. But better days are ahead...the sky's the limit."

35 Michael F——g Jordan

Kevin Garnett's head hung as his clinched left hand rested on his temple. He stared dejectedly at the night's final stat sheet while seated behind a microphone at the interview room table.

The Thunder had just stormed into Boston's TD Garden on the final day of March 2010 and captured a 109–104 victory over the Celtics. And Garnett couldn't believe what he had just seen.

"I thought we were playing Michael F——g Jordan tonight the way he was getting the whistle," Garnett griped into the mic. "Durant damn near shot more free throws than our whole team."

To understand the magnitude of that moment, you must first understand the point in which Durant stood on his career arc. This was the tail end of Durant's third season, long before he was an All-Star and scoring champion many times over, long before he led the Thunder to the NBA Finals, and long before he captured three gold medals and a league MVP Award. Back then, Durant mostly was still regarded as a smooth but scrawny scoring savant who'd someday challenge LeBron James for league supremacy. Back then, the Thunder wasn't a perennial power but a team putting together a surprising march to the postseason following a 23-win season the year prior.

Durant and the upstart Thunder stood toe to toe with the veteran-laden Celtics—who had embarrassed them with an 18-point drubbing in early December's first meeting in OKC—for 36 minutes before delivering the knockout punch in the fourth period. The Thunder did it by shutting down Boston's offense with smothering defense at one end and sinking clutch shots at the other. By the time it was over, the victory went down as the best of the then two-year Thunder era. On the second night of a back-to-back, the Thunder blitzed a championship contender, doubled their win total from the previous season, and proved once and for all both they and their turnaround were real. And here came Garnett, then a 13-time All-Star and former league MVP who was two years removed from winning the NBA title, likening the new kid on the block to "Michael F——g Jordan" all because he and his aging Celtics mates couldn't stop him. In shooting a dig at the officials, Garnett inadvertently sent a statement to the league: Durant is the real deal. It was one of the early acknowledgments that Durant had turned his promise into dominance and become a force. Garnett's grumbling about the officiating felt like the only way a once-transcendent but supremely bullheaded superstar knew how to pass the torch.

The NBA fined Garnett $25,000 for publicly criticizing game officials and "using inappropriate language" during a postgame interview. But at least the truth was on his side.

Durant shot 15-for-15 at the free throw line that night. Boston was 13-for-17 as a team. Durant finished with a game-high 37 points, carving up the Celtics from not just the stripe but from all over the court.

"We've grown up," Durant declared after the game.

Garnett hadn't gotten the memo. That was the 14th time that season that Durant was awarded at least 15 foul shots. He took 15 or more attempts 16 times that year and ended the season in a first-place tie with James for foul shots per game at 10.2. Durant sank 1.4 more per game, giving him a league-best 9.2 made foul shots that season. Durant had been doing his damage from the foul line all year. His résumé didn't warrant such treatment at that stage of his career, yet he was firmly entrenched as a league darling and recipient of superstar calls.

Garnett, however, wasn't the only proud champion to question how Durant was officiated that season. Two weeks after Garnett's outburst, then-Lakers coach Phil Jackson suggested Durant received preferential treatment.

"Yeah, by the calls he gets, he really gets to the line a lot, I'll tell ya," Jackson said.

Durant responded to the criticism by admitting he felt disrespected.

"Because it's taking away from what I do," Durant said. "That's a part of my game, getting to the free throw line and being aggressive. If you say that I get superstar calls, or I get babied by the refs, that's just taking away from how I play. That's disrespectful to me."

36 The Ovation

Mike Breen said he had never seen anything like it. Scott Brooks said it simply doesn't happen. Mark Jackson said seeing it on television wouldn't do it justice.

On April 30, 2010, Thunder fans cemented their status as the league's best when they responded to their team's season-ending 95–94 Game 6 loss to the Los Angeles Lakers by showering the Thunder with a hearty standing ovation. It was the final game of a storybook season in which Oklahoma City, then in its second season, enjoyed a 27-win improvement before standing toe to toe with the defending champions in the opening round of the playoffs.

Thunder fans already had built a reputation for showing up early, packing the house, standing until the home team scored its first basket, and cheering like crazy. But what unfolded on that Friday night on the final day of April was one of those rare sports moments you know is special the second it happens.

This one happened almost immediately after the final buzzer sounded.

With 0.5 seconds left following Pau Gasol's putback, Thabo Sefolosha threw in to Russell Westbrook in the right corner. In one continuous motion, Westbrook caught it, turned, and fired. His desperation heave hit the front rim, triggering a collective sigh from the 18,342 that filled the Ford Center for the 31st sellout that season.

The Lakers celebrated their survival. Jeff Green doubled over near halfcourt, with his face buried in his palms. Kevin Durant collapsed to the court, slamming his hand on the hardwood twice in disappointment.

Then it happened, three seconds after the final buzzer. Thunder fans, clad in complimentary blue shirts that covered their seats upon entry, and already on their feet for a fascinating finish in which neither team led by more than four for the final 4½ minutes, erupted in applause.

"And listen to these fans," Breen, ESPN's play-by-play man, exclaimed during the broadcast. "Right away giving their team a standing ovation."

In an instant, gratitude had replaced grief. Hope had replaced heartbreak. Anticipation had replaced agony.

"I've never seen anything like that," Breen remembered before the start of the following season. "Because it happened right away. It's like, the buzzer sounded. Game was over. Heartbreak. And within seconds, they're on their feet."

With the entire Thunder roster shown huddled behind Kobe Bryant's postgame interview with Lisa Salters—Kevin Durant declaring to his teammates in that huddle, "Next season starts now"—the crowd remained standing. Nobody moved. Nobody left. They just kept cheering.

Salters asked Bryant what he told Durant and Russell Westbrook during their respective embraces.

"I just said they're incredible basketball players," Bryant said. "And for them to keep working. They're going to be a team that we're going to have to deal with for years to come."

As Bryant finished his first answer, the huddle behind him broke and Thunder fans roared. Some players turned and gave waves of thanks. Some reciprocated and applauded the crowd.

"I've never seen a response like that," Thunder coach Scott Brooks said. "That *never* happens. It was heartfelt, and our guys appreciated it."

For two-and-a-half minutes, Thunder fans poured out their hearts and expressed their appreciation for the up-and-coming Thunder until the final player had exited the court.

"It was as good a scene as I've seen in all my years of playing and covering the NBA," said Jackson, ESPN's color commentator for the game. "The best fans in basketball, energetic, enthusiastic, and they acknowledged how hard their team fought and competed. It was really great to watch and to be in the building. I don't think watching it on TV would do the justice that we were able to witness seeing it firsthand."

Eric Maynor, a reserve point guard on that 2010 team, also said he'd never seen anything like it. Not in high school. Not in college.

Not after a loss.

"You kidding? No way. Everybody'd be leaving," he said. "For our fans to do what they did just shows us they really care. We care about them also."

37 Community

Christine Berney was shopping in Whole Foods when she heard someone shriek her name. Startled, she turned and spotted a pleasant surprise.

It was Tyler Ryan. Five years earlier, he had been honored during a Thunder game as the recipient of the Devon Community Hero Award. Ryan, an Edmond resident, saved a man's life as he helped him change a flat tire. But after pushing Morshed Khandaker out of harm's way as an out-of-control vehicle barreled toward them, Ryan was struck. He sustained fractured vertebrae in his lower back, multiple breaks in both his legs, and countless lacerations and contusions. Paramedics rushed Ryan to the hospital, where doctors operated on him throughout the night. He needed nine surgeries and ultimately lost his left leg after it required an above-the-knee amputation. "They really didn't know if he would make it or not," said Ryan's mother, Shirley Coleman.

So you can imagine the joy Berney was overcome with when she ran into Ryan as he approached his 30th birthday. As the Vice President of Community Relations for the Thunder, Berney is responsible for overseeing initiatives like the Devon Community Hero Award. Although that program was discontinued, Berney felt the impact of countless other community outreach efforts. She's been with the team since the beginning, and after nearly a decade with the franchise, similar encounters became commonplace. "Pretty much anywhere anybody in the organization goes, there's someone who has had some interaction with the Thunder in some way," Berney said. "And that's a pretty special feeling."

It's a credit to the Thunder's dedication to serving the community. The Thunder has more than a dozen community outreach

Quotable

"I feel like Oklahoma City is kind of like the Green Bay Packers. It's kind of like a small town where the fans really are just all about the team. They support you no matter what, win or lose, so it's almost like you know you'll never hear a boo in the arena because they're really with you. They're not there to watch you. Growing up, being a Packers fan, I think it's very similar. I think it makes you play better. It's an energy in the building."

—Steve Novak, a Milwaukee native,
following the 2014–15 season.

programs, initiatives ranging from literacy and health and fitness for children to feeding needy families for the holidays. Each one is designed to give back. "We wouldn't be playing basketball here if the fans didn't embrace the team like they have," Berney said. "We're a part of this community because of those fans.… Hopefully we're making a little bit of a difference in a positive way."

Since 2010, the Thunder have renovated or built 15 basketball courts in underprivileged neighborhoods. Since 2009, they've handed out more than 130,000 books to children who have boarded their mobile Book Bus. They've annually passed out dinners to families for Thanksgiving and taken others on shopping sprees for Christmas. And that's just the team initiatives. Multiple players have personal foundations that give back to the community throughout the year. The NBA requires players, upon request, to make at least 12 promotional appearances each season. But Berney said the Thunder typically rank in the top three among all teams for player appearances.

"All of the community work that we do, we want it to be an experience," Berney said. "We don't want it to just be, 'We're just stopping in.' We take those connections really seriously. And so we work hard to make whatever we're doing in the community a really great experience for everybody that's involved."

Thunder General Manager Sam Presti typically targets players he believes would not only fit well in the Oklahoma City community but also be an ambassador to it. Presti has made it clear that not every NBA player would be a good fit with the Thunder, and incoming players must understand what it means to put on an Oklahoma City jersey. In Presti's eyes, that's being part of the community. "That's a very important part to playing here," Presti said.

Presti has gone a step further by calling himself and those he works with "caretakers" of the organization. It's their job, he said, to build a franchise the community can be proud of. "We want people who are with us to have their work last well beyond their tenure with the organization," Presti said. "We all realize we are caretakers of the organization and its values. We understand how rare it is to put the foundation in place for an organization and what the work signifies for our community now and in the future. We see it as much of a responsibility as a privilege."

Kevin Durant once credited the character of Thunder players on and off the court for the city's connection to its lone pro franchise. "We show a lot of maturity," Durant said. "We show a lot of class. And people here are drawn to that."

The Thunder doesn't take community engagement lightly. It's something that starts at the top with ownership and trickles down to management to the coaches and to the players.

"I feel extremely lucky to work for an organization that values that so much," Berney said. "It's pretty special."

It's one of the franchise's most overshadowed aspects. While they were perennial contenders on the court, the Thunder have long been champions in the community.

38 Sustained Success

From the moment he was appointed general manager, Sam Presti had a plan, a vision for how he wanted to build the Thunder franchise.

It wasn't always the most popular approach, but in Presti's mind it was the most enduring. It was a long-term view, and reaching his desired destination would take patience and prudence. It would require trusting the process and sticking to clearly defined principles.

"As we established the core values of the Thunder in 2008, we wanted to build an organization that was capable of sustained success and organizational endurance," Presti said.

That phrase, "sustained success," practically became the franchise's motto. It would shape every move Presti and the Thunder made. When observers charged the organization with being cheap, Presti's retort was he was calculated. When fans screamed for the team to make short-sighted moves, Presti instead stuck to being shrewd.

"We don't want our championships to be making the playoffs," Presti said in his first month on the job back in Seattle. "What we want is sustained success. We want long-term growth, and we want the opportunity to see our group growing within an aligned timeline."

The more measured, methodical approach meant building organically through the draft rather than blowing money overpaying free agents. It called for stockpiling assets, using salary cap space strategically, and being opportunistic whenever possible. Some didn't understand the blueprint or why Presti was so devoted to his belief in it. In their minds, the Thunder general manager didn't place winning a championship as his No. 1 priority.

"Like every team in professional sports, our goal is to win a championship," Presti countered. "We believe in order for us to achieve sustained success, we first have to put ourselves in position where year-in and year-out we are positioned to be among a handful of teams that believe that if they execute and have a little good fortune along the way can impact the postseason and be the last team standing."

Think of it as a math equation.

"It is essentially trying to improve your odds of achieving your goals by allowing yourself increased opportunities," Presti said.

Kevin Durant and Jeff Green played their rookie seasons in Seattle before serving as the original cornerstones for the Oklahoma City Thunder.
(AP Photo/John Froschauer)

Fans and media could spend years debating whether it was the proper approach, and some did. But one thing the Thunder always avoided was reactionary, knee-jerk decisions that might have marginally improved the team's chances in the short term while handicapping the franchise's chances in the long term.

"Part of our job is to always look for ways to maximize the present while also staying vigilant and aware of what will ultimately allow the Thunder to endure and thrive in the future," Presti explained. "There are so many variables that come into play in professional sports, and many of them are out of your control at the end of the day. However, as an organization we put a strong premium on sustainability within our market and, therefore, the future is a daily part of our process."

Injuries, player movement, and collective bargaining agreement limitations are all among those critical and sometimes crippling variables. Those challenges and others—most notably Oklahoma City's small market size—are why Presti chose to be consistent with his established organization-building principles. Year after year, he layered the Thunder's roster so that it could withstand both inherent challenges and the test of time.

"To be able to accomplish the goal of sustainable success, you have to demonstrate that your organization possesses the trait of emotional resiliency," Presti said. "Success is not linear, and lasting success is often the product of the ability to recover from the unforeseen events and adversities that exist in sports. You have to have the resolve, optimism, and belief to continue your march forward."

Survive and thrive.

"It is our hope that as time passes on, we create lasting memories and experiences for multi-generations," Presti said, "and that we can become part of the fabric of the community that supports us consistently."

39 Russell Westbrook's Turning Point

Everyone tried to downplay it.

Russell Westbrook. Kevin Durant. Thabo Sefolosha. Scott Brooks.

They wanted to sweep it under the rug, claim it was being overblown, chalk it up as natural over the course of an NBA season.

But it happened, and it was real.

On December 28, 2011, Westbrook and Durant got into a heated sideline dispute and had to be separated. It happened on a Wednesday night, during a second quarter timeout in an eventual three-point win at Memphis. It was the third game of the lockout-shortened season.

Westbrook was horrible that night, suffering through the worst game of his career: a four-point, 0-for-13, six-assist, four-turnover stinker. Equally bad was that Westbrook was outplayed by Jeremy Pargo, a rookie point guard who scored 15 points with seven assists and only one turnover while filling in for the injured Mike Conley.

With 3½ minutes remaining in the first half, frustration bubbled up. It boiled over when Westbrook drove into the paint, fired a pass to Sefolosha in the corner, and then scolded him for turning down an open three-pointer. "Shoot the f---ing ball!" Westbrook woofed at Sefolosha.

During an ensuing pair of free throws, Sefolosha and other teammates, including Durant and Kendrick Perkins, attempted to settle down Westbrook. But he was steaming, and the exchange spilled over to the bench in a subsequent timeout one minute later. Durant again tried to calm Westbrook, but Westbrook appeared to take exception to how the message was delivered. In a matter of seconds, Durant went from peacemaker to aggressor. Tensions

A challenging two-game stretch in late December 2011 proved to be a turning point for Russell Westbrook in his development into an NBA superstar.
(Jerome Miron/ *USA TODAY* Sports)

rose. Tempers flared. Shouting started. Teammates and coaches stepped in just as the two appeared ready to square off.

"We're going to disagree sometimes, like I've always been saying," Durant said after the game. "But I'm behind him 110 percent, and he's the same way with me."

Said Brooks: "When you have an intense game, you're going to have arguments. I have no problem with it. I think it's healthy. I think you learn from it and you get better with it. That's just part of an NBA game."

This dispute felt different. It didn't originate with Durant and Westbrook yet quickly dissolved into infighting between the two. The bickering also appeared to have little, if anything, to do with basketball and everything to do with emotions. It all just seemed strange, shocking even.

For the better part of the previous three seasons, many observers wondered whether the Durant-Westbrook tandem was a good fit. They questioned whether a shoot-first point guard could coexist with a natural born scorer. They questioned whether the Thunder's two stars actually liked each other. Much of it was nonsense, of course. But when the sideline spat at Memphis occurred, naysayers pounced.

The next night the Thunder hosted Dallas in a nationally televised TNT game. Back home, facing a larger group of media, Thunder players were bombarded with questions about the previous night's incident. TNT sideline reporter David Aldridge welcomed viewers back from the first timeout with a report on the dust-up, but the network's replay of the incident cut off just before it reached its climax.

"It was a really tough time for me," Westbrook later admitted to *Sports Illustrated*. "I was hearing a lot of things."

Westbrook's poor play spilled over against the Mavericks. Through 41 minutes, he had nine points, four assists, and seven turnovers. He was 3-of-11 from the floor.

"He was playing so bad that night against Dallas, I mean really struggling," Thunder Assistant General Manager Troy Weaver told *Sports Illustrated*.

But then something special happened in the final four minutes.

A Kendrick Perkins steal led to a transition dunk by Westbrook. He was fouled by Jason Terry on the play, and as Westbrook stood at the foul line with 3:17 remaining, Thunder fans did something they had never done.

"Our crowd wouldn't leave him. They just stayed with him," Weaver said. "I remember this one kid, up in the Loud City section, chanting 'Rus-sell! Rus-sell!' and then everybody started chanting it."

Westbrook yanked down an offensive rebound on the next possession and nailed a jumper to push the Thunder's lead to three. He got a steal, then another jumper to push OKC's lead to five.

After two straight nightmare games, Westbrook was back. With an assist from his home fans, he had come alive when his team needed him most and set up Durant's buzzer-beating, game-winning three-pointer.

It was an emotional victory for the Thunder.

It was a turning point for Westbrook.

"I think his career changed that night," Weaver said. "I think it was the defining moment."

40 The Closer

There were occasional glimpses of how special James Harden could one day be.

There was his eye-popping 13-for-14 night at the foul line against Golden State on December 7, 2009, a 26-point outing that came in only his 20th career game and foreshadowed how he would so easily weave his way to the basket and manufacture points. There was Game 3 of the 2010 Western Conference first round, when he bounced back from consecutive scoreless performances on the road against his hometown Los Angeles Lakers with a superb 18-point, five-rebound, three-assist night in the first home playoff game in Oklahoma City history. And there was Game 5 of the 2011 Western Conference finals, when, even in defeat, Harden delivered his first defining moment by taking over early in the fourth quarter at Dallas.

But the moment James Harden arrived came on May 5, 2012, a Saturday night in which he was simply marvelous. It happened on the road, in Game 4 against Dallas in the opening round of the Western Conference Playoffs. In a game that featured Kevin Durant, Dirk Nowitzki, Russell Westbrook, and former Sixth Man of the Year Jason Terry, Harden easily was the best player on the floor.

With the Thunder facing a 13-point, fourth-quarter deficit, Harden captained a critical comeback in the closeout game. Working with the ball in his hands as the de facto point guard, Harden terrorized the Mavs in every way possible.

"He beat us in individual drives, beat us in pick and rolls," Mavs coach Rick Carlisle said. "He got up a head of steam and was great. We tried everything, five or six different coverages going. We needed to be better, but it was more about how good he was."

Harden scored 15 of his team-high 29 points in that final period. He dished three assists, all leading to three-pointers, for an additional nine points for which he was responsible in the final frame. Harden exploited Dallas' defense and got whatever he wanted, whenever he wanted, and seemingly with ease.

It was the first time the world saw how deadly Harden could be. More significantly, it had become unequivocally clear what a perfect buffer Harden was between Durant and Westbrook, who that night combined for just 36 points on 12-of-30 shooting—Westbrook going 3-of-12 and Durant committing five turnovers.

The performance was amazingly similar to the one that had come just short one year earlier in the West finals. This time, Harden finished what he started.

"If you want to be an elite team in this league, you got to have two or three guys who can go off at any time," Nowitzki continued. "And I just thought they had more weapons than us."

Two rounds later, San Antonio ran into the same buzzsaw. The end result was Harden's signature moment in a Thunder uniform.

The clock was ticking inside the final minute of a pivotal Game 5 of the West finals. OKC nursed a tenuous two-point lead. The Spurs faithful, 18,581 strong, implored the home team for defense. And their best defender, Kawhi Leonard, was in position, isolated on the left wing against Harden. The Thunder were scrambling. The Spurs were suffocating. Still, Harden stepped up and supplied arguably the biggest shot in Thunder history.

Manu Ginobili showed a hard double team, racing at Harden with seven seconds remaining on the shot clock before quickly retreating to Thabo Sefolosha in the left corner. Harden reset, dribbled once between his legs, faked to his right and then picked up his dribble as he stepped behind the three-point line and fired over an off-balanced Leonard. The ball splashed through with three seconds remaining on the shot clock, 28.8 seconds showing on the game clock. It put the Thunder up five and propelled OKC to a 108–103 win. Harden scored 12 of his 20 points in the fourth quarter, connecting on 6-of-11 shots for the game while adding four rebounds and three assists against zero turnovers. He finished with a game-high plus-24.

Two nights later the Thunder closed out the Spurs at home with an eight-point win to advance to its first NBA Finals.

Just like that, a star was born.

41 Slim Reaper

The best individual stretch of scoring Thunder fans will ever see came midway through the 2013–14 season.

It was a jaw-dropping stretch that began in early January and lasted through early April. That's the legendary tear in which Kevin Durant scored 25 points or more in 41 consecutive games.

Oscar Robertson (46 straight games in 1963–64) and Wilt Chamberlain (all 80 regular-season games in 1961–62) own the only two longer such streaks in NBA history.

Durant's streak started in sensational fashion, with him scoring at least 30 points in 12 consecutive games. For Durant, an apt nickname arose from those 12 spectacular performances as well as the 29 others that soon followed, "Slim Reaper."

Only one problem: Durant didn't care for it.

"I'm here to shine a bright light. I'm not here to be a guy of, I guess, death," Durant said.

Durant told fans he preferred KD and said they instead could call him "The Servant," although he would later say he was only joking.

But Durant was downright dominant. During his 41-game stretch, he had 17 30-point games, nine 40-point games, and two 50-point explosions. This wasn't just a streak in which Durant narrowly netted a nightly 25 points. He averaged 34.8 points on just 22.2 shot attempts per game in that span.

And this wasn't some disgusting display of shot-jacking and selfishness. Durant wasn't going out each night gunning for 25 points. He hoisted 25 shots or more only 12 times during his 41-game onslaught. Instead, he was scoring sensibly and efficiently, carving up opponents with back-breaking stepbacks and pull-ups, curls and backdoor cuts, transition buckets and freebies at the foul line. He produced points within the flow of the offense, on lightning-quick flurries and by taking and making one improbable "heat-check" shot after another.

Equally impressive is how Durant's scoring outbursts came complete with crazy efficiency. He connected on 51.5 percent from the field, 39.5 percent from beyond the three-point arc, and 86.5 percent at the foul line. At the same time, Durant had quietly morphed into one of the league's best all-around players, with complementary averages of seven rebounds, 6.1 assists, and 1.1 steals to go with stretches of stellar individual and team defense.

Durant was also carrying the Thunder to wins. His scoring tear started two days after Christmas, which coincided with the world learning Russell Westbrook would miss significant time after undergoing a third knee surgery. Durant dropped 30 points or more in four of the six games leading up to the start of his 41-game streak of at least 25 points, and he was averaging 29 points, 8.3 rebounds, and five assists in the 34 total games preceding the stretch. So it's not like KD wasn't already crafting a career year. But when he was needed most, Durant answered the call and kept the Thunder afloat as the team's All-Star point guard healed. Durant captained

OKC to a 27–14 record over that 41-game stretch, including a 17–7 mark when Westbrook wasn't by his side.

No performance within his 41-game streak of scoring brilliance depicted Durant's new moniker like what he did on a chilly mid-January night in Oklahoma City. Winners of 11-of-13, the upstart Golden State Warriors were in town seeking to avenge a one-point overtime loss inside Chesapeake Energy Arena two months prior. Westbrook stole the show in that one, scoring a game-high 34 points and sinking an improbable corner three-pointer with 0.1 seconds remaining. This time, Westbrook was in street clothes.

Without him, Durant worked over the run-and-gun Warriors for 44 minutes, beating them at their own game by splashing in shots and lighting up the scoreboard. By halftime, he had 29 points on 11-for-14 shooting. He scored 10 in the third quarter and 15 in the fourth, including 13 straight inside the final nine minutes to put the game away. The end result: a career-high 54 points. The final score: Thunder 127, Warriors 121.

In snatching the Warriors' collective soul, the Slim Reaper needed only 28 shots of which he made 19. It marked the first time since Michael Jordan in 1988 that a player scored at least 54 with at least five assists while shooting 65-plus-percent. On his best scoring night, Durant needed only 68 touches and had the ball in his hands for only 3 minutes, 17 seconds of game time.

When Durant stepped to the free throw line to put OKC ahead 14 with 2:45 left to play, the Chesapeake Energy Arena crowd showered him with its loudest and most in-unison chant of "M-V-P" to that point. Durant was starting to lengthen his lead over reigning back-to-back winner LeBron James in the MVP race, and the 25-point scoring streak ultimately is what enabled Durant to slam the door shut.

The streak reached its unceremonious end on April 8, 2014, a 15-point road win at Sacramento. Durant finished with 23 points on 8-for-13 shooting, sitting the entire fourth quarter after OKC entered the final frame with an eight-point lead.

"I was getting so many texts after every game," Durant said, "I'm glad that's over with."

42 Perfection

It was a night to remember, a performance for the ages, yet Serge Ibaka wanted to forget it.

"I know it was an incredible performance," Ibaka sheepishly admitted. "But I don't think it's good for me to keep thinking about.... I think about it more as a game we won. It was big for us."

It was June 2, 2012, the night Ibaka put on a perfect shooting display against San Antonio in Game 4 of the Western Conference finals. The Thunder's power forward stunned the Spurs with a playoff career-high 26 points on 11-of-11 shooting. The Thunder won 109–103 inside Chesapeake Energy Arena.

"We needed every basket," Thunder coach Scott Brooks said. "If he was 10-for-11, we might not have won."

With the win, the Thunder evened the series at 2–2 before taking the next two games to advance to the NBA Finals. Oklahoma City became only the 15th team in NBA history to climb out of a 0–2 hole and win a best-of-seven series.

Ibaka narrowly missed tying the NBA postseason record for most field goals made without a miss. Larry McNeill went 12-for-12 in 1975. Scott Wedman in 1985 went 11-for-11, the only other player in NBA playoff history to do so.

"I didn't know [during the game]," Ibaka said of his flawless accuracy. "I just kept shooting. I had confidence. I was hot. And my teammates…kept passing the ball, and I kept shooting."

"And he made tough shots," Brooks added. "He made shots with guys in his face. He made jump shots. He made inside shots. They weren't all gimmes."

Ibaka had one field goal in the opening quarter, five in the second, three in the third, and two in the fourth. Nine of his 11 field goals came off assists—three from Kevin Durant, two from James Harden, and one apiece from Derek Fisher, Kendrick Perkins, Thabo Sefolosha, and Russell Westbrook. Seven of Ibaka's field goals came with the margin standing at seven points or less, and six of his baskets were from 15' and beyond.

Marv Albert and Reggie Miller, who called the game for TNT, grew more mesmerized with each subsequent shot, Albert emphasizing each syllable in "Serge Ibaka" as only he can. Ibaka, meanwhile, grew more confident.

He pointed to Kendrick Perkins following his first basket, as if to say thanks for the assist. He clapped his hands with a more determined look while backpedaling on defense after his third make, his second straight jumper. He flashed his patented "Air Congo" wings after his fourth bucket, a dunk set up by Fisher. He left his follow through hanging just a tad longer after knocking down his sixth field goal, a baseline jumper set up by Durant. He popped the front of his jersey following his eighth straight field goal, enlarging the "THUNDER" emblazoned across his chest.

"He was relaxed and settled in and did what we needed him to do," Perkins said. "But I thought we got him the ball early, which got him some easy buckets and got him going which will help anybody's confidence."

Not to be taken for granted is how Ibaka worked to get good looks. He was patient but assertive, a force by fitting into the flow of the offense rather than being the focal point. He set screens, moved without the ball, flashed to the passer with fluid cuts, and floated into open spaces.

"Eleven-for-11 in Game 4 of the conference finals is not easy to do," Spurs guard Manu Ginobili said after the game. "I understand if he runs the floor for transition dunks or [scores] on drop-offs when we help. That can happen. But he made five to six jumpers, and that's something we were willing to give up. But he was impressive today."

Ibaka also made all four of his free throws to finish with 26 points in 41 minutes. He added five rebounds and three blocked shots, but his scoring was huge because it helped compensate for an off night from Westbrook, who had just seven points on 2-for-10 shooting.

"The good thing about it," Ibaka said, "is it was the right moment, a moment where my team needed it; a big moment, a conference final."

Led by Ibaka, the Thunder's big man trio of Ibaka, Perkins, and Nick Collison combined to shoot 22-for-25. Perkins was 7-for-9. Collison was 4-for-5.

"If you did a shooting drill with nobody guarding you, I don't think you could do that," said Spurs coach Gregg Popovich, who later said every time he sees Ibaka or hears his name, he thinks "11-for-11."

Ibaka had assembled a handful of highly efficient shooting performances prior to that Game 4. He netted 18 points on 9-for-10 shooting at Phoenix on February 4, 2011, and went 9-of-12 for 22 points against Dallas in the opening round of the 2012 playoffs. Two seasons later, during the 2013–14 season, Ibaka scored 25 points on 12-for-12 shooting in a 25-point win at Brooklyn.

But this was perfection in the postseason, a moment when potential turned into production and 41 magical minutes left everyone salivating over what was in store for the future.

"To me the sky's the limit for Serge," Perkins said. "I feel like all he's got to do is just continue to work and continue to try to get better.

"If he gets it in his mind that he wants to be one of the top power forwards in the league, it's not hard for him."

43 Marathons with Memphis

Oklahoma City and Memphis met in the playoffs three times in a four-year span from 2011–14.

All three showdowns came complete with comebacks and captivating position battles, twists and turns, and countless wild and crazy quirks that would define each series and put the two franchises on a path to becoming fierce rivals.

Their playing styles were polar opposites. The Thunder had a high-octane offense powered by two superstars with sensational one-on-one skills. They liked to play fast and free, feasting in transition and on isolations. The Grizzlies were more methodical. They built their identity with shutdown defense and a punishing inside attack on the offensive end. Little about the clashing philosophies made for a pretty matchup. Games were largely slow-it-down, grind-it-out, defensive dogfights. But that created some crazy contests and some fantastic finishes.

When the two met in the 2011 conference semifinals, the Thunder prevailed in seven games. Game 4 became an instant classic, a three-hour, 52 minute, three-overtime thriller in which the Thunder crawled out of an 18-point first-half hole and outlasted the Grizzlies 133–123 inside FedEx Forum. Russell Westbrook and Kevin Durant combined for 75 points that night, the most the duo ever scored in a playoff game. But that series had an average margin of 13.4 points. No contest was closer than eight points. But 2014 was a different story.

After losing to the Grizzlies in five games while playing the 2013 conference semifinals without Westbrook, who was lost for the playoffs after the infamous Patrick Beverley play that tore Westbrook's meniscus, the Thunder made it clear they wanted revenge. "Memphis put us out [last year]," Westbrook said. "Now it's our turn to come back."

"Now that we healthy, we get a chance to get a little get-back." Kendrick Perkins added.

The teams collided in the first round, the Thunder owning homecourt after securing the No. 2 seed, the Grizzlies coming in confident as a 50-win 7-seed. Memphis hit a two-month storm early in the year when center Marc Gasol, the league's reigning Defensive Player of the Year, missed 23 games with a knee injury. The Grizzlies went 10–13 without him. They were 40–19 with him. In other words, they weren't your typical 7-seed. Memphis rolled into the postseason winners of 18 of their final 25 games, including a franchise-record 14 straight at home. The Grizzlies' last home loss came before the All-Star break, on February 5, and their overtime win over Dallas in the regular season finale enabled them to draw the Thunder rather than a dreaded first-round matchup with San Antonio, a team that had whipped them in 14 of their last 16 meetings. The Grizzlies had their preferred matchup, momentum, confidence, and health.

And they got demolished in the opening game. The Thunder never trailed and led by as many as 25 before holding off a furious Grizzlies second-half rally to take a 100–86 victory. But the next four games would be epic battles. Games 2 through 5 were decided by a combined 13 points. Each of the four contests went into overtime, setting an NBA record for consecutive overtime games in a playoff series.

The Thunder trailed by five with 18.1 remaining in regulation of Game 2. Durant then hit one of the most miraculous shots in Oklahoma City playoff history, a desperation corner three-pointer that he flung to the basket while falling out of bounds and on his bottom. He was fouled by Gasol on the play and made the ensuing free throw for a four-point play that pulled the Thunder within one with 13.8 seconds left. "Some guys are just special," Grizzlies guard Tony Allen said after the game. "That was just one of those special plays." Mike Conley split a pair of free throws, and Perkins converted a buzzer-beating putback off a missed 3 by Westbrook to send it to overtime. Memphis then clamped down, holding the Thunder to six points on 2-for-8 shooting in the extra frame. Durant scored all six points, giving him a game-high 36 point, 11-rebound, four-assist stat line that masked the number Memphis had done on him.

Allen, who starred at nearby Oklahoma State a decade earlier and had evolved into the league's premier perimeter defender, hounded Durant all night. He glued himself to Durant, locking and chasing him on screens, holding his ground in the post, and contesting shots as best he could despite yielding at least five inches. Durant entered the fourth quarter with 16 points on 18 shot attempts. He went 6-for-10 in the fourth quarter and overtime to finish 12-for-28, still below the crazy-efficient standard he had set. Twelve of Durant's shot attempts came from three-point range, illustrating how far away from the basket Allen muscled Durant and how much Durant settled for jumpers after everything else had been disrupted. The same dogged defense Allen displayed that night had long been a tough test for Durant, and it once again would shape the complexion of the matchup and the series.

In Game 3, the Thunder dug itself out of a 17-point, fourth-quarter hole but again saw the game slip away in overtime, this time 98–95 inside FedEx Forum. Durant and Westbrook combined for 60 points on 19-for-53 shooting. They were 4-for-21 from three-point range, with Durant going 0-for-8. Allen again supplied a steady dose of defense, but he also chipped in an unexpected source of offense. His 16 points off the bench were seven more than the Thunder's reserves had combined. Meanwhile, a disturbing two-game trend had developed in the series' first two overtime frames—Durant and Westbrook were reverting to hero ball, having hoisted 19 of the team's 20 overtime shot attempts.

But the Thunder showed no signs of panic. "A lot of positives," Thunder coach Scott Brooks said of the defeat. "One of the positives is we've been here before. Matter of fact, we've been here before with this Grizzlies team." In their 2011 playoff clash, the Thunder fell into a 2–1 hole against the Grizzlies but tied the series with that thrilling triple-overtime victory in Game 4 at Memphis. OKC ultimately advanced in seven.

The Thunder offense, however, still couldn't get untracked in Game 4. Durant and Westbrook combined for just 30 points on 11-for-45 shooting. They had 12 turnovers against 11 assists. On most nights, the Thunder would have gotten trounced in a playoff game had their stars performed that poorly. Fortunately

What Tony Said

Following the hotly contested 2014 first-round series between the Thunder and Grizzlies, Memphis guard Tony Allen was asked about Kevin Durant during a local radio interview. Although complimentary, Allen shared his thoughts on how Durant could be more dangerous. His comments echoed what many observers by 2014 had come to realize.

"I think if Kevin Durant had the mentality that three things are going to happen, 'I'm going to score, get fouled, or get an assist and put the pressure on [defenders] like Westbrook,' his mentality, I think the series go a whole different way," Allen said. "I don't think Durant be aggressive enough. It should be smooth sailing for him.... I just think he gifted. He's 6'10" with a jumper like that and a handle like that. I just believe you could put more pressure on a defense."

for the Thunder, reserve guard Reggie Jackson rescued them from falling into a dreaded 3–1 hole. Jackson scored 17 of his game- and playoff-career-high 32 points in the fourth quarter and overtime to power OKC to a season-saving 92–89 victory. He took over down the stretch, first with two monumental baskets in the final minute of regulation to help force overtime, and then with eight points in overtime. His final four points came on free throws in the last 13 seconds to extend the Thunder's lead to three each trip. As Jackson stood at the stripe, Durant stood in front of his bench barely able to watch. He turned his back and spoke with an assistant coach on the first attempt. He doubled over and snuck a peek at the second. When he saw it splash in, Durant gave a fist pump.

Back in OKC for Game 5, longtime referee Joey Crawford became the center of attention in the closing minute. Before he did, the Thunder stormed back from a 20-point, third-quarter deficit and forced overtime courtesy of one of the best and most pivotal plays of Westbrook's career. Trailing 90–88 with 15 seconds remaining in regulation and a five-second differential between the game and shot clock, the Thunder didn't need to foul. Conley orchestrated Memphis' offense from high above the three-point arc. As the shot clock ticked to seven, he called for a Gasol screen and started to his left. Westbrook fought over the pick. Durant's show of help thwarted a drive. The shot clock trickled to three. Conley went back right. Westbrook stuck out his left arm. His fingertips grazed the ball and poked it away from Conley's possession. Westbrook scooped it and scooted the other way for a game-tying uncontested dunk with four seconds left. A Zach Randolph layup came just after the buzzer.

In overtime, Durant stood at the free throw line with 27.5 seconds left and a chance to tie the score with a successful second foul shot. But after throwing him the ball for the second attempt, Crawford raced in and interrupted Durant just before he went into his patented routine. Crawford strolled over for a conversation with the scorer's table, making sure the foul count was displayed properly yet stopping Durant's rhythm and leaving a packed house that was already on pins and needles confused. When he finally got the ball back, Durant missed. The scoreboard never moved again. Grizzlies 100, Thunder 99. "I was just trying to stay focused and knock the free throw down," Durant said after the game. "I don't know what happened. But I got to make that free throw."

The interruption became a convenient excuse for fans. But the Grizzlies had just held the Thunder under 40 percent shooting for the fourth straight game, which coincided with Durant appearing completely out of sorts. His poor play led to *The Oklahoman's* infamous "Mr. Unreliable" headline. Also in that Game 5, Mike "Thunder Killer" Miller came off the bench to score 21 points, splashing in 5-of-8 three-pointers in 30 minutes. He added six rebounds, three assists, and three steals. For Thunder fans, it was a frustrating flashback to Game 5 of the 2012 NBA Finals, when Miller stroked seven threes in a show of storybook sharpshooting during Miami's championship-clinching win over OKC.

Durant, however, exorcised his demons and responded in Game 6 with a signature performance—36 points on 11-for-23 shooting with 10 rebounds in the Thunder's 104–84 victory. The game marked the first time since inserting Westbrook into the starting lineup in 2008 that Brooks switched his starting lineup by choice rather than necessity. He started Caron Butler in place of Thabo Sefolosha, a tactic designed to kick-start the Thunder's stagnant offense and prevent the Grizzlies from continuing to hide Conley on Sefolosha. Though few knew it at the time, the league office was also reviewing Randolph's actions from a mild altercation with Steven Adams. On the day between Games 6 and 7, the league announced Randolph would be suspended for Game 7 for punching Adams in the face in the fourth quarter of Game 6.

Without Randolph, the Grizzlies jumped out to a nine-point lead after the opening quarter of Game 7. But the Thunder outscored Memphis 67–45 in the second and third quarters to cruise to a 120–109 victory.

The Thunder advanced to face the Los Angeles Clippers in the conference semifinals, taking that series in six games before losing in six to San Antonio in the West finals.

44 Nick Collison

At the start of the 2016–17 NBA season, three players had been with their respective franchises for 15 or more seasons. All three were champions, multi-time All-Stars, and locks for the Basketball Hall of Fame—Dirk Nowitzki, Tony Parker, and Manu Ginobili.

Then there was Nick Collison.

Through relocation and rebuilding, six coaches and two general managers, injuries and aging, losing and winning, two ownership groups and a lockout, Collison was the one constant in the Sonics/Thunder franchise. His 14 seasons with the same organization tied him with Miami forward Udonis Haslem for fourth among active players.

"I know it's really rare," Collison said, "for somebody to be able to stick that long."

Particularly role players.

Collison, though, wasn't your average role player. Thunder General Manager Sam Presti often labeled the 6'10" power forward a "founding member," giving Collison equal footing as perennial All-Stars Kevin Durant and Russell Westbrook. "He represents the type of player that we want to ultimately have our organization embody," Presti said.

Nick Collison (4) was drafted by the Thunder franchise in 2003 when the team played in Seattle. He spent his first 15 seasons with the same franchise, earning the nickname "Mr. Thunder." (AP Photo/Jeff Roberson)

"Who knows? Sam might have had me in a trade that fell apart last second seven years ago," Collison countered in 2014. "I think by being able to be here so long I've been able to find that niche, whereas if I was bouncing around different teams I'd be just another guy."

Another place might not have reserved the same respect and appreciation for Collison. With the Thunder, though, Collison's commitment to the team on the court, on practice days, and game nights as well as the everyday example he set in the locker room and as a community leader, helped Oklahoma City establish an identity and create a culture.

"He's the definition of Thunder basketball," Westbrook said. "He's been here since Day One. He's seen the ups and the downs, the ins and the outs. He does his job every day consistently. He never complains about nothing. He's one of those class act kind of guys."

Thunder fans came to know Collison as a blue-collar player, the consummate teammate who dutifully did the little things that went into winning. He had a knack for drawing charges and setting textbook screens to free shooters. He focused not on scoring but playing defense and pulling down rebounds. And when he couldn't grab rebounds, he gladly boxed out the opposition so a teammate could. When a loose ball was on the floor, you could bet Collison would be the first to dive after it. In Oklahoma City, Collison's selfless approach always was admired and acknowledged by the fans. They would erupt in a roar whenever Collison provided one of his patented hustle plays. When his minutes dwindled as the years went on, they showed their appreciation by showering him with applause at the mere sight of his sporadic strolls to the scorer's table.

"I feel like they really appreciate what I do, and I know that's rare for a player like me," Collison said. "A role player like me who averages four [points] and four [rebounds] or whatever it is, no one really thinks twice about him. But I know that I have kind of a special place here. So I really appreciate that."

There was a time when Collison was the star. At Iowa Falls High in 1999, he was a McDonald's All-American. At Kansas in 2003, he was the Big 12 Player of the Year and the National Association of Basketball Coaches (NABC) Player of the Year. With the help of longtime friend Kirk Hinrich, Collison led the Jayhawks to back-to-back Final Fours in 2002 and 2003, losing to Carmelo Anthony and Syracuse in the 2003 title game. But after being drafted 12th overall in 2003 by the Sonics, Collison missed his rookie season because of a shoulder injury.

He began to alter his game, reverting to basics he was taught in his formative years by his father, who doubled as his high school basketball coach. As a young pro, Collison focused on doing anything he thought would keep him on the court. It was all the little things Thunder fans came to know and love. That was the genesis of Collison turning himself into a glue guy.

"He's a great role model for all of our players to look up to and see, 'That's how you have to be to be an NBA player,'" former Thunder coach Scott Brooks said. "Every team needs a Nick, and we're not giving him up."

Added Presti: "His fingerprints are all over the success of the organization, and those fingerprints will have a lot of staying power."

The Most Miserable Season Ever

For one night, things finally were going well.

For one night, the Thunder escaped another slow start, another series of turnovers, another string of missed free throws. For one night, Oklahoma City finally cleaned up the comedy of errors that had plagued it all season and crafted a performance so overpowering it was setting up the franchise's first ever runaway victory.

It was December 10, 2008, a Wednesday night in Oklahoma City, the 23rd game in Thunder history. The Memphis Grizzlies were in town.

The Thunder led by six at the end of the first quarter, only the sixth time that season OKC held a lead after the opening period. A 13–0 run in the second frame pushed the margin to 19, and a Nick Collison dunk off an assist from Russell Westbrook bumped the Thunder's advantage to 21 with 5:07 left in the first half.

But there were 29 minutes to be played, and what transpired next summed up the Thunder's inaugural season.

After missing 21 of their first 29 shots, the Grizzlies roared back with nine straight points. They used an 18–4 run over the final five minutes of the second quarter to get within 55–48 at halftime. The Thunder's lead remained at seven entering the fourth quarter. The Grizzlies, with a group of reserves led by second-year point guard Mike Conley, then outscored the Thunder 32–19 over the final 12 minutes. With Kyle Lowry and O.J. Mayo (the team's leading scorer), glued to the bench in the final period, Conley erupted for 14 points to power Memphis and send the Thunder to a fifth straight loss that dropped them to 2–21.

In a season full of bad losses, this one went down as the worst.

"This is the most miserable season I've ever been a part of," forward Nick Collison deadpanned after the game.

Collison never was the type to spew hyperbole. As one of the team's leaders and elder statesmen, he carried a professional demeanor and was no-nonsense when he was on the clock. He was a quiet but insightful figure who largely kept his head down and humbly went about his business. But when he spoke, Collison said what he meant and meant what he said.

His statement carried greater significance given the chaos he was subjected to the year prior, in the franchise's final season in Seattle. But Collison was like most that season who couldn't believe how bad the Thunder were each night and, worse, couldn't see an end in sight.

Two nights before that disheartening loss to Memphis, the Thunder suffered an almost equally bad home defeat to Golden State. Against the Warriors, who had lost nine straight and were playing the final leg of a three-game trip without scoring leaders Stephen Jackson and Corey Maggette, the Thunder never led and trailed by as many as 21. Golden State got 17 points and 21 rebounds from Andris Biedrins and overcame a game-high 41 points from Kevin Durant in a 112–102 victory.

"The Golden State game was about as bad as it could be. But tonight, to be up 20 and then to lose to Memphis, it's tough," Collison continued. "I don't really know what to say at this point. It's been the same thing every game…. We're just not very good right now."

Oklahoma City lost 16 of its first 17 games that season, and with a 3–29 record through December 29 was on pace for the worst season in NBA history. The Thunder lost 34 games by double digits, five of them coming by at least 20 points, three of them by at least 30 points, and a 42-point thrashing.

"That was a tough little stretch for us, but it made us into the team we are now, made us into the players we are now because of going through those tough times," Durant said years later.

Thunder coach Scott Brooks insisted to both his team and the fans that those early tough times wouldn't last.

"The only way to attack it is to go through it," Brooks said. "You have to either go through it or around it or over it. But there's no way you let it stop you from getting to where you want to go."

The Thunder showed great improvement in the second half of the season, going 20–30 over the final 50 games. Their 23–59 record was the league's fourth worst, but the season that went down as the most miserable ever played an important role in who the Thunder are and what the franchise is built on.

"We weren't winning games," Brooks said, "but we were learning how to win games."

46 30 Points, 30 Shots

Criticism of Russell Westbrook was never more severe than in the 2011 playoffs.

Prior to that point, much of the uproar about Westbrook centered on whether he was a true point guard and if he was the right fit for the up-and-coming Thunder.

But there was a different tone to the Thunder's journey to the 2011 Western Conference finals. The third-year point guard got picked apart by fans, media, and legendary players turned commentators. Everything he did was scrutinized. If Westbrook shot too much, he was labeled selfish and a ball hog. If he didn't shoot enough, they said he was too passive, pouting even. It was constant condemnation.

"Russ' [criticism] lasted throughout the whole playoffs," Kendrick Perkins said. "No matter if he played good or bad, he still was getting criticized on something."

The start of the attacks came during the first round against Denver. They began in earnest following Game 4, a three-point Thunder loss on April 25, a Monday night in The Mile-High City.

That was the night Westbrook famously scored 30 points on 30 shots.

His performance that night, and his nightly shot count for the remainder of that playoff run, became the league's most hotly debated topic of that postseason until LeBron James vanished in the NBA Finals.

"OKC would have won tonight if they would have given the ball to their best player," TNT's Chris Webber said. "Their best player is Durant."

Westbrook made only 12-of-30 shots. Kevin Durant, meanwhile, pumped in 31 points on 8-for-18 shooting. The world couldn't understand. The shot count didn't compute. Why wouldn't the Thunder's point guard just keep things simple and feed his two-time scoring champion?

"He's a star, too," Durant said, coming to Westbrook's defense back in Oklahoma City the next day. "He's shown he can win games for you. You can't be mad at him because he missed a few."

Westbrook had hoisted 30 shots or more twice in his career prior to that Game 4. But both instances came in the regular season, and both were overtime contests in which Durant was unavailable for all or the majority of those games. This time, Westbrook's 30-shot night came with the world watching and the Thunder fielding their full complement of players. Taking 12 more shots than Durant was one thing. But when Westbrook launched only two fewer attempts than Durant, Serge Ibaka (nine), and James Harden (five) combined, critics pounced.

"Did he take too many shots? Absolutely," Thunder coach Scott Brooks agreed before also expressing support for his point guard.

"His heart and his determination is always in the right place, and that's all I care about with Russell," Brooks added.

Westbrook, then a 27 percent three-point shooter for his career, went 0-for-7 from beyond the arc. Three of Westbrook's misfires from deep came in the final 30 seconds, each of them launched when the Thunder was within two or three points. In the final five minutes, Westbrook went 1-for-8 with one assist and one turnover.

Lost in the echo chamber was the fact Oklahoma City held a commanding 3–1 lead. But the damage was done. Westbrook had become a lightning rod for criticism, both locally and nationally, by fans and media.

Publicly, Westbrook absorbed it all with poise and positivity.

"Regardless of what I do, it doesn't matter. I can't do no right," he said. "So I just go out and play."

In Game 5, Westbrook played a more passive role. He took only 15 shots, missing 12, and scored just 14 points in 36 minutes. Charles Barkley said Westbrook appeared to be pouting. The Thunder, though, won by three and advanced to play Memphis. By then, the floodgates had swung open.

Critics fired shots at Westbrook after Game 1 against the Grizzlies when he took two more shots than Durant in a 13-point loss. Westbrook then took the brunt of the blame for the Thunder's offense stalling in the second half and overtime of an eight-point Game 3 loss in which the Thunder scored just 17 points in the final 17 minutes. He was ripped for another second-half collapse by the Thunder in Game 6; Westbrook had three costly fourth-quarter turnovers. And in Game 2 of the West finals at Dallas, Westbrook again was at the center of controversy when he was benched in favor of Eric Maynor for the entire fourth quarter of OKC's only win of the series.

"It's kind of crazy how the last two series happened with all the stuff he had to go through," Nick Collison said. "It kind of hit everybody by surprise because, for us, it didn't seem like anything was different. We love Russell, and we love what he brings. And we realize without him this year we wouldn't be a playoff team. We wouldn't be anywhere near as good as we are."

47 Kendrick Perkins

Dwight Howard had just concluded morning shootaround with his Orlando Magic, and as he towered over reporters he marveled at what that night's opponent, the Oklahoma City Thunder, had done a day earlier.

"They're up there now," Howard said. "They have a legitimate chance of winning a title."

The Thunder had just acquired Kendrick Perkins in a stunning deadline-day trade with the Celtics. The specifics were Perkins and Nate Robinson to the Thunder; Jeff Green, Nenad Krstic, a future first-round pick (which became Fab Melo), and cash to the Celtics. Reaction in both cities was swift and severe. Boston fans expressed great outrage over losing their 26-year-old defensive-minded center. Oklahoma City fans expressed great disappointment in losing a favorite in Green. But people in the NBA, and those charged with covering the league, hailed the deal a steal for the Thunder.

"I think Oklahoma City is going to remember this day as the day they took a step up to be a true championship contender in the NBA," TNT analyst and NBA.com reporter David Aldridge wrote.

"For three-and-a-half years, the Thunder have been a team of the future. Today, they became a team of the present," wrote John Hollinger, who was with ESPN.com at the time.

Three days after the trade, Kobe Bryant chimed in by calling Perkins the best low-post defender in basketball.

It seemed the Thunder had finally landed their long-awaited legitimate center.

Perkins immediately changed the makeup of the Thunder. He brought toughness and physicality that Krstic never could. Krstic was a finesse floor spacer. Perkins was a bruising and unapologetic enforcer. In Boston, Perkins had tag teamed with Kevin Garnett to transform the Celtics into the league's best defensive team for the better part of four seasons. He now was being paired with Serge Ibaka to do the same for the Thunder.

Many observers concluded the Thunder made the deal solely to contend with the Los Angeles Lakers' twin towers of Pau Gasol and Andrew Bynum. The truth is the Thunder brain trust long believed in amassing ample size so the roster could adapt to any playing style, big or small, fast or slow. The philosophy quickly paid off, as Perkins delivered strong playoff performances as a primary defender against the likes of Nene, Bynum, and Gasol, Zach Randolph and Marc Gasol, DeAndre Jordan and Tim Duncan. Perkins wasn't always successful, but he was going against the league's best low-post scorers on the game's biggest stage and he won more battles than he lost.

In Boston, Perkins was light on his feet. He served as a shot-blocking rim protector and an occasional source of offense, shooting a high percentage by running the floor and converting alley-oop dunks and putbacks. But the Thunder acquired Perkins just as his body began breaking down. Perkins tore his ACL in Game 6 of the 2010 NBA Finals and was never the same.

With the Thunder, Perkins dealt with a long list of ailments that included a sprained MCL in his left knee, a torn ligament in his left wrist, a partially torn right groin, a strained left groin, and additional surgery on his already surgically repaired right knee. He didn't register his first double double in a Thunder uniform until his 44th game. He finished with only two as a member of the Thunder.

In 273 games in OKC, Perkins averaged 4.2 points, 5.9 rebounds, 1.2 assists, and 0.9 blocked shots in 23.1 minutes per night.

"He's somewhat of an easy target because of his stats," Thunder coach Scott Brooks said. "He's never going to be a statistical guy. He brings toughness. He brings experiences. He brings things that help you win. He makes winning basketball plays."

Frustrated fans grew tired of hearing about Perkins' intangibles. For all of his strengths, Perkins' weaknesses were much more pronounced, his failures much more noticeable than his successes. He struggled in the 2011 Western Conference finals against a superior athlete in Tyson Chandler. He was out of place against Miami in the 2012 NBA Finals. And in 11 playoff games in 2013, his minus–0.6 Player Efficiency Rating marked the worst in postseason history among players who logged at least 200 minutes.

Critics became more vocal. Many spent three years imploring the Thunder to waive Perkins via the league's amnesty clause, a one-time chance each team had under rules of the new collective bargaining agreement to release a player without his salary counting against the team's payroll. Perkins had signed a four-year, $34 million extension five days after arriving in OKC. But Thunder General Manager Sam Presti never saw the benefit in essentially paying Perkins to go away (players still received their salaries, the money just wouldn't count on the books) only to then be forced to find a suitable replacement.

Instead, the Thunder defiantly defended Perkins, often pointing to the team's success with him in the lineup. It was sound logic supported by mounds of evidence that was hard to argue against.

The Thunder's ascension to an elite defensive team coincided with Perk's arrival. Before him, the Thunder was allowing 104.9 points per 100 possessions. After Perkins joined the team, that number fell 2.6 points in his first season and never rose above 101 points per 100 possessions in his final 3½ seasons, ranking in the

With Kendrick Perkins in the lineup, the Thunder went 191–82, giving him a 0.699 winning percentage that solidified him as one of the Thunder's all-time winningest players. (AP Photo/Mike Stone)

top 10 every season. Oklahoma City also ranked in the top five in opponent field-goal percentage for Perkins' entire tenure.

Most impressive was the Thunder's 191–82 record with Perkins in the lineup. That success ran counter to Perkins' individual stats, but for all his flaws, Perkins' 0.699 winning percentage solidified him as one of the Thunder's all-time winningest players.

48 Visit Thunder Alley

A must for any Thunder fan attending a game in Oklahoma City is a visit to Thunder Alley, the lively pregame festival held during select home dates. This is where Thunder fans come together as one and enjoy world-class entertainment before being thrilled by the team's world-class athletes.

Thunder Alley sits on Reno Avenue, the street that runs between Chesapeake Energy Arena and the Cox Convention Center. A one-block stretch of Reno Avenue is barricaded between South Robinson Avenue and E.K. Gaylord Boulevard whenever the Thunder hosts their Thunder Alley festivities. There, fans will find a boisterous block party that includes live music, food and drink, interactive games, inflatables, sport courts, face painting, and many more entertainment options. Thunder Girls, Thunder Drummers, and Storm Chasers annually liven up Thunder Alley with appearances and performances.

During the playoffs, the Thunder typically erects a stage in Thunder Alley, where the team's customary *Thunder Live* pregame show is broadcast before a huge crowd of onlookers. The show begins one hour prior to tip-off.

Thunder Alley opens three hours prior to tip-off for most games. For noon games, Thunder Alley opens at 10:00 AM.

"It's a chance in a safe, family-friendly environment for our fans to embrace the Thunder experience and get ready for the game," said Dan Mahoney, Thunder Vice President of Broadcasting and Corporate Communications. "For those with tickets, they can enter the arena when doors open. Other Thunder fans can enjoy the pregame entertainment and then go to their favorite viewing establishment to watch the game."

Looking for last-minute tickets to see the Thunder play live? Thunder Alley is also home to the Thunder Rewards Zone, which gives fans a game-day opportunity to win specially designated tickets. Each game, the Thunder raffles off 50 pairs of Loud City tickets. In the team's early days, fans had to register for the drawing just outside the arena and be present to win. But prior to the start of the 2016–17 season, the team streamlined the process with an online registration system. Entry closes seven hours prior to tip-off, and winners are notified via email at least four hours before tip-off. Registration is free, but participants must be at least 18 years old and can register only once per home game.

49 No More Watch Parties

Minutes after the Thunder's series-clinching victory over the Los Angeles Lakers in Game 5 of the Western Conference semifinals, delight turned to dread.

More than 6,000 had gathered in Thunder Alley, where the team began hosting watch parties during the 2012 playoffs, allowing fans without tickets the opportunity to take in each game on the 74' wide, 20' tall videoboard mounted alongside the northwest corner of Chesapeake Energy Arena. Crowds had grown larger each game. A playoff tradition was being established. But on this night, May 21, 2012, chaos ensued. As 18,203 fans filed out of the arena, joining the thousands already on the street, gunfire rang out just three blocks east of the arena, on Reno Avenue between Mickey Mantle Drive and Joe Carter Avenue. Eight people were shot. A pregnant woman was injured.

Thunder Alley was never the same.

Oklahoma City officials, in conjunction with the Thunder, permanently shut down the wildly popular watch parties. "This ever-growing game night crowd that gathers on the street outside the building, that can't continue," Oklahoma City Mayor Mick Cornett said a day later. "There are too many public safety concerns. As much as we love the expression of enthusiasm, it's no longer a workable situation."

In a statement released by the team, Thunder Vice President of Broadcasting and Corporate Communications Dan Mahoney said the team was saddened to hear of that night's violence and said the team's top priority always is to make games and Thunder Alley a safe, fun environment for fans. "We will continue to work closely with law enforcement and the city to review security and crowd control procedures, and we stand ready to make any necessary changes to ensure safety," Mahoney said.

Police said Avery Myers, 16 at the time, confessed to shooting into the crowd. Myers in 2014 was sentenced to 25 years in prison after pleading guilty to eight counts of assault and battery with a deadly weapon.

Leanna Marshall, mother of two of the alleged victims, said Thunder Alley needed to end. "You go down there thinking you're going to do something friendly and fun and you come out with bullet wounds, and that's not okay," Marshall said. "This was supposed to be something for them to experience, something new.... I would rather see them close that down than to have something like that take place again."

Others had hoped that the actions of a few wouldn't ruin the fun for everyone.

"It's crazy how many people were outside and how many people come and support," Russell Westbrook said. "So I think they'll be a little disappointed. So hopefully they don't cut it off."

Thunder Alley festivities now conclude when games begin.

50 Meet a Super Fan

At every Wednesday night home game during the inaugural season, the Thunder went hunting for their biggest fan.

They partnered with Oklahoma City–based Love's Travel Stops & Country Stores on an in-game promotion they labeled "Love's Ultimate Thunder Fan." From the start of the season through March 4, one fan was selected as the winner based on the roar of the crowd when candidates were shown on the big screen. Online voting at the team's website determined eight semifinalists. Four finalists were then revealed during a home game against Chicago on March 18, 2009. The grand-prize winner received an all-expenses-paid trip to Boston to see the Thunder take on the Celtics.

The promotion flooded the Ford Center with the wildest, wackiest, and craziest costumes you'll ever find in an NBA arena. But it was that promotion that gave birth to some true super fans. The grand-prize winner from 2008–09, for example, was a fan from Ada, Oklahoma, who went by the name Thunderhead. Josh Newby, as his mother named him, attended games wearing a giant

Thunder logo covering his entire head. The promotion returned for 2009–10, with the grand-prize winner walking away that season with 2010–11 season tickets in the South Terrace Suites, a package valued at $10,000. The organization encouraged fans to let their imaginations run wild, and fans didn't hesitate to rise to the challenge. They showed up dressed as robots and Rumble, wrestlers and superheroes. Before there was a Rumble in that first season, they were the team's mascots. They became a staple of Thunder games, and their unbridled passion became a part of the unique home game experience.

Here are a few of their stories.

Thunder Princess

Nauzi Jagosh never intended on being a long-term fan. She just wanted to see what the hype was about. But after buying a ticket in Loud City for opening night, she was hooked. She caught Thunder fever during the pregame festivities, with NBA Commissioner David Stern welcoming Oklahoma City to the NBA and Oklahoma City mayor Mick Cornett emceeing the unveiling of a blue Thunder flag in the rafters.

"It was the first time I felt like in Oklahoma everyone could love one thing," said Jagosh, who you might know better as the woman who sits behind the basket closest to the Thunder bench wearing a tiara, a tutu, and a glittery custom No. 85 Thunder jersey with "Princess" in place of a player's last name.

Jagosh attended 28 games in the inaugural season. She became a season ticket holder the second year. She even traveled alone to Los Angeles to attend the Thunder's first playoff game against the Lakers. But she blossomed into a costume-wearing die-hard during the Love's Ultimate Thunder Fan contest that first season. She remembered only one other female fan winning the contest. So toward the end of the year, she decided to increase the ratio. And she wanted to make a statement. "I just wanted to be the super girly and ridiculous option," she said. "What's more girly than a princess with a big flowy skirt, a tiara, and I used to wear glittery heels but I'm older now. I can't do that no more."

The tiara and tutu remained essential. Other fans began expecting it.

"People love it," she said. "I feel like if I don't come in it I'm letting somebody down, and I don't want to do that."

Lady Blue

Angela Love always liked basketball. She was a Celtics fan in the '80s and a Hornets fan when they were in OKC. She appreciated the limited number of players on rosters. She could learn every player's name, face, and personality. When the Thunder arrived, players soon learned hers.

Love sits in Section 119, the seats near the tunnel that the Thunder comes out. She's the woman with the blue hair, the only other woman to win the Love's Ultimate Thunder Fan contest in the first season. "When we got our team I thought, 'I'll just show them I can do something crazy,'" she said. Love has worn the blue hair ever since. "It stands out and it's easy to do," she said.

Back in 2008–09, Love had a more elaborate costume. She wore a feathery boa and a blue T-shirt declaring herself as the "temporary mascot" since Rumble the Bison had yet to debut. She dropped the boa, but the blue hair is a keeper. "I never did it for the attention," Love said. "Sometimes I wonder when I'm walking to the game, 'Why are people staring at me?' I don't even hardly think about it anymore."

In a way, Love is living out her childhood fantasies. She is like most Oklahomans of a certain age who could only dream of having a major league sports team as a child. While she thoroughly enjoys the Thunder, she says she's jealous she didn't have a team to call her own as a kid. "I just want to tell everybody, 'Appreciate this.' When I was a kid in the '80s, the thought of this was just inconceivable," she said. "The '80s, if you told someone you were going downtown, they'd say, 'Why? You got a court date?'"

Brickman

Derrick Seys wanted to get inside Kobe Bryant's head. Six games before Bryant played the Ford Center, the Lakers legend had erupted for 81 points against Toronto, the second most points scored in NBA history. "I said, 'When he comes into our arena, he's not going to do that,'" Seys remembers vowing.

It was February 2006. Oklahoma City was home to the Hornets then. Seys was crafting a new hand prop to distract opposing players at the free throw line when he realized his latest work would fit as a hat. He put it on and learned it was large enough to cover his head. Just like that, Brickman was born. From his seats in Section 120, behind the basket closest to the Thunder's bench, Seys covers his head with a Styrofoam brick during opposing free throws and prides himself on being a possible nuisance for unsuspecting opponents. "If I could catch their eye for a second I just might get in their brain a little bit and create just enough of a mental lapse that maybe they'll brick one for us."

Seys has more than 300 handmade signs, many of them poking fun at stars using OKC's Bricktown District as a pun: Welcome to Bricktown. Brick Mamba. LeBrick James.

A new job required Seys to move to Illinois in 2010. But you don't think 740 miles and an 11-hour drive would stop this super fan, do you? Seys remained a season ticket holder and continued to travel by car to a dozen games a year. He'd leave his home 12 hours before tip-off and often turn around and head back shortly after the game. He put between 15,000 and 18,000 miles on his Toyota Corolla each year before passing it down to his 16-year-old daughter in 2017 with more than 217,000 miles on it.

Seys enjoys enhancing the game and fan experience. Best of all, though, is when an opposing player steps to the free throw line and tosses up a brick. "It was never one of my career goals, aspirations, or even on the bucket list," he said. "It just happened."

Thundor

Garrett Haviland remembers getting cable television. He couldn't believe his eyes when he found ESPN. All the sports. All the highlights. He was in sixth grade, and after seeing another middle-schooler highlighted on "SportsCenter" for making a halfcourt shot, he wondered if he could ever make it on television. But when his basketball career concluded as a high school freshman, Haviland figured it would never happen. Boy, was he wrong.

Haviland rose to fame as Thundor, the big-bellied, mask-wearing, megaphone-carrying super fan who delights Thunder crowds and forces opposing players into double takes. Haviland always loved sports and making people happy. He also never cared about making a fool of himself. So when the Thunder began searching for the ultimate Thunder fan in 2008, he broke out a luchador wrestling costume he happened to have from Halloween. On December 10, 2008, he wore it and earned Ultimate Fan of the Game. He was cemented as Thundor.

Haviland became a season ticket holder in 2010–11, the Thunder's third season, and evolved as the team did. His full body suit gave way to ripping off his shirt, Hulk Hogan style, and soon he did away with shirts altogether. Pasties and belly art became his staples. So too did his hand-sewn cape, armbands, Thunder-colored knee-high socks, and suspenders attached to jersey shorts. "Every year it seems like it gets more and more ridiculous," he said.

The persona blossomed into more than Haviland ever imagined. He's received pictures of himself on a Buenos Aires poster, has been featured in a French magazine, and has a following in Japan and China. A local car dealership filmed two commercials with him. U.S. Fleet Tracking did, as well. The company even invited him to its president's birthday bash and, naturally, Haviland showed up in a Hula Skirt and a coconut bra with "Happy Birthday, Cindy" painted on his torso. He was an extra in the infamous "Thunderstruck," participated in a Russell Westbrook Air Jordan commercial, got interviewed on set by the *Inside the NBA* crew following Game 3 of the 2014 Western Conference finals, and has had a complete stranger ask him to attend his wedding.

"It's been a really crazy ride," Haviland said, "I would just hope to one day see the Thunder hang a championship banner while I'm painted up half naked and happy."

51 Meet the Thunder at the Airport

They were there when the Thunder clinched a playoff berth for the first time.

They were there when the Thunder played their hearts out and won a triple-overtime marathon at Memphis.

They were there when the Thunder fell in the NBA Finals and fell short of making the postseason.

Since 2010, Thunder fans have been there, waiting at Will Rogers World Airport to welcome their team home after huge wins and heartbreaking losses. No matter the time, weather, or result, Thunder fans will be there, showing their passion and support by traveling to the General Aviation Terminal to stand along a chain link fence and greet players, coaches, and support staff upon their return.

What began as a grassroots effort is now one of the fans' biggest and best traditions.

"Win, lose, or draw, they're there," former Thunder guard James Harden once said. "It shows the support they have for us and the love they have for us."

The airport greetings helped establish Thunder fans as arguably the best in the NBA.

"I played in Boston for eight years, and I thought they were the best fans in the world until I got to OKC," Kendrick Perkins said. "Now I see what it means to be a part of something special."

Most remarkable about the rambunctious receptions is they're organic. The Thunder has never announced when the team plane would land. Through Internet searches, social media, word of mouth, and deductive reasoning, fans decipher the team's travel schedule and quickly spread the word. Some wait for hours to get a good spot and a good glimpse of the team.

Royce Young, founder of the popular fan site DailyThunder. com, spawned the idea with help from his readers. Together, they started a movement. A few hundred fans showed up on the night of April 3, 2010, when the Thunder clinched a playoff berth for the first time following a 121–116 win at Dallas. The event exploded from there, with more fans journeying to the airport after each subsequent postseason road trip.

"In the fourth quarter, people will already start tweeting at me, 'Hey, airport time? You got a time?'" Young said. "People are dying to know. And it's really become this kind of tradition of welcoming the team back to Oklahoma. It's become a cool thing."

Even cooler is the appreciation Thunder players have for the show of support. Rather than simply walking to their vehicles, several Thunder players generally stroll over and express gratitude by giving high-fives through the fence.

One of the most impressive showings came following Game 4 of the 2011 semifinals. The Thunder outlasted Memphis in a 133–123 triple-overtime slugfest to even the series at two games apiece. The contest took 3 hours, 52 minutes. With an 8:30 PM tip-off, the Thunder didn't land until approximately 3:00 AM. Still, Thunder fans were there—on a Monday night.

A year later, after a 103–100 road win in Game 4 of the semifinals against the Lakers, inclement weather delayed the team charter. The Thunder didn't arrive until 5:15 AM. Despite heavy rain, wind, and lightning, Thunder fans kept the tradition alive. Some had been there since 1:30 AM.

"It's not normal," Nick Collison said.

Thunder Bolts

In 2008, Royce Young was in his last semester at the University of Oklahoma when team chairman Clay Bennett unveiled "Thunder" as the nickname for Oklahoma City's new NBA franchise. And Young hated it. So he launched a website where he could write about his disdain.

That's how DailyThunder.com was born. It has since become the most popular fan site for the Thunder community. Young, a journalism major at OU, modeled the site's mission after a popular Chicago Cubs fan blog, Bleed Cubbie Blue. But unlike the long-established MLB team he rooted for, the Thunder was a new team in a new pro market. And no one had carved out a niche with the fan community. Young gave it a shot by covering the team from a fan perspective but with a professional eye.

"I'm not going to sit here and say I was good at it. I didn't know what I was doing," Young said. "I think it did help that I went to journalism school and at least had an idea of the industry a little bit."

Young, who once thought it a longshot to break into journalism but now covers the team for ESPN.com, considers the growth and popularity of his site "pure luck." But Young worked diligently by posting daily content while other upstart Thunder blogs struggled with consistency, and fans ultimately chose Daily Thunder as their preferred blog to comment and build a community. "That, as much as anything else, helped me," Young said. "People picked my little site to talk."

The team name Young preferred instead of Thunder?
Barons.
But Daily Barons just doesn't have the same ring to it.

It became the norm in OKC.

"At first we were talking amongst ourselves, 'Do you think they're going to be here?' 'Nah, it's 3:00 in the morning. They're not going to be here,'" remembered guard Thabo Sefolosha. "And then we'd come out the plane and 'Oh, they're here!' After a while we just figured, 'Okay, they're going to be here.' It was just a great feeling."

The largest gathering came on an excruciatingly hot and humid June day, when more than 4,000 fans braved the elements—as well as a traffic jam—to meet the Thunder. It was the day after the team's Game 5 loss to Miami in the 2012 NBA Finals, a Friday. They came with signs and team flags. They dyed their dogs and risked going into labor.

They did it all to see and support the home team.

"I would just be sad if I went into labor because I couldn't make it to see the team," said Rosala Erwin, a pregnant Thunder fan who was due 11 days later and said she had an early contraction on the way to the airport that day.

Atop a temporary stage erected in an open field just off Terminal Drive and Amelia Earhart Lane, Thunder players, one by one, began addressing the crowd. As each player spoke, he was flanked by teammates and coaches recording the crowd. They were cheering and chanting, hooting and hollering.

At no point did it feel like the Thunder had just seen their season end in the NBA Finals.

"Last night was one of the toughest times we ever had as a group," Kevin Durant said. "But coming back home, we knew we'd get to see you guys in the morning."

Former Thunder coach Scott Brooks labeled the raucous airport greetings "exciting times."

"We're really appreciative of the fans we've got," Collison said. "It speaks to the consistency that they've shown, in good times and bad. I think that's the most rare thing about our fan base."

52 Russell Westbrook at All-Star Weekend

Here's a year-by-year look at Russell Westbrook's trips to All-Star Weekend.

2009: Playing against teammates Kevin Durant and Jeff Green in the Rookie Challenge, Westbrook scored 12 points in 18 minutes off the bench. Westbrook and the Rookies fell 122–116. This year was also the closest Westbrook came to competing in the dunk contest. Fans got to vote for this year's fourth participant alongside Dwight Howard, Nate Robinson, and J.R. Smith. Rudy Fernandez won the fan vote over Westbrook and Joe Alexander. Westbrook never again expressed interest in competing in the contest, even as fans clamored to see him. "If they wanted to see me in it, they would have voted me in it when I was [a candidate]," Westbrook joked in 2012. In 2015, Westbrook elaborated on why he doesn't participate, saying the dunk contest had become too gimmicky. "I just dunk on people in the game," Westbrook said. "That's it."

2010: Westbrook scored 29 of his game-high 40 points in the second half of the Rookie Challenge, but his Sophomore squad fell 140–128. Westbrook was also selected as the replacement for Derrick Rose in the Skills Challenge, the timed obstacle course event. Competing alongside Steve Nash, Deron Williams, and Brandon Jennings, Westbrook finished last with a disappointing time of 44.1 seconds.

2011: Westbrook's first All-Star Game appearance came courtesy of West coaches selecting him as a reserve. In his native Los Angeles, he scored 12 points with five rebounds and two assists in 14 minutes. His West squad won 148–143. Westbrook also had a better showing in the Skills Challenge. This time fans voted Westbrook among three other players—Stephen Curry, Derrick Rose, and John Wall—to compete alongside Chris Paul. Westbrook made the final round with a first-round-leading time of 30.0 seconds. But he struggled to get a bounce pass through a net in the final round against Curry and finished with a time of 44.2 seconds.

2012: In his second All-Star Game, Westbrook came off the bench and scored 21 points with five rebounds, two assists, and two steals in 28 minutes. For the third straight season, Westbrook participated in the Skills Challenge. Tony Parker, Rajon Rondo, Deron Williams, John Wall, and Kyrie Irving were his competition. Westbrook narrowly missed the cut for the final round, finishing with a time of 33.8 seconds.

2013: In his third straight appearance as an All-Star reserve, Westbrook scored 14 points with four rebounds, three assists, and one steal in 18 minutes. He also competed in the Shooting Stars Competition. Team Westbrook featured Westbrook, Minnesota Lynx forward Maya Moore, and seven-time NBA champion Robert Horry. After advancing to the final round with a time of 29.5 seconds—just 4.4 seconds off the course record set in 2006—Team Westbrook did not finish in the allotted time. After the event, Horry raved about Westbrook, saying, "I love the guy. I hope he continues to be successful because he definitely has the potential to be one of the best point guards ever." Westbrook also coached the East Celebrity All-Stars. His team lost 58–38 to the James Harden–coached West Celebrity All-Stars.

2015: After missing the 2014 All-Star festivities due to injury, Westbrook walked into Madison Square Garden and showed the world he was back and better than ever with a dazzling 41-point performance that led the West to a 163–158 win. He won the All-Star Game Most Valuable Player. His point total was one shy of Wilt Chamberlain's All-Star Game scoring record. "I missed about six or seven layups," Westbrook lamented. "I definitely could have had it." Westbrook's 27 first-half points—23 of which came in his first seven minutes—and 11 made first-half field goals set All-Star records for a half. Westbrook again participated in the Shooting Stars Competition, joined this year by the Indiana Fever's Tamika Catchings and NBA legend Anfernee "Penny" Hardaway. After advancing to the final round, Team Westbrook went 0-for-26 on the halfcourt shot and did not finish in the allotted time. Hardaway, like Horry before him, heaped praise on Westbrook. "I respect his game so much," Hardaway said. "He's definitely one of my favorite guys. He has the mindset of a Michael Jordan. He really does. Michael, he wasn't making friends out there when he played. He was ready to take your heart out, and that's how Russell is."

2016: Westbrook again took home MVP honors after scoring a team-high 31 points with eight rebounds, five assists, and five steals in just 22 minutes. The West won 196–173. Of Westbrook's 23 field goal attempts, 17 were three-pointers, of which he made seven. Westbrook joined Bob Petit as the only players to win consecutive All-Star Game MVP Awards. "Any time you can be able to be in the history books, it always means something special to me," Westbrook said.

2017: Despite averaging a triple double, Westbrook was not voted as an All-Star Game starter by the fans. He came off the bench behind Stephen Curry and James Harden but still had a chance to become the first player to win three straight All-Star Game MVP Awards. Westbrook scored 41 points, making 16-of-26 shots, including 7-of-13 three-pointers. But New Orleans Pelicans star Anthony Davis stole the show in his host city, delighting the Smoothie King Center crowd with a record 51 points to lead the West to a 192–182 win.

Kevin Durant at All-Star Weekend

Kevin Durant participated in almost every event at NBA All-Star Weekend. The only two events he didn't enter as a member of the Thunder were the Slam Dunk Contest and the Skills Challenge. "I'm going to try to do everything before I'm done," Durant once joked. Here's a year-by-year look at each of Durant's trips to All-Star Weekend.

2008: Durant scored a team-high 23 points for the Rookies in the Rookie Challenge. But the Sophomores won 136–109.

2009: Durant was named MVP of the Rookie Challenge after scoring a record 46 points, shattering Amar'e Stoudemire's 2004 mark of 36 points. Durant scored 30 in the second half to power the Sophomores to a 122–116 victory. Durant also won the weekend's first H-O-R-S-E competition, beating out Joe Johnson and O.J. Mayo.

2010: Durant's first selection as an All-Star came in Dallas, Texas, where the league held the game before a record-setting crowd of 108,713 inside Cowboys Stadium. Durant was selected as a reserve by Western Conference coaches. He scored 15 points with five rebounds in 20 minutes. Durant also defended his H-O-R-S-E title by knocking off Rajon Rondo and Omri Casspi. The NBA then discontinued the event. "I've got a little bragging rights," Durant joked. Durant also served as an assistant coach under Adrian Dantley for the Rookie Challenge.

2011: Durant was voted by the fans as a starter for the first time, receiving more than 1.7 million votes. He scored 34 points in 30 minutes, but Kobe Bryant won MVP honors after scoring a game-high 37 points in the West's 148–143 win. After previously saying he'd pass on the three-point contest, explaining he didn't see himself as a three-point contest type of player because of a poor showing at the 2006 McDonald's All-American festivities, Durant entered the 2011 field. He hit just five of 25 shots, the fewest since Vladimir Radmanovic in 2005.

2012: Durant scored 34 of his game-high 36 points in the first three quarters and won All-Star Game MVP honors following the West's 152–149 win. Durant also redeemed himself in the three-point contest. He was named an injury replacement for Joe Johnson and finished second behind Kevin Love. But as coach of the West Celebrity All-Stars, Durant's team suffered an 83–54 loss. "It was bad," Durant said. "I won't be the next Scotty Brooks, I know that."

2013: Durant scored a game-high 30 points in the All-Star Game and became the first player to score at least 30 points in three straight All-Star appearances. He bumped his All-Star Game scoring average to 28.8 points, the highest in the game's history. With 115 total points in his first four All-Star Game appearances, Durant scored the most of any player through his first four All-Star contests. "I'm just out there having fun," Durant said. "I've played a lot of street basketball. I've played a lot of celebrity games. This is my type of ballgame."

2014: Durant scored 38 points in the All-Star Game, sharing game-high honors with Blake Griffin, and finished four points shy of Wilt Chamberlain's All-Star record set in 1962. Durant attempted 17 three-pointers, including a record 11 in the second half. Durant also participated in the Shooting Stars Competition, a four-team, three-person-per-team timed shooting event. Team Durant was comprised of Durant, Tulsa Shock guard Skylar Diggins, and NBA great Karl Malone. They took second place.

2015: Despite missing 27 games due to injuries, Durant was selected as an All-Star reserve by the West coaches. It was the first time since 2010 that Durant was not a starter. Critics questioned Durant's inclusion, saying other players were more deserving. But the Thunder were 17–9 in games Durant played, and he averaged 25.9 points, 6.6 rebounds, and four assists in those contests. Foot soreness and lingering discomfort from a sprained left big toe, however, limited Durant to 10 uneventful minutes. He scored three points on 1-for-6 shooting.

2016: In his final All-Star Game appearance as a member of the Thunder, Durant scored 23 points in the West's 196–173 win.

54 Serge Ibaka's Slam Dunk Contest

Serge Ibaka first expressed interest in the Slam Dunk Contest at NBA All-Star Weekend in February 2010. He watched the marquee event of All-Star Saturday night live that year in Dallas, Texas, and it was largely forgettable. "I feel like I can compete with them," Ibaka said.

Ibaka won a dunk contest in Spain in 2008 and claimed he could dunk from the free throw line. With several highlight dunks over his first 1½ NBA seasons, Ibaka earned the nickname "Air Congo" and was a worthy candidate.

The NBA granted Ibaka's wish in 2011, selecting him to participate alongside Blake Griffin, JaVale McGee, and DeMar DeRozan. Griffin was the heavy favorite. He exploded onto the scene thanks to his monstrous dunks and nightly double doubles. "I watch his highlights," Ibaka admitted. "He goes high, and he can dunk. He goes hard." But Ibaka wasn't backing down. "It's a slam dunk contest," he said. "[The rim] is 10', and I can dunk, too."

Each participant was paired with a dunk coach assigned to assist his respective player. Griffin was paired with Kenny Smith. McGee worked with Chris Webber. DeRozan, named a replacement for the injured Brandon Jennings, was coached by Darryl Dawkins. Ibaka teamed with Kevin Durant. "That's Serge's problem right there," Thunder coach Scott Brooks said. "KD has one dunk, the one-handed tomahawk. That's all he brings to the table. That's not going to be championship dunk ready, either. I'm serious. I don't know what he's going to do. I'm worried."

Ibaka, though, didn't disappoint. For his first dunk, Ibaka exhibited his showmanship, marching out of the tunnel flanked by a parade of giant green flags with "NBA Africa" printed on them. He then backed up his boast and took off from the foul line, his

Serge Ibaka, shown here at the 2010 Slam Dunk Contest, captured Thunder fans' hearts for seven seasons with his high-flying dunks and momentum-changing shot blocking. (AP Photo/Mark J. Terrill)

toes just barely touching the line as he soared for a one-handed dunk. The slam scored only 45 out of 50 points from the panel of judges. On his second dunk, Ibaka used a 10-year-old and a small Rumble the Bison doll as props. With the doll hanging from the front of the rim, Ibaka promised the kid he'd get his doll. Coming from out of bounds along the baseline behind the basket, Ibaka snagged the doll with his mouth before throwing down a sideways tomahawk. He then returned the doll to the kid. But the dunk garnered only 45 points, giving Ibaka 90 for the first round. It was the lowest first-round score, eliminating Ibaka.

DeRozan finished third after also being eliminated in the first round with a total score of 94 points. His first dunk, a between-the-legs throwdown off a stanchion pass from teammate Amir Johnson, received a 44. He garnered a 50 for his second dunk, a highly thrown bounce pass to himself which he cupped before ducking under the rim and slamming in a reverse. McGee and Griffin advanced to the final round with a 99 and 95, respectively. Griffin received a 49 for his first dunk, a 360-degree slam, and McGee got a 50 for dunking two balls on two different baskets. Griffin's second dunk took seven tries but ultimately was an impressive windmill after catching a pass from teammate Baron Davis off the side of the backboard. McGee then threw down three basketballs in one sequence, carrying the first two and catching a lob pass from teammate John Wall on the third.

Griffin was the eventual winner, jumping over a car for his final dunk with the Crenshaw Elite Choir singing, "I Believe I Can Fly" at halfcourt. Griffin, however, jumped over "only" the hood of the sedan, leaving many largely unimpressed. "I hate to say this," Charles Barkley said, "but that wasn't the greatest dunk."

Fans determined the champion via text messaging, and it felt like the most popular player, not the night's best dunker, won.

55 The Curious Case of James Harden

No one saw it coming.

James Harden had been too good for too long.

But on the game's biggest stage, when most figured he would have his finest hour, Harden assembled the worst performances of his career.

It was the 2012 NBA Finals, and it became a forgettable experience for the Thunder's sensational sixth man. Not just because the Thunder lost in five games to LeBron James and the Miami Heat, but also because Harden's struggles largely led to OKC falling short.

Harden had won the Sixth Man of the Year Award that season after averaging 16.8 points, 4.1 rebounds, and 3.7 assists. He was even better in the first three rounds of that postseason against Dallas, the Los Angeles Lakers, and San Antonio. But against the Heat, Harden couldn't replicate the stuff that made him so special.

In the five-game series, Harden averaged 12.4 points, 4.8 rebounds, 3.6 assists, and 1.2 steals. But he shot 37.5 percent from the field, 31.8 percent from three-point range, and 79.2 percent from the foul line. Each of those percentages was far lower than his regular season and postseason averages.

After failing to score in double figures only four times in 62 of that season's 66 regular season games, Harden had three Finals games with less than 10 points.

He had a five-point, 2-for-6 shooting night in Game 1, barely getting involved in the offense as Kevin Durant and Russell Westbrook dominated in the Thunder's lone win. Game 2 was his only quality game, a 21-point, four-rebound, two-assist effort in which he scored 10 of the Thunder's 15 first-quarter points and netted 17 by halftime. In Games 3 and 4 he shot a combined 4-of-20 and totaled just 17 points. His only other double-digit scoring performance came in the Heat's 121–106 series-clinching Game 5 blowout, when he scored 11 fourth-quarter points after Miami entered the final frame ahead by 24.

"It's tough," Harden said after the series. "Shots didn't fall. The shots that felt good, that usually go in, didn't go in. They were hitting back rim or rimming in and out. It starts to take a toll on you. You start to think about it a little bit."

Everything about Harden looked off. A player who was supremely confident had become stunningly passive. A playmaker who was decisive and dangerous had become hesitant and harmless. Much of it had to do with Miami. Unlike the Mavs, Lakers, and Spurs, the Heat trotted out smaller lineups that sent hard traps at Harden. Quicker defenders helped neutralize Harden's effectiveness using a ball screen and hounded him into forcing the action or passing off. He never found his rhythm.

"They were so aggressive defensively," Scott Brooks said of Miami. "They were challenging every dribble, they were challenging every pass, and they were challenging every shot. They really played a physically intimidating brand of basketball."

The Thunder tried to encourage Harden. Sam Presti, the team's general manager, reminded Harden why he selected him third overall in 2009. Serge Ibaka gave Harden a heartfelt pep talk.

"He said I have to go out there and attack, be a beast, be a monster out there on the court," Harden later relayed. "That really meant a lot."

Daequan Cook tried, too.

"I told him, 'There's no reason for you to not have confidence every time you shoot the ball,'" said Cook, a reserve shooting guard on that 2012 team. "'You've been doing it all season for us. You look for it. You miss a shot? Oh well. We know what you're capable of doing, so don't allow that to affect your play.'"

Said Nick Collison: "We all have faith in James. We're always supportive of our guys. We really do believe it. It's not just to play mind games with him to have a better game. We really do believe in him. We know without him playing well, we all wouldn't be here."

Steve Kyler, editor and publisher of *Basketball Insiders*, later claimed late nights on the town in Miami contributed to Harden's disappearing act, as well as to the Thunder's decision to trade him prior to the start of the 2012–13 season.

"It was a lot more about James and James' mindset," Kyler said. "You're kind of seeing it play out now in Houston, is what the Oklahoma City Thunder were afraid of, and that is, if you rewind back to the NBA Finals run, James was kind of a ghost in the NBA Finals. In Miami, there were rumors that he was out late on South Beach."

Maybe the rumors were true. Maybe not.

Maybe a 22-year-old player in his third season simply struggled on the game's biggest stage, against the best player of his generation.

It happens.

"It's a learning experience," Harden said.

56 See a Halfcourt Shot

How about this for an interesting stat?

The Thunder are 5-for-130 all-time on shots from 40' and beyond. In the year 2013, Thunder *fans* went 5-for-47 on halfcourt shots.

Take in a game inside Chesapeake Energy Arena and you never know what you might see.

With a nightly chance to win $20,000 as part of the team's promotional deal with MidFirst Bank, Thunder fans have become surprisingly good at halfcourt heaves. There have been 10 made halfcourt shots by fans since the team relocated to Oklahoma City. The first dropped on December 12, 2010, on the 97th fan attempt. The second happened just seven days later. A flurry of fan makes then came in 2013, as five fell from March 5 to November 21. The final two in that five-game stretch happened in back-to-back home games over a four-day span.

How do you get a crack at the halfcourt shot? First, you've got to get lucky. A set of fans is selected randomly prior to tip-off. The earlier you arrive, the better your chances. The chosen pair then goes head-to-head in a free throw contest at opposing baskets. The fan with the most free throws in an allotted amount of time—ties are broken by a coin flip—gets $100 and the opportunity to let one shot fly from halfcourt. Another $500 is awarded just for hitting the rim or the backboard. But the real money comes only when the ball goes through the net.

Whenever the improbable shot goes in, the arena immediately cues up "I'm So Excited," the 1982 hit by The Pointer Sisters. The Chesapeake Energy Arena crowd goes wild. The winning fan freaks out and typically takes a euphoric victory lap.

Winners of the contest have come from all over the state and region, and carried all kinds of interesting backstories. Amazingly, many said they came close to turning down the opportunity. Ultimately, they all thrilled sellout crowds and helped fellow fans leave with a lasting memory. Their names are: Robert Yanders, Todd Lafferty, Roman Owen, Heath Kufahl, Justin Dougherty, Larry Hill, Cameron Rodriguez, Brad Brucker, Shane McKinzie, and Tony Juarez. Here are some of their stories.

Robert Yanders
The date: December 12, 2010
The opponent: Cleveland
Yanders was the first fan to knock down a halfcourt shot. What we didn't know was Yanders actually was a professional basketball player overseas. He had competed in college at Missouri State before playing nine seasons in Great Britain, where he teamed with NBA forward Luol Deng and guard Ben Gordon on the Great Britain National Team the summer before sinking his shot. A Springfield, Missouri, native, Yanders was in town visiting a friend on the Cavaliers' coaching staff. He estimated it was his first NBA game in about eight years. The tickets, he said, were a Christmas gift. He used over half the prize money to start a nonprofit basketball program. "We do a lot of good work in the community," Yanders said proudly. "I'm paying it forward."

Heath Kufahl
The date: March 5, 2013
The opponent: L.A. Lakers
There hasn't been a more touching story behind a Thunder fan's halfcourt shot. And there probably never will be. Some knew Kufahl, 37 at the time, as the volleyball and boys basketball coach at Christian Heritage Academy in Del City, Oklahoma. But after

sinking his halfcourt shot and telling his story, the world came to know Kufahl for the heartache happening in his home. His wife, Jenni, was diagnosed with Stage III appendix cancer only three months earlier. The $20,000 prize would be set aside for their mounting medical bills. With seven children at home, the money was much needed. The Kufahls became a story of inspiration and garnered national attention. Heath and Jenni appeared on ESPN. CNN aired the family's story. Prominent websites wrote about it. It's exactly what Jenni, a stay at home mom, wanted—to give others hope. "It just came at a great time," Jenni said. "It really gave us good encouragement to see that the Lord is in control. It wasn't luck that he made that shot. We really believe it was the Lord." After finding temporary relief following the shot, Jenni's cancer returned. Doctors told her there was nothing more they could do. Jenni passed away in August 2014. She was 39.

Justin Dougherty
The date: March 24, 2013
The opponent: Portland
Then a 24-year-old sports reporter at a television station in Springfield, Missouri, Dougherty's girlfriend, Sydney Friar, bought him tickets to the game for his birthday. When his shot went in, he unleashed the best celebration Chesapeake Energy Arena had ever seen. Dougherty enticed Kevin Durant to join him at midcourt. Durant obliged and playfully tackled Dougherty. "He called me out there, and I am glad he made it," Durant said. "When it left his hands, it looked like it was short, but it went straight in. I was happy for him, and then I turned around and he was calling me over. I had to run out there."

Cameron Rodriguez

The date: November 18, 2013

The opponent: Denver

The fourth Thunder fan in the 2013 calendar year to sink a halfcourt shot became the most controversial. Rodriguez was a member of the Southwestern College (Winfield, Kansas) men's basketball team and was prohibited from making money off his athletic ability, per NAIA rules. Rodriguez initially was informed that if he kept the prize money he would lose his amateur status. But his school appealed, and nearly a month later the NAIA ruled Rodriguez could use the winnings as scholarship money. A sophomore at the time, Rodriguez was required to maintain his amateur status throughout the remainder of his eligibility. Rodriguez said he would have forfeited the money before giving up his eligibility.

Brad Brucker

The date: November 21, 2013

The opponent: L.A. Clippers

Then a 33-year-old business teacher at Piedmont High School, Brucker thought someone was peddling something when he felt a tug on his arm and heard the question, 'Hey man, do you shoot baskets?' After responding with a quick "Nope," his companion at the game told him it was probably the $20,000 halfcourt shot contest. After making the shot, Brucker began leaving the floor only to be greeted and congratulated by recording stars Beyoncé and Jay Z, who watched from courtside seats next to Durant's family. Brucker said the experience "didn't feel real." "I walked over and shook his hand, and he kind of pulled me in for a hug," Brucker said of Jay Z. "I wanted to shake hands with Beyoncé, too, but I went over to shake her hand and she kind of stepped back. I didn't want to be trucked by their security." It was the second straight home game that a fan drilled a halfcourt shot. Durant joked after the game, "We might go broke after these guys, they're hitting every halfcourt shot."

And here's the best part of all the fan halfcourt shots. If you see one drop, you'll probably see a runaway Thunder victory. Oklahoma City is 9–1 when fans make the halfcourt shot. The lone loss was a three-point defeat against Phoenix on December 19, 2010. In the nine wins, the Thunder has enjoyed a 16.2-point average margin of victory.

57 Kid Clutch

Midway through the 2011–12 season, the NBA launched an ad campaign promoting the upcoming playoffs. The theme, "Big things are coming," was a cool concept that highlighted nine players and one team.

Individual words quickly flashed in sequence to form sentences and questions while showing slow-motion action shots of the players. Dirk Nowitzki, Rajon Rondo, Ricky Rubio, Ty Lawson, Chris Paul, Blake Griffin, LeBron James, Kobe Bryant, and the Chicago Bulls were featured in separate 30-second commercials.

The ninth player was Kevin Durant. His spot began as he stepped into a pull-up jumper. The cleverly presented subtitles appeared in white capital letters as the camera followed the trajectory of the shot until it splashed through the net.

"Let's check in on Kid Clutch. From OKC. The knockdown shooter with a golden touch. We all know where this is headed. Arriving at our destination shortly. Home sweet home."

As Durant turned and trotted back on defense, the audience is told three things. *"He is automatic. He is the* real McCoy. *He is BIG."*

Durant Daggers

Here's a quick look at some of Kevin Durant's biggest shots.

February 20, 2010: Thunder 121, New York 118 (OT)

Down 105–102 with six seconds remaining in regulation at Madison Square Garden, Durant buried a straight-on three-pointer to tie it. He then hit the go-ahead shot with 16 seconds left in overtime. Durant later ranked the buckets among his biggest.

January 22, 2011: Thunder 101, New York 98

With the game tied at 98-all with 6.5 seconds remaining, Durant made a fadeaway three over Danilo Gallinari from just in front of the Knicks bench. It was Durant's second buzzer-beating game-winner and the first time Oklahoma City fans got to see him be the hero. "After so many times of trying to hit game-winners, I finally hit one," he said. "It gave me a lot of confidence as well."

December 29, 2011: Thunder 104, Dallas 102

Trailing 102–101 with 1.4 seconds remaining after allowing a go-ahead three-pointer to Vince Carter, Durant caught an inbounds pass, squared, and fired a rhythmic three-pointer. The ball splashed through the net as time expired, sparking pandemonium inside Chesapeake Energy Arena. It was Durant's third buzzer-beating, game-winner of his career.

April 28, 2012: Thunder 99, Dallas 98

Durant shook off an off-shooting night and willed in the game-winner, a one-handed push shot over Shawn Marion and Ian Mahinmi with 1.5 seconds left. The shot rescued the Thunder from a seven-point

It was the perfect commercial at the perfect time for the perfect player. Only one problem—Durant didn't like the nickname. "I'm not a kid," the then 23-year-old deadpanned, shooting down yet another in a string of seemingly perfect monikers.

But clutch he was. That much no longer could be disputed.

By his fourth season, Durant had evolved into one of the NBA's most lethal late-game performers, consistently carrying his team in fourth quarters and coming up, well, big, when the Thunder needed him most late in games.

deficit with $2\frac{1}{2}$ minutes remaining and lifted OKC to a 1–0 series lead. "It's the playoffs," he said. "No matter how it gets done, you've got to do it."

May 19, 2012: Thunder 103, L.A. Lakers 100

Durant walked into a straight-away three-pointer over Metta World Peace with 13.7 seconds remaining. The shot broke a 98-all tie and lifted the Thunder to a commanding 3–1 series lead in the semifinals. Durant said after the game, "It left my hand [and] I was thinking, 'If this doesn't go in, it's going to be a terrible shot.'"

March 21, 2014: Thunder 119, Toronto 118 (2OT)

Durant captained an improbable comeback after the Thunder trailed by eight with 49.3 seconds to go. His dagger came on a deep three-pointer with 1.9 seconds left. Durant once listed the game-winner as his all-time favorite shot.

December 21, 2015: Thunder 100, L.A. Clippers 99

Durant drained a 19' jumper with 5.8 seconds left before blocking a potential game-winning 18-footer by Chris Paul as time expired. "No doubt, the block was good for our team," Durant said. "But as a kid, I wanted to hit the game-winner all the time. So I'll take the game-winner over the block."

February 3, 2016: Thunder 117, Orlando 114

Durant hit a three-pointer with just a half-second on the clock to give the Thunder a wild win. Durant's buzzer-beater capped his 37-point night.

In the same season the NBA released its catchy campaign, Durant became king of the closers. He led the league in fourth-quarter points per game for the first time, his 3.8-point average ranking him in the top five for the second of six straight years. In moments categorized as "clutch time," when the game's margin is five or less with less than five minutes to play, Durant led all players with 4.7 points per clutch time situation. That season, he scored 145 points in 152 clutch time minutes. He was even better in 2012–13, pumping in 154 points in 145 clutch-time minutes.

When Durant arrived in Oklahoma City, however, he showed up with little late-game experience. "In high school, we were always really good so I really didn't have to," he said of hitting big shots. "Either we lost by 10 points or we won by 30 points." In his lone season at Texas, Durant's first big shot came 29 games into his 35-game college career. And in his rookie season in Seattle, the Sonics won only 20 games and lost by a league-worst 8.8 points per game. But his first buzzer-beating game-winner came that season on a deep three-pointer on November 16, 2007, at Atlanta.

Through his first 1½ seasons with the Thunder, Durant struggled to close games. On January 2, 2009, he hit a three-pointer similar to the dagger he nailed as a rookie at Atlanta and gave the Thunder a one-point lead over Denver with 2.7 seconds remaining. But Carmelo Anthony stole the game with a three-pointer with 0.1 seconds left. Durant then had his share of hard luck and heartbreak with last-second letdowns, leading to some Thunder fans questioning his clutch gene. He missed a potential game-tying 20-footer with 9.3 seconds remaining against Houston on January 9, 2009. The Rockets won by two. One night later, he missed a potential game-winning 22-footer with 1.9 seconds left in regulation at Chicago. The Thunder ultimately won in overtime. Two nights after that, he missed a go-ahead 20-footer with 36.5 seconds left in regulation at New Jersey. The Nets prevailed by four in overtime. "Very rarely do guys come straight out [of college] and just hit game-winners," Durant said. "It even takes a lot of courage to go out there and shoot those shots."

By 2011–12, Durant had found enough success to confidently say the clutch gene was real and it indeed ran through his veins. "I think you do have it," Durant said. "It's not overrated. I think knowing the importance of a basketball game and wanting to win every single game, especially late in the game, is what you dream about doing."

58 The Craziest Game of Kevin Durant's Career

A sellout crowd of 19,800 packed the Air Canada Centre to witness it, and those who stayed all three hours and 17 minutes got a real treat.

It included a 50-point eruption, a 30-point performance, and four 20-point efforts. It saw two players get slapped with technical fouls and three get disqualified after fouling out. It had 12 ties, 23 lead changes, a late and improbable comeback, and took two overtimes.

"That was the craziest game I've ever been a part of," Kevin Durant proclaimed following the Thunder's 119–118 double-overtime victory at Toronto on March 21, 2014.

Playing on the second night of a back-to-back, on the final leg of a three-game road trip, the Thunder played a forgettable first half. Oklahoma City trailed 46–42 at halftime. The Thunder shot just 32.6 percent in the opening 24 minutes. Durant in particular was out of sorts. He sat on 13 points on 3-for-12 shooting with four turnovers at the break. But just when the Thunder needed him most, Durant transformed into the Slim Reaper.

A scary collision between Russell Westbrook and Kyle Lowry knocked Westbrook out of the game midway through the third period. It was an innocent play. Westbrook made a slight jab-step beyond the three-point line on the left wing, and as he held his left pivot foot in place, Lowry inadvertently bumped into Westbrook's right knee while closing on the ball. Westbrook's knee bent inward, and he immediately called a timeout, slamming the ball to the court upon doing so. The enormity of the scene cannot be overstated. Westbrook had missed 27 consecutive games that season and 31 to that point while recovering from a third knee surgery, each one a byproduct of Patrick Beverley crashing into his leg during the 2013 playoffs. It was only his 12th game back, and Westbrook was still on a minute restriction as well as being held out of one game during back-to-back sets. With assistance from teammate Hasheem Thabeet and trainer Joe Sharpe, Westbrook limped off the court and to the locker room, where he remained for the rest of the contest.

While Thunder fans everywhere worried sick about the team's All-Star point guard, Durant went to work. He put on a dazzling display the rest of the way, shaking off his subpar first half and responding with 38 points on 12-for-20 shooting in the final 34 minutes. His pair of free throws on the Thunder's first possession without Westbrook gave him 25 points and extended his streak of 25-plus-point games to 34. He'd pump in 14 points in the third period. He then scored or assisted on 6-of-8 Thunder points during an 8–0 run that put OKC ahead seven, its largest lead of the night, three minutes into the fourth quarter.

From there, it felt like every possession included some sort of twist, turn, lucky bounce, tough break, bad call, or big play. You had the Raptors double teaming Durant at the end of regulation, forcing him to feed Derek Fisher, who couldn't get off a shot before time expired. You had Durant's tiebreaking three-pointer and subsequent block on Amir Johnson's post-up late in the first overtime. You had Caron Butler fouling out with 20 seconds left in the first overtime, joining Andre Roberson (and later Raptors guard Greivis Vasquez) among the disqualified. You had Derek Fisher's mammoth three-pointer with 15 seconds remaining in double OT that gave the Thunder hope. And you had John Salmons missing a pair of free throws and leaving the door open when he could have given Toronto a four-point lead with 9.7 seconds remaining. Then you had the Slim Reaper show up and put the Raptors to sleep.

The Thunder trailed by eight with 49 seconds remaining in double overtime. Durant drilled a quick three-pointer out of a timeout with 46.3 seconds left. A Raptors shot clock violation set up Fisher's monster three, and Salmons' empty trip to the foul line set up one last shot for Durant. Fisher inbounded the ball to Jeremy Lamb, who fired it to Durant but saw the deflected pass ricochet out near halfcourt. Durant gathered, took two dribbles left and pulled up from 31' out on the left wing. Splash. Thunder 119, Raptors 118 with 1.7 remaining.

"We couldn't go another overtime, so I had to live with whatever happened," Durant said. "We had to get out of there. I wasn't trying to go to another overtime. So I pulled up for it. It looked good when it left my hands, and God guided that thing in the basket."

Durant then forced DeMar DeRozan into a contested fadeaway that fell well short, capping the craziest contest of Durant's career. Durant left the arena that night with the game ball. He asked each of his teammates to sign it to commemorate the contest. Durant at one point ranked his dagger that night as his all-time favorite shot.

"That was the most memorable one probably because that arena was so electric, just being down eight points with 45 seconds to go," Durant said. "A lot went into that game, and that's one of the last memories I have with Derek Fisher as well. So that meant a lot—Derek being my brother—that kind of connection we had in that game was different from what I've ever felt before from him."

Durant finished with a game-high 51 points, his second 50-point game that season, and added 12 rebounds and seven assists.

"If you got Kevin Durant on your team, you're safe," said Raptors guard Greivis Vasquez, a high school teammate of Durant's. "He's like Jesus in this league."

59 Thabo Sefolosha

Tony Parker was having his way. In a matchup of two of the league's best at their position, he was outclassing Russell Westbrook and running the overzealous young guard ragged. Oklahoma City needed to find a solution and fast. Time was running out.

That's when Coach Scott Brooks turned to Thabo Sefolosha. Brooks sicced his defensive ace on San Antonio's crafty point guard, and it changed everything.

This wasn't the 2012 Western Conference finals. This was a mid-March contest in the inaugural Thunder season. This was Sefolosha's 11th game in a Thunder uniform.

Down two with 18 seconds remaining inside a sold out Ford Center, the Spurs inbounded to Parker, the man with the hot hand. He sat on 28 points and now had a chance to tie or take the lead. But there was Sefolosha, glued to Parker as he had been since Brooks made the switch midway through the third quarter. Sefolosha smothered Parker, forcing him into a contested 19' jump shot that bounced off the front of the rim with 5.9 seconds showing. Then, after Michael Finley rebounded the miss and fired it back out to his point guard, Sefolosoha partially blocked Parker's desperation three-point attempt from the left corner.

Thunder 78, Spurs 76.

"Thabo played great," Jeff Green said. "His defense on Tony Parker was amazing."

Three years later, Sefolosha changed the complexion of the conference finals and powered the Thunder past the Spurs and into the NBA Finals after Brooks famously made the same defensive adjustment in Game 3. After losing the first two games, the Thunder won the next four to become only the eighth team in NBA history to win a best-of-seven series with four consecutive wins after trailing 2–0. Parker went from averaging 26 points, 5.5 rebounds, and seven assists on 61.1 percent shooting in the first two games to 19.3 points, three rebounds, and six assists on 41.2 percent shooting in the final four games. Sefolosha again made all the difference. But the Thunder's shutdown shooting guard announced his presence and proved his worth in Oklahoma City long before those pivotal final four conference finals games.

Fans first just had to learn who he was.

Thabo Sefolosha arrived in Oklahoma City as an unknown young prospect. He quickly developed into a pivotal All-Defensive player. (Jerome Miron/ USA TODAY Sports)

Sefolosha was in his third season with Chicago when the Thunder acquired him on February 19, 2009, the day of the trade deadline. OKC sent the Bulls a 2009 first-round pick, which they used to select Taj Gibson, who, as fate would have it, the Thunder acquired from the Bulls at the 2017 trade deadline. Chicago drafted Sefolosha 13th overall out of Switzerland in 2006. He played sparingly as a rookie before becoming a spot starter in his second and third seasons. But consistent minutes were hard to come by with the Bulls, who during Sefolosha's stay fielded a wing rotation of Kirk Hinrich, Ben Gordon, Luol Deng, Chris Duhon, Andres Nocioni, and Larry Hughes. The day before agreeing to the deal, Chicago also acquired John Salmons from Sacramento. In Oklahoma City, Sefolosha's chief competition was rookie guard Kyle Weaver. Veteran swingman Desmond Mason had been lost for the season after hyperextending his knee. "I see it as a fresh start, coming into a young team where I really think I can fit in. I'm really excited about that," Sefolosha said, still just 24 when the trade was made. "They have a spot for me over there. Even if it's not in the starting five, I really hope to bring something to this team."

Sefolosha became a consolation prize following the Thunder's failed pursuit of C.J. Miles, who signed a restricted free agent offer sheet with OKC in the summer of 2008 only to see Utah match and retain his services. But in Sefolosha, the Thunder got a player who brought a much-needed defensive disposition. At 6'7', he possessed prototypical size for a shooting guard. He had ample athleticism, long limbs, and a willingness to sacrifice shots and supply dirty work. It made him a natural pest for opposing perimeter players. Sefolosha was gritty, too. He embraced the nightly task of defending the opponent's best wing scorer. To Sefolosha, it never mattered who that player was, what his credentials were, or how much he scored in a given game. Sefolosha would keep coming back, keep digging deep to secure stops. It quickly became clear Sefolosha was a fantastic complement to the immense offensive talents of Westbrook and Kevin Durant, and he soon became a fixture in the Thunder's starting lineup. Sefolosha came off the bench in his Thunder debut but was inserted into the first string in his second game. He then started 367 regular season games from 2009–14.

Following the trade, Sefolosha appeared in 23 games and averaged 8.5 points, 5.2 rebounds, two assists, 1.7 steals, and 1.1 blocked shots in 31.2 minutes. Prior to the 2009–10 season, the Thunder extended Sefolosha's rookie contract for four years and $14 million. That year, he played all 82 games and earned All-Defensive Second Team honors.

Perimeter shooting was a struggle for Sefolosha and was all that prevented him from being a perfect solution at shooting guard. He made only 27.5 percent of his three-pointers in 2010–11 but worked diligently to improve his outside shot and connected on a career-best 43.7 percent in 2011–12. He followed that with a 41.9 percent clip in 2012–13 but fell back to 31.6 percent in 2013–14.

Nagging injuries also hampered Sefolosha. He missed 23 games due to right foot soreness in 2011–12 and 20 games during 2013–14 because of a left calf strain and a sprained right knee. His calf strain coincided with the Thunder signing veteran forward Caron Butler for the remainder of the season on March 1, 2014. When he returned to the lineup for the final six games of the regular season, Sefolosha found difficulty regaining his rhythm, and his playing time plummeted. His struggles spilled over into the postseason.

Against Memphis in the opening round of the 2014 playoffs, Sefolosha averaged 3.4 points on 33.3 percent shooting in the first five games. Brooks benched him in Game 6, inserting Butler into the starting lineup in hopes he would bring more balance. It was the first time since 2011 that Brooks altered his starting lineup despite his preferred first string of Westbrook, Sefolosha, Durant, Serge Ibaka, and Kendrick Perkins all being healthy. The lineup change stayed the same for Game 7. The Thunder won both games. Sefolosha didn't step foot on the floor for either. The same happened two rounds later against San Antonio in the 2014 Western Conference finals. Sefolosha started the series going 0-for-9 in the first two games. He was benched for Games 3 and 4 and never saw the court. OKC won both. Sefolosha then played only eight minutes in a 28-point Spurs rout in Game 5 before his Thunder tenure ended unceremoniously in Game 6, when he played only the final five seconds of San Antonio's series-clinching victory.

Sefolosha could sense his time with the Thunder had come to an end. "The last month of basketball was a little bit tough and head-scratching for me, going from the starting five to not playing at all," he said. "It had been a pattern a little bit going on, me playing in the starting five but not playing for the rest of the game, basically.... I thought it was maybe time for me to move on and find a new place."

In July 2014, Sefolosha signed a three-year, $12 million contract with Atlanta. A wildly successful 5½-year run had come to an end. Sefolosha came to town as a 24-year-old finding his way. He left as a 30-year-old who came into his own as an elite perimeter defender who was vital to the Thunder's transformation into a perennial title contender.

"It was just incredible to be a part of what we were building and what we were doing at that time," Sefolosha said. "Looking back, and just knowing I had a big role in the success of this team, it's special."

60 What Is a Zygomatic Arch?

Russell Westbrook clearly was trying to conceal his face.

As he walked out of the visiting locker room inside the Moda Center, past a small crowd of reporters waiting in the arena's amazingly narrow hallway, he kept one hand attached to his face. Hidden behind his hand, however, was a nickel-sized dent that sat between the back of his right eye and just in front of his right ear. It looked like something out of a cartoon.

The Thunder had just lost a three-point decision at Portland on February 27, 2015, and Westbrook sustained the injury in the final seconds. Teammate Andre Roberson attempted to hurdle Westbrook as he rose to his feet, but Roberson couldn't clear him and inadvertently kneed Westbrook in the side of the face. The impact of the collision knocked Westbrook back to the floor, and as the team's All-Star point guard laid on the court, flat on his stomach, his face buried into his arms, it was impossible to not think the worst. The Thunder had already limped along in a season ravaged from the start by injuries. Now it appeared Westbrook, who already was reduced to a spectator for 14 games earlier that season because of a broken right hand, would again join the walking wounded.

"Definitely scary," Westbrook later admitted. "When you feel your face and it feels a little deformed, it's definitely a different feeling, definitely scary."

Further complicating the matter was how well Westbrook had been performing. He was in the middle of his first career string of triple doubles, having dropped 40 points, 13 rebounds, and 11 assists against the Blazers that night, marking his third straight triple double. It capped a fabulous February in which Westbrook, while guiding the Thunder to a 9–3 record, averaged 31.2 points, 9.1 rebounds, and 10.3 assists to capture his first career Western Conference Player of the Month honor.

The team didn't make Westbrook available to the media after the Blazers game. His medical examinations took what felt like an eternity and kept the Thunder in a holding pattern at the arena well over an hour after the last player had dressed and exited the locker room.

The next day, a Saturday in Los Angeles, Westbrook underwent surgery to repair a fractured zygomatic arch, or as it's more commonly called, a cheekbone. He missed Sunday's game against the Lakers, and the Thunder didn't provide a timetable for when Westbrook would return to the lineup. Three days and one game later, he was back.

His injury mandated he wear a protective mask, and the news alone set the Internet on fire. No one was sure what in the world Westbrook, an unabashed fashion risk-taker, would have up his sleeve. Fans photo-shopped possibilities and braced for something we'd never before seen.

"Fortunately for all of us, he does not get to choose his own color of the mask," then Thunder coach Scott Brooks said. "It's going to be a clear mask."

Not even a mask could slow Westbrook. In a 123–118 overtime victory over Philadelphia, Westbrook scored 49 points, grabbed a career-high 15 rebounds, and dished 10 assists. He became the first player since Michael Jordan in 1989 to register four straight triple doubles and joined Wilt Chamberlain, Oscar Robertson, Magic Johnson, and Maurice Stokes as the only players in NBA history to record four consecutive triple doubles.

When the Thunder fell behind 32–17 just 8½ minutes into the game, it was Westbrook who energized his squad. Out of an inbounds play that he received a step inside the baseline boundary, Westbrook streaked the length of the court, using just five dribbles to weave his way through traffic, before powering down an improbable two-handed dunk. It ignited the crowd and sparked a 20–2 Thunder run to close the quarter. Westbrook had a hand in 13 of those points. The coast-to-coast dunk stands as one of Westbrook's signature plays.

In the final 8½ minutes of regulation, Westbrook scored eight points with three rebounds and two assists. He had the final six points for the Thunder, his last two in regulation coming at the foul line, where he gave OKC an eight-point lead with 1:32 remaining. As he stood at the stripe, Westbrook was showered with the loudest "M-V-P" chants he'd ever received. He then scored 10 of the Thunder's 13 points in overtime and added two rebounds and his 10th assist.

"For those of you, including myself, who thought Russell might need a couple of games to get used to a mask, we were wrong," Brooks said. "He was all over the floor."

The next night at Chicago, Westbrook scored a game-high 43 points and became the first player in Thunder history with three straight 40-point games. Three nights after that, against Toronto, he registered 30 points, 11 rebounds, and 17 assists, his fifth triple double in six games.

In 16 games with a mask, Westbrook averaged 30.1 points, 8.6 rebounds, 10.1 assists, and 2.4 steals.

61 Jeff Green

He was affectionately referred to as "Uncle Jeff."

It was a nickname LeBron James coined because, even in his early days, Jeff Green was bigger, stronger, and better than most of his peers—and there wasn't much they could do about it.

"He's like that uncle you used to play basketball with at the Y who will punish you down on the blocks and you get mad," James explained during the 2009 Rookie Challenge at NBA All-Star Weekend.

For two-and-a-half seasons, Green was a fan favorite in Oklahoma City, the main running mate to Kevin Durant before Russell Westbrook blossomed into a megastar.

Green was drafted with the fifth overall selection of the 2007 NBA Draft, three slots after Durant back when the franchise was in Seattle. On draft night, the Sonics traded Ray Allen, then a seven-time All-Star, to Boston for the draft rights to Green, point guard Delonte West, forward Wally Szczerbiak, and a second-round pick.

In his final season at Georgetown as a junior, Green was named Big East Player of the Year after averaging 14.3 points and 6.4 rebounds while helping the Hoyas reach the Final Four. He was now being partnered with Durant as the building blocks for the franchise.

"What we see in these players is tremendous versatility," GM Sam Presti said. "We see guys that are skilled with the ball and have a great size-to-skill ratio."

At 6'9", Green was capable of playing multiple positions, mostly the two forward spots. He began his career as a small forward while Durant primarily played shooting guard. As a rookie, Green quickly established a reputation as a do-it-all player who could score, rebound, pass, and defend. He wasn't particularly great at anything but was functional at everything. "He's one of those intangible guys," James said.

Green averaged 10.5 points, 4.7 rebounds, and 1.5 assists in his first season and joined Durant on the All-Rookie First Team. In his second season, the franchise's first in Oklahoma City, Green slid over to power forward when first-year coach Scott Brooks deployed Durant at his natural small forward position. It's where Green spent the bulk of his minutes with the Thunder, and it was far from a perfect fit as a long-term solution. Green suddenly was

The Aneurysm

Jeff Green missed the 2011–12 season after undergoing heart surgery to repair an aortic aneurysm. Boston detected the aneurysm during his training camp physical, one day following the conclusion of the 161-day NBA lockout. Had the lockout continued and the aneurysm gone undetected, it could have cost Green his life.

In June 2012, then NBA Commissioner David Stern punished the Thunder by ordering them to send a second-round pick to Boston as compensation for Green missing the season. A statement released by the league read: "Stern found that there was no evidence of bad faith or any intent to withhold information on the part of Thunder management or its physicians, but that Oklahoma City's cardiologists were in possession of information about Jeff Green that was not shared with Thunder management and that should have been disclosed to the Celtics in connection with the trade of Green in February 2011."

The Thunder were forced to surrender the 2013 second-round pick they acquired from Charlotte in the 2011 deal that sent Byron Mullens to the then Bobcats. Privately, the punishment irked Sam Presti, and the GM quietly found a way to pooh-pooh the penalty. First, Houston acquired the selection from Boston in the 2012 trade that sent Courtney Lee to the Celtics. The Thunder then reacquired the selection as part of the 2012 trade that sent James Harden to the Rockets. And with the 32nd overall pick in the 2013 NBA Draft, the Thunder selected Alex Abrines from Spain.

an undersized four before the league's small-ball craze hit. He went from defending perimeter players to facing nightly mismatches against the likes of David West, Amar'e Stoudemire, and Zach Randolph. But Green never complained publicly about his role. Instead, he averaged 16.5 points, 6.7 rebounds, two assists, and one steal while playing 36.8 minutes in 2008–09.

One of the best moments of Green's tenure came on January 21, 2009. The Thunder were at Golden State. Two teams that were a combined 42 games under .500 found themselves in a wildly entertaining shootout. And Green was the hero, banking in a turnaround 16-foot jumper at the buzzer to lift the Thunder to a 122–121 victory. "Yeah, I called it," Green insisted that night.

The 2009–10 season saw Green begin taking more of a backseat to the emerging Westbrook. Meanwhile, the Thunder added a rookie named Serge Ibaka, who was a natural power forward. Still, Green accepted his role—not exactly the toughest pill to swallow given his career-high 37.1 minutes per night—and averaged 15.1 points while playing all 82 games. He helped the Thunder reach 50 wins, a 27-game improvement, and their first playoff berth.

Prior to the 2010–11 season, however, Green and the Thunder reached an impasse in negotiations to extend his rookie contract. The two sides failed to reach an agreement before that year's November 1 deadline, meaning Green would be a restricted free agent in July 2011. He never reached that day as a member of the Thunder. On February 24, 2011, the trade deadline, the Thunder sent Green, center Nenad Krstic, and a first-round pick to Boston in exchange for Kendrick Perkins and Nate Robinson. Green later signed a four-year, $36 million contract with the Celtics.

It was the first major trade in Thunder history, the first time a core player was sent packing. Fan reaction fell somewhere between heartbroken and furious. No one, however, took the trade harder than Presti, the GM who pulled the trigger and grew teary-eyed while discussing Green in a farewell news conference. "I have unbelievable respect for Jeff Green," Presti said. "I value him greatly."

After four seasons in Boston, Green became a journeyman, playing with the Memphis Grizzlies, Los Angeles Clippers, and Orlando Magic.

No matter where he went, to Thunder fans he was still Uncle Jeff.

62 Eric Maynor

The Thunder's backup point guard position was a mess.

In two seasons, starting with the franchise's final year in Seattle, eight different players had a shot at holding down the spot. In order, they were Delonte West, Luke Ridnour, Earl Watson, Mike Wilks, Russell Westbrook, Chucky Atkins, Kevin Ollie, and Shaun Livingston.

Then came Eric Maynor.

Oklahoma City acquired Maynor on December 22, 2009. He was in his rookie season with Utah, which had selected him with the 20th overall pick in the 2009 draft, making him the first player out of Virginia Commonwealth to be chosen in the first round. As a college sophomore, Maynor drilled a game-winning shot to lift the No. 11–seeded Rams to an upset victory over sixth-seeded Duke in the first round of the NCAA tournament. As a junior and senior, Maynor earned Colonial Athletic Association Player of the Year honors. He left VCU as the school's all-time leader in scoring, assists, and free throws made. The school ultimately retired his No. 3 jersey and inducted him into its Hall of Fame.

In exchange for Maynor, the Thunder sent Utah one of those quasi assets that never amount to anything, in this case the rights to 2002 draft pick Peter Feshe, a second-round pick out of Germany who might as well have been a ghost. Oklahoma City took advantage of a necessary cost-cutting move by the Jazz and took on injured forward Matt Harpring's expiring $6.5 million contract. Naturally, the Thunder also received a small trade exception. But the real prize was Maynor.

Maynor arrived in Oklahoma City as a spirited 22-year-old who spoke with a country North Carolina drawl, slow and thick. He had an old soul and was wise beyond his years, especially on a basketball court.

That's where Maynor immediately provided the Thunder with elusive stability and long-term security behind Westbrook. He was magnificent at managing the second unit, controlling the flow of the game by playing with great patience and precision, poise and pace. He wasn't ultra-athletic and was far from physically imposing, but he was super smart, had an amazing ability to dictate tempo, and he possessed a killer floater that remains the best in Thunder history. His best skill, however, was creating easy buckets for his teammates.

In his first season with the Thunder, Maynor played 55 games and averaged 4.5 points, 1.7 rebounds, and 3.4 assists against one turnover in 16.5 minutes per game. He finished the 2009–10 season with a 3.13 assist-to-turnover ratio that ranked him 10th among all players. The Thunder went 37–18 after Maynor arrived.

"It's amazing that he's come into the games controlling the games as well as he has," Scott Brooks said only eight games into Maynor's tenure. "You can tell the guys that follow the league and are gym rats because he came in and knew exactly what our guys liked and where they like it. That's a great thing to have."

Maynor had point guard pedigree. His father, George Maynor, played the position for East Carolina in the 1970s, and George always told Eric he would be a point guard. By the time Eric Maynor reached the NBA, he was savvy enough to enter every game with a four-item checklist for what would please his coaches—which was funny considering his first NBA coach was the man who cut his father from the Chicago Bulls, Jerry Sloan.

"Get guys shots. Take care of the basketball. Score when you need to. And defend," Maynor said.

Maynor made most of them look easy. He was a limited defender, but when it came to orchestrating offense Maynor quickly established himself among the league's best backups.

"He's so poised," Kevin Durant said. "He's been like that ever since he got into the league and that's not going to change. His pace is great for a young point guard. He's coming out there and controlling the team."

Maynor played all 82 games for the Thunder during the 2010–11 season. His statistical averages almost were identical to the previous year. His impact, though, could not be ignored.

"Offensively," Brooks said, "he's pretty much flawless in leading our team."

63 Eric Maynor Goes Down

Everything was going so well.

The Thunder came out of the 2011 NBA lockout with a stacked young roster. They had just marched to the Western Conference finals. They began the 2011–12 campaign with six wins in their first eight games. And they had been incredibly healthy—until the night of January 7, 2012.

It was game No. 9 of that season, a Saturday night inside Houston's Toyota Center. With just under eight minutes left to play, Eric Maynor attacked the basket, dribbling right as Goran Dragic defended. After two hard dribbles, Maynor planted his right leg. His knee buckled. He immediately collapsed to the court, clutching his right leg. Minutes later, teammates Kendrick Perkins, Serge Ibaka, and Lazar Hayward carried Maynor off the floor.

The diagnosis a day later was a torn ACL. Maynor would miss the rest of the season.

"Seeing one of our brothers hurt like that is tough on all of us," Kevin Durant said.

Maynor's injury, not Russell Westbrook's fluke injury from the 2013 postseason, became the first in a string of yearly devastating Thunder injuries. By then, the Thunder had built shared experience navigating a coaching change and constant losing, emotional trades and early success. What the team had not yet exhibited was an ability to overcome a key injury.

But the Thunder aced that test, and their resolve set the standard for how the franchise would respond in the face of future setbacks. Oklahoma City plugged in rookie Reggie Jackson before signing and shifting to veteran Derek Fisher. The Thunder adjusted and adapted, finishing 47–19 in the truncated season before journeying to the NBA Finals.

That January night, though, marked the last time we'd see the real Eric Maynor.

Maynor worked hard to regain his form and even assembled an encouraging 2012 preseason. But when the regular season started, Maynor provided only marginal impact. He simply wasn't himself, and by mid-November it had become clear a change was needed. In what eventually became a 25-game trial run to maintain his position, Maynor averaged 3.5 points on 30.9 percent shooting. He averaged only 2.4 assists against 0.9 turnovers. Unlike previous seasons, when he made playmaking look so easy, Maynor struggled to initiate the offense and set up teammates for easy scores. His assist rate plummeted, in part, no doubt, due to the emergence of James Harden and his ability to facilitate, but also because of his own ineffectiveness.

Routine things became a chore. Opposing point guards such as Leandro Barbosa, Eric Bledsoe, and Jarrett Jack began pressuring Maynor the length of the court, causing him to fumble the ball and flirt with eight-second violations. Maynor's lack of athleticism and explosiveness went from a minor issue to a major problem. In an early game against New Orleans, Maynor's diminishing mobility prevented him from beating 6'10" forward Ryan Anderson off the dribble. And nobody ever confused Anderson for a defender. Maynor soon began settling for more long-range attempts rather than knifing into the lane looking to create.

And so on December 20, 2013, Scott Brooks brought an end to the Eric Maynor era. It happened at halftime of a road game against Minnesota. Brooks benched Maynor in favor of Jackson. The next game, a Christmas Day showdown at Miami, Maynor was completely out of the rotation. He appeared in only 11 more games with the Thunder. All of them were the definition of garbage-time appearances, as OKC won those contests by an average margin of 21 points.

On February 21, 2013, Maynor was traded to Portland for the same thing the Thunder gave up to get him—nothing. A ghost of a draft pick named Giorgos Printezis. Of course, the Thunder received a trade exception.

Maynor went on to become a steady hand behind that season's eventual Rookie of the Year, Damian Lillard. In the summer of 2013, Maynor signed with Washington before being traded to Philadelphia and ultimately bouncing around in Europe.

"At one point," Blazers General Manager Neil Olshey said, "Maynor was considered the premier backup point guard in the NBA."

64 Derek Fisher

Derek Fisher was desperate for another championship.

The Thunder were desperate for another steady guard.

Desire met opportunity in March 2012, when the two worlds collided and a three-year marriage was consummated.

Fisher joined the Thunder for the first of three stints when the team signed him as a free agent on March 21, 2012. One week earlier, Fisher had been traded from the Los Angeles Lakers to the Houston Rockets. Two months before that, Thunder backup point guard Eric Maynor suffered a season-ending knee injury only nine games into the lockout-shortened season. After a trip to the Western Conference finals in 2011, the Thunder had championship hopes. Behind the incredibly steady Maynor, however, was unproven rookie Reggie Jackson. Meanwhile, the Rockets were a relatively young team scraping to make the eighth seed. Fisher never reported to Houston, instead agreeing to a buyout that allowed him to join the Thunder.

"Everything that I had observed from this particular team fit right into what I felt like was what I wanted to be attached to, what I wanted to be a part of," Fisher said before making his debut against the L.A. Clippers. "Being a part of success and winning, it's not easy to let go. And so when you see an opportunity to be a part of something that is special and feel as though you can add to it, that was really what was the deciding factor in terms of me coming here."

Oklahoma City was happy to have him. Thunder coach Scott Brooks said Fisher "has winner all over his DNA." Thunder GM Sam Presti said Fisher, even at 37, was too good to pass up. "It's not often that an opportunity like this comes about at this point in the season," Presti said. "We felt like it was something we had to pursue."

Fisher had won five NBA championships as a member of the Lakers. He also carried a reputation as a clutch shooter, a bulldog defender, and a tough competitor. He appeared in 20 games down the stretch of 2011–12, averaging 4.9 points, 1.5 rebounds, and 1.4 assists in 20.4 minutes.

Fisher's first nine games, however, foreshadowed what was to come in his Thunder tenure. Brooks showed unwavering support in Fisher even when the veteran's production proved undeserving. Fisher made just nine of his first 40 shots and only three of his first 17 three-pointers. Still, he got the nod over guards Daequan Cook and Royal Ivey, both of whom had been extremely productive coming off the bench. In only his second game with the Thunder, Fisher logged a season-high 36 minutes. In his ninth game, Fisher played 27 minutes despite going scoreless with two rebounds, one assist, and five fouls. In the 2012 playoffs, Fisher averaged more minutes than Nick Collison and the same as starting shooting guard and defensive ace Thabo Sefolosha. In the 2012 Finals against Miami, Brooks played Fisher 25.6 minutes per game. "He just does all the little things that help you win games," Brooks said.

In 2012–13, Fisher signed with Dallas in late November. But with the Mavericks floundering around .500, Fisher again orchestrated an exit. Citing difficulty being away from his California family, Fisher asked for his release. Mavs owner Mark Cuban granted it on December 22, 2012. Two months later, Fisher was back in Oklahoma City, where the Thunder were rolling at 41–15. For the Thunder, the move made sense. At the 2013 trading deadline, OKC traded Maynor, who struggled to regain his form, to Portland. Fisher provided insurance behind Westbrook and Jackson, experience, leadership, perimeter defense, and familiarity. But in his 24 games with the Thunder, Fisher averaged 4.1 points in 14.4 minutes—0.2 minutes more per game than the emerging Jackson. Despite providing sturdy defense, Fisher shot just 33.3 percent from the field and during one seven-game stretch missed 18 consecutive shot attempts. He also had a comical tendency to have a toe on the three-point line, which turned would-be threes into forehead-slapping long twos. But Fisher elevated his performance in the postseason and was huge in helping the Thunder survive Houston in the first round after Westbrook was lost to a knee injury. In 11 playoff games, Fisher averaged 8.7 points on 45.7 percent shooting. He made 47.1 percent of his three-point shots.

It was enough for the Thunder to re-sign Fisher to a third season on July 24, 2013. He was two weeks shy of turning 39. In his final NBA season, Fisher appeared in 81 games with the Thunder and averaged 5.2 points, 1.5 rebounds, and 1.4 assists in 17.6 minutes.

65 Reggie Jackson

It probably will be a long time before a player comes along and ruffles the feathers of Thunder fans like Reggie Jackson managed to do during his 3½ seasons.

Jackson's tumultuous tenure saw him go from unknown draft pick to questioned rookie to scrutinized emergency starter to disgruntled backup to Public Enemy No. 1.

Drafted 24th overall out of Boston College in 2011, Jackson's NBA dream was put on hold just one week after he thought it came true. The NBA lockout was to thank. By the time the labor dispute lifted, Jackson walked into his rookie season without the summer league experience, without a full training camp, and without a complete preseason schedule. He also nursed injuries and faced another brief delay while his contract got ironed out. He had less than two weeks to get acclimated before the season opener came on Christmas Day 2011. Then, just nine games into the year, Eric Maynor went down, thrusting Jackson into the fire. Predictably, he struggled leading the bench only a month into the job.

After two-and-a-half months of subpar play from Jackson, the Thunder brought in veteran guard Derek Fisher to alleviate the pressure. But Jackson still had big dreams. He wanted to be a big-time player. One of the greatest ever. And because he was supremely self-confident, he openly shared his desires. But that's where his problems in Oklahoma City began in earnest. There was room for only one star point guard, and his name was Russell Westbrook. Everyone from fans to media to the team felt Jackson needed to fall in line. But Jackson had blossomed into more than a backup by his third season. He had grown into a capable starter.

In 2013–14, Jackson appeared in 80 regular season games, 36 as the starter as Westbrook bounced in and out of the lineup while recovering from multiple knee operations. Jackson averaged 13.1 points, 3.9 rebounds, 4.1 assists, and 1.1 steals in 28.5 minutes per game. After struggling to close games as the team's go-to guy in the regular season, Jackson delivered his defining moment during Game 4 of the opening round of the 2014 playoffs at Memphis. With the Thunder facing a 2–1 series deficit and Westbrook and Kevin Durant combining to score 30 points on 11-of-45 shooting, Jackson stepped up and scored 32 points and nine rebounds on 11-for-16 shooting in 37 minutes off the bench. The Thunder won 92–89. OKC went on to win the series in seven games.

But 2014–15 began with Jackson professing his desire to be a starting point guard. It came on the heels of him turning down a reported four-year, $48 million extension to remain the sixth man. "I want to be a starter," Jackson declared at the team's media day.

"I've always wanted to be a starter. I've always wanted to be great. All the greats I've seen started, so that's kind of the mold." The situation turned acrimonious when a sprained ankle kept Jackson out of the team's first three regular season games. Many questioned the severity of Jackson's injury. He fueled conspiracy theories prior to the third game, the team's home opener, when he told reporters he probably wouldn't play that night against Denver. Immediately after his interview, Jackson grabbed a ball and threw down a drop-step windmill dunk. It was a defiant act that came at a time when the team was limping along with only eight healthy players. Two nights later, Jackson made his season debut at Brooklyn and teammates Kendrick Perkins and Serge Ibaka at times froze out Jackson, refusing to pass him the ball. Still, in 13 games as the starter while Westbrook nursed a broken hand, Jackson proved his star potential, averaging 20.2 points, 5.2 rebounds, and 7.8 assists in 38.9 minutes per game.

Jackson's defense, however, often was brutal, and his attitude rubbed teammates the wrong way. He had grown completely disgruntled and wanted out of Oklahoma City. When the Thunder acquired Dion Waiters on January 5, 2015, the situation turned toxic. Thunder coach Scott Brooks no longer needed to rely on Jackson. He had a new toy. Jackson averaged only 20 minutes in his final 18 games. On February 18, 2015, one day before the trade deadline, a report surfaced that Jackson's agent had requested a trade. When asked directly whether he wanted to remain with the Thunder, Jackson replied, "I would love to play basketball." A day later, just minutes before the 2:00 PM deadline, the Thunder traded Jackson to Detroit as part of a three-team deal. Jackson then delivered a parting shot that again ticked off Thunder fans when he tweeted just 2½ hours after the trade, "Crying tears of joy," with the hashtag, "God is great."

Appearing on a Yahoo! Sports podcast a day after the trade, Jackson offered his take on his tumultuous tenure in OKC.

"I wasn't always perfect, nor was the situation, but I became the brunt of the blame there," Jackson said. "Everything bad that happened, I was the scapegoat."

66 Andre Roberson

The Minnesota Timberwolves entered the 2013 NBA draft owning the 26th overall selection. They received the pick from Memphis via Houston. By the end of the night, the selection belonged to Oklahoma City via Golden State.

In real time, there was mass confusion surrounding which team actually possessed the pick. There was also mass confusion about Andre Roberson, the mystery player who ultimately was taken with that selection and traded to the Thunder.

Few fans in Oklahoma City were familiar with Roberson. A 6'7" forward, Roberson was an early entry candidate who averaged 10.9 points and 11.2 rebounds before earning Pac-12 Defensive Player of the Year honors as a junior at Colorado. Thunder fans in Oklahoma, however, had no reason to pay attention to the Buffaloes after they bolted the Big 12 for the Pac-12 in 2011. Colorado basketball wasn't exactly must-see TV before their move. But Roberson was quietly an intriguing prospect. He finished fourth in the nation in rebounds per game as a sophomore and second as a junior. He was the only CU player ever to register 1,000 points and rebounds, 150 blocks and steals, and 100 assists. He was also the first Buffaloes player to lead the team in rebounding, blocked shots, and steals for three consecutive seasons. "We think he's a unique player," Thunder GM Sam Presti said on draft night.

Most mock drafts projected Roberson to go early in the second round. The Thunder, who entered the draft in possession of picks No. 29 and No. 32, liked him enough to trade up three spots to get him. The decision was both strange and unpopular. Denver and San Antonio held the 27th and 28th picks, respectively, and there were rumblings the Spurs coveted Roberson, a San Antonio native. Still, the selection was met with apathy at best by the fan base and anger at worst. "I think people are disappointed more because they don't know the names," said Kevin Durant, who admitted he was also unfamiliar with Roberson, as well as the team's 12th overall pick, Steven Adams.

Roberson was said to have a great nose for the ball, tremendous instincts, and the ability to defend multiple positions. Advanced analytics also spoke favorably of Roberson. "He's one of those players that brings energy to the floor," Thunder Assistant GM Troy Weaver said on draft night. OKC hoped Roberson would develop into a "three-and-D" wing player, someone who could knock down three-pointers as a spot-up shooter and lock up opposing perimeter players with sturdy defense. After a rookie season spent backing up starting shooting guard Thabo Sefolosha and bouncing between the Thunder and D-League, Roberson stepped into a starting role in 2014–15 following Sefolosha's departure. He quickly established himself as a defensive pest. His length, athleticism, and tough-mindedness made him a prototypical stopper. He was Sefolosha reincarnated, a vital complementary piece between Durant and Russell Westbrook, a selfless player who made it his mission to take on the league's best perimeter scorers.

The offensive side of the ball was a different story. Roberson spent his first four seasons struggling to find his offensive rhythm. He sacrificed touches and deferred to the team's stars. But when the ball swung his way, he rarely looked comfortable or confident making a play. His three-point shooting was a liability. For all his natural gifts as a defender, Roberson's overall lack of offense often hampered the Thunder in halfcourt sets, as defenses sagged off him and packed the paint to discourage drives from Durant and Westbrook. When the stars kicked it out to Roberson, defenders dared him to shoot.

That all changed late in the 2016 playoffs. It became Roberson's breakout moment and served as the blueprint to how he could become an offensive weapon. In the final eight games of the Thunder's run to the Western Conference finals, Roberson averaged 9.6 points on 53.4 percent shooting. He made 47.8 percent of his three-pointers over that stretch and added 7.4 rebounds, 1.1 assists, 1.4 steals, and 1.3 blocked shots in 30.2 minutes per game. He was a terror in transition, a threat cutting off the ball, a more confident slasher using one and two dribbles, and a source of offense through sheer hustle plays. Meanwhile, he was providing pivotal resistance against the likes of Kawhi Leonard and Klay Thompson. Roberson finally flashed two-way player potential. "I felt like it was my job and the staff's job to try to figure out the way to incorporate him offensively where he can play to his strengths rather than just be a floor spacer standing in the corner," Thunder coach Billy Donovan said.

But it didn't last. After failing to come to terms on an extension to his rookie scale contract before the October 31 deadline in 2016, Roberson struggled with consistency throughout 2016–17. He remained a stout defender, but his shooting percentages plummeted. With the sensational scoring ability of Durant no longer bolstering the lineup, Roberson's suspect offense began negating his spectacular defense. But after bolstering the roster with the blockbuster Paul George deal, the Thunder and Roberson agreed to a contract extension for three years and $30 million on July 5, 2017.

67 The Invocation

The lights dim and the players line up, standing shoulder to shoulder from sideline to sideline, the home team sprawled across one free throw line, the visitors stretched along the other, both facing halfcourt.

A spotlight shines on the individual standing in the middle of the court, microphone in hand. The public address announcer politely asks those congregated, "Please rise and remove your hats for tonight's invocation."

"Almighty God, we ask Your blessing upon all gathered here, and especially the players on both teams. Help them to play well and safe. We always remember that in following You, we are all winners with the gifts You have given us. May we never cease to praise You and give thanks for our blessings. In Your holy name we pray. Amen."

That, in essence, is how the Thunder begin every game.

A short pregame prayer has been the team's tradition since the franchise made its Oklahoma City debut at the start of the 2008–09 season. The Thunder is the only team in the NBA with an invocation, which has been covered by *The New York Times* and *USA Today.*

"Notwithstanding your affiliation," Thunder chairman Clay Bennett said, "we thought it was a reflection of the values of Oklahomans."

NBA fans in Oklahoma City have never known anything else.

The idea was introduced by George Shinn, the former New Orleans Hornets owner who sold Oklahomans on NBA basketball when his franchise played two seasons in Oklahoma City following Hurricane Katrina in 2005. Shinn established the tradition with the Charlotte Hornets in 1988 before relocating to New Orleans and continuing the ritual there. Shinn explained the pregame prayer stemmed from a promise he made to God. As the story goes, Shinn grew anxious while on a trip to New York City to pitch Charlotte as an expansion city to then–NBA Commissioner David Stern and league officials. He found a church and prayed, telling God he would give Him the honor if his bid was approved.

"I told David that I made a pact, I promised the Lord," Shinn said. "I said I would honor Him, and I'm going to do the prayer."

Charlotte never revived the custom after acquiring the expansion Bobcats in 2004. New Orleans discontinued the practice prior to the 2011–12 season, less than a year after Shinn sold the team. The Carolina Panthers of the NFL are believed to be the only other team across North America's major men's professional sports to include an invocation as part of its pregame presentation.

Bennett, despite growing up Jewish, immediately embraced the tradition when he and his fellow owners rebranded the Seattle SuperSonics in Oklahoma City.

The Thunder uses a variety of clergy to deliver the invocation and maintains a short but strict list of guidelines: keep it to 30 seconds, refrain from using inappropriate language, and stick to nondenominational prayer. The team also requests and reviews drafts of each prayer prior to handing over the mic.

"We feel people's faith is important to them. It's an important part of their lives," said Dan Mahoney, the Thunder's Vice President for Broadcasting and Corporate Communications. "And as they gather in our arena to support our team each night, we feel it's appropriate to build in that invocation as a prayer or silent reflection or whatever they want it to be. Our fans appreciate it."

Occasionally, the Thunder encourages clergy to include a mention of tragedies or the passing of someone from the NBA family. The team made such requests for the April 2013 passing of NBA official Greg Willard, the 2015 terrorist attacks in Paris, and the 2016 Brussels bombings, among others.

Every so often, a spiritual leader will inject a sense of humor.

Rev. Ronnie Fields, while a minister at First Christian Church in El Reno, prayed for world peace prior to a game against Sacramento late in the 2011–12 regular season. Two days prior, Los Angeles Lakers forward Metta World Peace, whose birth name is Ron Artest, left Thunder sixth man James Harden concussed after a vicious elbow to the head.

"We are called to pray for our enemies, and I believe God has a sense of humor," Fields said.

Some fans haven't found the invocation funny. Mahoney acknowledged the Thunder occasionally receives negative feedback. But the majority of fans, Mahoney said, report they are proud to be home to the pregame prayer.

"Our position is it's a moment of silent reflection, however they choose to use that moment," Mahoney said. "We're not insisting that people pray. We're not insisting that people join in a prayer. Most of our fans partake in it and want to be part of it. If someone doesn't think it's appropriate based on their beliefs, they can use it as their own moment of reflection however they see fit. Or they can just not be in their seats yet."

No player from the Thunder or an opposing team has ever publicly disapproved. While sprawled along the free throw line, many bow their heads and close their eyes.

"I think every team should do it, recognize God before a game," Kevin Durant once said.

68 The Ghost of LeBron James

By the end of the 2012 NBA Finals, two things had become clear about the Oklahoma City Thunder—they had a LeBron James problem, and they had no earthly idea how to solve it.

After his Miami Heat dropped Game 1 in Oklahoma City, James toyed with the Thunder while powering his team to victory in the next four games. His averages in the five-game series: 28.6 points, 10.2 rebounds, and 7.4 assists.

That Finals series epitomized James' mastery over the Thunder. It also began a streak of six consecutive victories by James over the Thunder, with the Heat sweeping the two 2012–13 meetings.

In 15 regular season games from the 2008–09 season through the 2015–16 season, James owns a 12–3 record in games he played against the Thunder. His Cleveland and Miami teams defeated Oklahoma City by an average margin of 12.1 points over that same span. James averaged 29.7 points, 6.5 rebounds, 7.3 assists, 2.3 steals, 0.9 blocks, and shot 52.3 percent in those games.

No other player comes close to owning OKC like James.

In fairness, James dominated most teams. But most teams didn't have Kevin Durant, who was widely considered the world's second-best player behind James for much of that eight-year stretch. Their head-to-head matchups, however, often (but not always), revealed how wide the gap was between the two. It was James' overpowering presence that in part led to Durant's famous quote from a 2013 *Sports Illustrated* cover story announcing he was tired of second place.

"I've been second my whole life," Durant said. "I was the second-best player in high school. I was the second pick in the draft. I've been second in the MVP voting three times. I came in second in the Finals. I'm tired of being second. I'm not going to settle for that. I'm done with it."

Durant finished second to James in MVP voting in 2010, 2012, and 2013.

James cast such a huge shadow over Durant, the Thunder, and the franchise's inability to solve him that some fans and media scoffed at Durant becoming workout partners with James in both the 2011 and 2012 off-seasons. Durant joined James in his native Akron, Ohio, for the workouts, which led to questions about Durant's competitiveness.

"You are owned by LeBron James," television personality Skip Bayless said of Durant. "Have fun in the NBA Finals finishing second again."

Bayless later posted to Twitter: "Wake up, KD: LeBron is keeping his friends close and his enemy closer. You're letting him own you."

During the 2011 lockout, Durant and James also hooked up to settle some playful social media trash talk by organizing teams and competing against each other in a flag football game. It took place in Akron and was broadcast live on Ustream. James' crew, "Team Bron," wore green and gold uniforms as a nod to his high school alma mater, St. Vincent–St. Mary. Durant's crew, "Team KD," wore burnt orange and white as a nod to his one season starring at the University of Texas. Both teams were outfitted in cleats, football pants with pads, gloves, and football jerseys. Naturally, James took that victory as well, with his team winning 70–63. With Team KD driving for a game-tying touchdown, James intercepted a pass inside the final 20 seconds to seal the game.

The game that best illustrated James' dominance over Durant and the Thunder, however, took place on February 14, 2013, Valentine's Day in Oklahoma City. It was a Thursday night, a marquee game on TNT's schedule and the final regular season matchup between the 2012 finalists. The Heat already had sent the

Thunder a message on Christmas Day, and this, the final contest before All-Star Weekend, was the Thunder's last chance to exorcise their demons before the two teams potentially met once again in June.

James strolled confidently into Chesapeake Energy Arena wearing all black, and by the end of the first quarter the game felt like a funeral. Fueled by James, the Heat opened a 15-point lead after the first period. LeBron had 11 points, five rebounds, two assists, and one steal in the frame. He also had a huge part in holding Durant to two points on 0-for-4 shooting. Durant missed his first seven shots that night in large part to James, and while Durant was out of sorts the Heat were pulling away, pushing their lead to 17 at halftime and as many as 23 in the third quarter.

Durant closed strong, making 11 of his final 13 shots before walking out with a game-high 40 points on 12-for-24 shooting. But it was James who captained the blowout, kept the Thunder at bay, and ensured OKC never threatened. James finished with 39 points, 12 rebounds, and seven assists. He made 14-of-24 shots in 40 minutes. By the end of the Heat's 110–100 thumping, James had shown once more the Thunder simply were powerless to stop him.

"Obviously they've been dominating us for the last six games," Thunder center Kendrick Perkins said after the Valentine's Day massacre. "So if we do meet again, it's just a problem that we got to deal with and figure it out."

For the Thunder, there would be no meeting that June. And for the final three years of the Durant era, there would be no solution to the franchise's biggest riddle.

69 Injuries Galore

The 2014–15 season was the team's most taxing. It was an injury-ravaged season that saw 15 players miss a combined 224 games and the Thunder miss the playoffs for the first time since 2008–09.

The Thunder's starting lineup of Russell Westbrook, Andre Roberson, Kevin Durant, Serge Ibaka, and Steven Adams missed a combined 115 games. Durant, coming off his MVP-winning 2013 season, was sidelined for 55 contests due to foot and ankle injuries. Ibaka missed the final 18 games because of right knee surgery. Westbrook and Roberson were knocked out of 15 games apiece, and Adams couldn't compete in 12 contests.

Oklahoma City played only 24 games with its customary starting lineup, going 16–8 in those contests. The Thunder's next most-used starting lineup—Westbrook, Roberson, Perry Jones, Ibaka, and Adams—took the court for tip-off in only 10 games. Four lineups started eight games apiece, and no other lineup started more than three games. The Thunder used 18 different starting lineups in 2014–15, matching the combined total from the previous three seasons and coming one shy of tying the Oklahoma City–era record from 2008–09.

The injury rash started early and spread quickly. All but six players on that year's squad missed time—D.J. Augustin, Kyle Singler, Sebastian Telfair, Lance Thomas, Ish Smith, and Dion Waiters. On opening night at Portland on October 29, the Thunder had six injuries that kept players sidelined. "There's that saying, 'If you don't laugh, you're gonna cry,'" Thunder coach Scott Brooks said. "Sometimes I feel like crying."

But the Thunder never used injuries as an excuse. They didn't have to. It was clear how shorthanded they were and the degree to which that weakened their chances each night. Instead, the team rallied around each other, and Brooks coached his butt off in arguably his finest season at the helm. With his main threats sidelined, Brooks no longer could rely on his rigid ways. He grew creative. He played small. He played zone. He played shrink. "He

Injuries

Here's a look at the Thunder's long list of player injuries from the 2014–15 season.

Player	Games Missed	Injury/Illness
Steven Adams	1	Migraine
Steven Adams	11	Right hand fracture
Nick Collison	9	Left ankle sprain
Kevin Durant	17	Right foot Jones fracture
Kevin Durant	6	Right ankle sprain
Kevin Durant	4	Sprained left great toe
Kevin Durant	28	Foot surgery
Serge Ibaka	18	Right knee surgery
Reggie Jackson	3	Right ankle sprain
Grant Jerrett	16	Left ankle surgery
Perry Jones	13	Right knee contusion
Perry Jones	1	Left ankle bruise
Perry Jones	3	Left ankle sprain
Enes Kanter	1	Right thigh contusion
Enes Kanter	1	Left ankle sprain
Jeremy Lamb	5	Lower back sprain
Mitch McGary	17	Left foot fracture
Mitch McGary	23	Periostitis left tibia
Anthony Morrow	7	Left MCL sprain
Anthony Morrow	1	Right shoulder soreness
Steve Novak	8	Appendectomy
Kendrick Perkins	1	Left knee contusion
Andre Roberson	8	Left foot sprain
Andre Roberson	7	Left ankle sprain
Russell Westbrook	14	Right hand fracture
Russell Westbrook	1	Zygomatic arch fracture

A Bad Run

Kevin Durant was sidelined for 55 games in 2014–15, so Russell Westbrook took over. He led the league in scoring for the first time at 28.1 points per game. But OKC missed the playoffs. The Thunder point guard was far from fulfilled when asked what his latest feat meant.

"S—t," Westbrook said. "It doesn't mean nothing. 'Good job. Hooray.' I'm at home, watching other teams play. It doesn't mean nothing."

rallied us," Durant said. "He made sure everybody was emotionally stable. It was a lot of guys in and out of the lineup, and he kept everybody together."

The drop-off in talent, though, was too steep. Westbrook did his best to carry the load, averaging a league-best 28.1 points, 7.3 rebounds, 8.6 assists, and 2.1 steals. But without Durant, the Thunder went 3–15 in games decided by five points or less. OKC finished 45–37 and on the final day of the regular season lost out to New Orleans for the eighth seed on a tiebreaker. A contested, double-clutch, buzzer-beating three-pointer by Anthony Davis inside Chesapeake Energy Arena on February 6, 2015, lifted the Pelicans to a pivotal three-point win that proved to be the difference.

"I couldn't be prouder in what they've done all year," Brooks said. "We just fought every game. We came down to the last game. We came up a game short. But we fought."

70 Steven Adams

Sometimes, sports are just unfair. Unfortunately for Steven Adams, he'll always be known as the biggest fish the Thunder netted in the controversial James Harden trade.

Adams, the affable 7' center from New Zealand, was taken 12th overall in the 2013 draft. At that spot, he was a steal, the product of the once-prized Toronto Raptors pick Oklahoma City received from Houston as part of the teams' blockbuster trade just before the start of the 2012–13 season. Of course, Adams was part of a much larger package that became Kevin Martin, Jeremy Lamb, Mitch McGary, Alex Abrines, and, through a subsequent Lamb trade, Daniel Hamilton. Yet hindsight doesn't shine a favorable light on OKC's end of the deal. Outside of Adams, the Thunder didn't land so much as another starter, never mind a star. Harden, meanwhile, became a superstar, developing into a perennial All-Star, an All-NBA performer, an MVP candidate, and a future Hall of Famer. Thunder loyalists might be the only segment of the basketball community capable of moving past Adams' connection to Harden.

But in his first four seasons, Adams did much to rewrite the narrative on the trade that forever will be debated. In short order, Adams transformed from a relative unknown out of Pittsburgh— the first New Zealander selected in the first round—into a rugged but versatile defensive anchor with gobs of offensive potential. As a rookie, he stepped onto a star-studded and veteran-laden team yet quickly carved out playing time with a no-nonsense approach centered on defense, rebounding, and just playing hard. He backed up Kendrick Perkins in 2013–14 and pushed the prideful but aging champion so much in practice every day that Adams said his

After years of searching for a stabilizing presence at the center position, the Thunder finally found Steven Adams with the 12th overall pick in the 2013 NBA Draft. (AP Photo/Jim Mone)

"welcome-to-the-NBA moment" came not on a game night but inside the team's training facility.

"I accidentally hit him. And then, like, he turned around and elbowed me in the ribs, and I'm like, 'Oh my God' [holding ribs]," Adams revealed after his rookie season. "Then he just yelled at me, 'I'm the only silverback!' I was like, 'What the...?' So that was a big [reality] check. It was like, 'We got some animals in the NBA.'"

Adams would soon show the league he too was an animal. In his rookie season, Adams unleashed a physical style that got under the skin of numerous opponents. Five players were ejected or suspended, or both, after altercations with Adams. Vince Carter threw an elbow to Adams' head. Larry Sanders threw multiple elbows to Adams' throat. Nate Robinson and Jordan Hamilton punched Adams in the chest. Zach Randolph punched Adams in the face. In subsequent seasons, Nick Young, Raymond Felton, and Hassan Whiteside also delivered elbows. Draymond Green delivered the blow of all blows, twice connecting on crotch shots in back-to-back games during the 2016 Western Conference finals, first with a knee and then with a kick. And somehow Green was neither ejected nor suspended, only fined.

Adams walked away from each incident without losing his cool. He never lost his cool. His nonchalant reactions endeared him to fans. "When he gets hit, it doesn't bother him," Nick Collison said. "He doesn't take it personally like a lot of guys in our league do, where they think someone is out to get them."

Asked how he would describe his style of play, Adams said aggressive. "Coach tells me to do one thing, then I'll just go do it. It's pretty simple," Adams explained. "Just go rebound or something simple like that. I just do the best I can. Just hustle." A *Los Angeles Times* survey of 24 anonymous NBA players during the 2015–16 season, however, identified Adams as the league's second-dirtiest player. Matthew Dellavedova was voted the league's dirtiest. Randolph and Young both publicly questioned Adams' tactics. Young labeled Adams a "sneaky, dirty player." Randolph vented, "Seven players have gotten suspended because of him. You've got to look into that. Why are players getting into it with this particular guy?"

"He's just aggressive," Carter countered. "Some can deem it borderline. He fits the mold and gives them a presence. He's one big human. That's just what they need down in the post. Perkins has been that type of guy for many years. So to have another guy being groomed into that role is great for them."

Adams, who Dirk Nowitzki once labeled the "white Kendrick Perkins," credited his toughness to his family. He is the youngest of 18 children. The males average 6'9". The females average 6'. His sister, Valerie Adams, is a world class shot-putter. She won Olympic gold in 2008 and 2012 and Olympic silver in 2016. She stands 6'4" and weighs 265 pounds. "She's strong," Adams said. "My family is really strong. So getting hit by them is really painful. But you can't say something about it, especially being the youngest. If you're the youngest and you say something, you'll get more hits."

Before long, Adams again changed the nationwide narrative, this time going from notorious goon to pivotal piece. He supplanted Perkins as the starter in 2014–15 and averaged 7.7 points, 7.5 rebounds, and 1.2 blocked shots. The next season, Adams showed he could soon be a star, stepping up when it mattered most. In the playoffs, he flashed mobility and versatility rarely seen from men his size, effectively defending everyone from Nowitzki to Tim Duncan to Stephen Curry. His signature sequence came in the closing seconds of a Game 2 road win over San Antonio in the conference semifinals. After the Spurs stole an inbounds pass, Adams hustled to single-handedly thwart a 3-on-1 break. He deterred two potential layups and closed out and contested a Patty Mills corner three-pointer. OKC escaped with a one-point win. Adams had 12 points and 17 rebounds, one of his six double doubles in 18 post-season games.

From then on, the basketball world couldn't stop buzzing about the biggest fish OKC got in the Harden trade.

"Steven is going to be a monster," Serge Ibaka said following the 2016 playoffs. "Give Steve two more years, he's going to be a monster."

71 Killer Collapse

For all the thrilling playoff moments, the big shots and the legendary performances and the heart-pounding victories, Oklahoma City also has seen its share of clunkers.

Not lopsided losses. Epic collapses.

The final minutes of Game 6 of the 2016 Western Conference finals against Golden State has been stained in the minds of most, and without question it holds the greatest significance in the story of the Thunder. But there were others. Several others.

In Game 3 of the 2011 Western Conference semifinals against Memphis, the Thunder led by as many as 16 and held a comfortable 13-point cushion at the start of the fourth quarter. With just more than 7½ minutes remaining, OKC still owned an 11-point advantage. But the Grizzlies forced overtime by closing the fourth quarter on a 15–4 run before outscoring the Thunder 15–7 in the extra period to take a 101–93 victory and a 2–1 series lead.

In Game 1 of the 2012 Western Conference finals against San Antonio, the Thunder blew a nine-point lead at the start of the fourth quarter and dropped a 101–98 decision inside the AT&T Center. OKC surrendered a staggering 39 fourth-quarter points and allowed San Antonio to shoot 12-of-16 from the field in the final frame.

And in Game 4 of the 2014 Western Conference semifinals, the Thunder led the Los Angeles Clippers by as many as 22 points and held a 16-point lead with 9:19 remaining. Oklahoma City then was outscored 35–17 over the final nine minutes. L.A. scored 24 points in the paint in the final period.

But those paled in comparison to what happened on May 23, 2011.

It was Game 4 of the Western Conference finals, a Monday night against the Dallas Mavericks. Kevin Durant drilled a three-pointer to put the Thunder ahead by 15 with 5:06 left to play. When the ball splashed through the net, the Thunder star looked toward his bench, put both hands in front of his waist, and motioned as if he was fitting his midsection with a championship belt.

Big shot. Big celebration. Big mistake.

While the Thunder's 20-somethings were busy celebrating, the cagey old Mavs were busy chipping away. Ten minutes later, the Thunder found themselves on the wrong end of a colossal collapse, a 112–105 overtime decision. Instead of knotting the series at two games apiece, the Thunder got outscored 28–6 in the final 10 minutes, 6 seconds and fell into the dreaded 3–1 deficit.

Following Durant's three-pointer, a bucket that put OKC ahead by its largest margin of the night, the Thunder missed eight of its final nine shots in regulation while turning it over twice.

It was a classic case of youth succumbing to experience. No play defined the Thunder's inexperience more than the final shot of regulation.

After the Thunder inbounded the ball at halfcourt, Durant settled for an early 30' heave from the right wing. Dallas forward Shawn Marion blocked the attempt, and the Mavs recovered with enough time to call a timeout with 0.7 seconds remaining. The

Mavs' lob pass to the basket on an inbounds play was batted away, and the Thunder survived only to die a slow death over five extra minutes.

"I didn't have anything else to do," Durant said of his final shot of regulation. "I caught the ball almost at the halfcourt line, seen three Mavericks in front of me, and had three seconds on the [game] clock. I didn't know what else to do. I tried to get a shot up. I didn't want to run into their defense and get another turnover."

The Thunder scored all of four points in the extra period, both coming off jumpers from unlikely offensive sources Thabo Sefolosha and Serge Ibaka. Durant and Russell Westbrook combined to shoot 0-for-5 in overtime and had both of the team's turnovers in the frame. Within the Thunder's offensive drought there were quick shots in addition to the turnovers, stagnant offense characterized by one-on-one play and, of all things, missed free throws. Westbrook came up empty on a trip to the stripe with 2:11 left in regulation that could have bumped the lead to nine.

In overtime, the Thunder then missed 5-of-7 shots, fouled when it shouldn't have, yet didn't when it needed to most, allowing 8.9 seconds to run off the clock before wrapping up Mavs guard Jason Terry in the final 30 seconds.

"There's no doubt it was a tough loss," Thunder coach Scott Brooks said after the game. "If this loss did not hurt, there's no such thing as a loss that can hurt you."

Unlike the blown leads in 2011 to the Grizzlies, 2012 to the Spurs, and 2014 to the Clippers, this collapse happened at home, inside the friendly confines of Chesapeake Energy Arena, where the Thunder were 36–13 that season when you included the previous eight postseason games. And unlike those other blown leads, the Thunder never recovered in the series. The Mavs closed out OKC in Game 5 back in Dallas, this time with a 17–6 run over the final 5½ minutes to send the Thunder into a summer of misery.

Dallas moved on to the NBA Finals, where the Mavs flustered LeBron James and the Miami Heat and captured their first NBA title.

The Thunder, meanwhile, were left waiting for next year.

"I let the city down," a sullen Durant said in his Game 4 postgame press conference.

72 Tulsa

Lewis Katz was a larger-than-life character, an affable New Jersey native who spoke with an unmistakably thick New Jersey accent and couldn't help but be a straight-shooter. As a minority owner of the New Jersey Nets in 2008, Katz was part of the NBA's seven-member relocation committee that would determine Oklahoma City's viability as a permanent NBA city.

When he traveled to Oklahoma City in March 2008 along with several other high-ranking league officials for a presentation on the city's potential, Katz unexpectedly became Oklahoma's most outspoken outside advocate. While the rest of the sports world was criticizing the NBA for even considering a move from Seattle to a much smaller market, Katz, when asked his concerns over the matter, critically analyzed it.

"Let me say this about small markets," Katz started, in an almost agitated and defensive tone. "Everybody keeps telling me that you think you're a small market. There's an hour and a half between Tulsa and Oklahoma City. That hour and a half has 2½ million people, or 70 percent of your state. Brooklyn, the fourth largest borough in America, has 2½ million people. This is not Oklahoma City [alone]. This is Oklahoma. And my view is 20 percent of your ticket sales [with the Hornets] came from the Tulsa market. I really didn't look at this as a small market. And I think the argument in the committee was that this is a state market with a history of people that love sports."

Put simply, without the city of Tulsa, there would be no Oklahoma City Thunder. Everyone involved with bringing the NBA to Oklahoma City knew it. If the franchise was going to succeed, it would need support from all corners of the state. No place was more critical than Oklahoma's second most populous city, which is connected to the capital city by an 88-mile-long trek along the Turner Turnpike.

Of course, there was a long history of a not-so-friendly rivalry between the state's two largest cities, and it led to questions of whether the two could collaborate. But the Oklahoma City–based ownership group of the Sonics was well aware of how critical it was to prove to the league its franchise could survive shifting from the country's 14th largest market to the 45th. When preparing to make their case to the relocation committee on March 25, 2008, Sonics owners and Oklahoma City officials invited anyone who was anyone to greet and speak with league executives. That included then Tulsa Mayor Kathy Taylor. She didn't hesitate to join the efforts. But Taylor and Oklahoma City Mayor Mick Cornett both admitted that 20 years prior it would have been unlikely that leaders from either city would have supported a major initiative of the other. The potential arrival of the NBA, however, was different than anything the cities ever vied for, and it launched a lasting partnership.

"It really puts Oklahoma on a national map, and that's what's important," said Taylor, an Oklahoma City native. "And it continues to grow the economy of Oklahoma City, which helps Tulsa. We are the two most significant contributors to the state economy. Anything that we can do to help Oklahoma City's economy expand is good for Tulsa."

When the franchise ultimately relocated, Thunder Chairman Clay Bennett made sure to make Tulsans feel a part of the journey at every step. In announcing the move on July 2, 2008, before the team even had a name, Bennett vowed to put games in Tulsa. "We want to make this Oklahoma's team," Bennett said. "This is a team that's going to play games in Tulsa, it's a team that's

Oklahoma vs. Oklahoma City

It wasn't all rainbows and butterflies between Oklahoma City, Tulsa, and surrounding areas. As the franchise's impending relocation crept closer, there was widespread consternation over whether the team's official name should be Oklahoma City or Oklahoma. NBA Commissioner David Stern recommended the team consider going with Oklahoma given its statewide appeal. Team owners and Oklahoma City civic leaders said no way.

After all, it was Oklahoma City that took on three MAPS renovations, Oklahoma City government and business leaders who did the heavy lifting luring the NBA, first with the New Orleans Hornets and then with the Sonics and Oklahoma City-area residents who would supply the bulk of the support. But there was an ulterior motive. "It's a branding issue," Oklahoma City Mayor Mick Cornett said. "Oklahoma City has traditionally not been protective of its brand. As a result, we find ourselves with identity issues when we try to market ourselves on the east coast or elsewhere."

Oklahoma City wanted to ride the wave that is the NBA's marketing machine and tell its story to the rest of the country and the world. And so on April 29, 2008, two months before the team's move became official, the Oklahoma City Council approved a contract between the city and the Sonics that stipulated Oklahoma City would be required to be in the team's name. It was buried in a revenue-sharing agreement focused on how the two sides would split arena concessions and restaurant revenues. But it ended all debate about Oklahoma vs. Oklahoma City. "We had allowed ourselves through the years to be branded through our tragedies," Cornett said. "I wanted Oklahoma City identified with something more positive...to increase Oklahoma City's identity and branding, which had never been done before."

going to promote in other markets and have appearances in other markets, and we really feel that bringing everybody together is a huge part of what this is all about." Later that month, the NBA announced the Tulsa 66ers of the NBA Development League would become the minor-league affiliate of the soon-to-be-named Thunder. It would further connect Tulsa to the parent club, as the team's young talent often was assigned to the 66ers to develop. "We're really pleased and thrilled about the opportunity to expand our basketball operation into Tulsa," Bennett said. "Tulsa has been an important part of our efforts to be successful in Oklahoma City with the NBA relocation. Ultimately, the team must be a statewide team, and we've committed to that and believe in that. We know it will work, but the first place we need to be is in Tulsa."

The 66ers spent nine total seasons in Tulsa—six as the Thunder's affiliate—before moving to Oklahoma City and becoming the Blue after the team's home, the SpiritBank Event Center, announced it would no longer hold major events. The Thunder were unsuccessful in landing a suitable replacement venue in the Tulsa area. But when Bennett unveiled the team's name and logo in September 2008 he said, "This is very much an Oklahoma organization." A month later, the Thunder's first game on Oklahoma soil was played inside Tulsa's BOK Center. It was a specially arranged preseason contest against Houston on October 13, 2008. More than 10,000 fans witnessed history. It was the start of a commitment by the franchise to hold one preseason game in Tulsa annually.

Once rival cities, Oklahoma City and Tulsa had found common ground, something joyous that finally brought the two communities together for a cause everyone could rally around. And it wasn't just Tulsa and Oklahoma City. Thanks to the Thunder, the same state pride could be found in all 77 counties. It was the lone thing on Bennett's mind when presented with the 2012 Western

Conference championship trophy following the Thunder's historic Game 6 victory over San Antonio.

"All I can think of," Bennett said, "is how this incredible group of young men has unified this city and this state as never before."

73 The Shot

The game was tied 118–118. Possession belonged to the Thunder coming out of a timeout with 29.5 seconds remaining. Klay Thompson had just converted a three-point play that once again gave Golden State new life when the Warriors long ago should have been laid to rest.

Thompson then hounded Russell Westbrook into missing a tough, off-balance jumper that would have given the Thunder the lead with eight seconds to play. The ball landed in Serge Ibaka's hands, but Draymond Green tapped it out and directly to teammate Andre Iguodala at the foul line. The clock was ticking…*eight, seven, six, five*. Iguodala spotted Stephen Curry, the reigning MVP, standing, waiting, on the wing to his left. Curry received the pass and patiently strolled up the court, the Warriors electing to not use their final timeout. Curry took three comfortable dribbles before gathering his feet just three steps past halfcourt, where he was level with the "E" in the THUNDER emblazoned at center court. He pulled up as he was parallel with the "R."

With the flick of his wrist, the greatest shooter the game has ever seen launched a bold but rhythmic, high-arcing jump shot. It traveled through the air for two seconds before it rained into the cylinder and broke Oklahoma City's back.

"Baaaaaaang! Baaaaaaang!" ABC play-by-play man Mike Breen exclaimed. "Oh, what a shot from Curry, with six-tenths of a second remaining!"

The moment, February 27, 2016, a Saturday night inside Chesapeake Energy Arena, will live forever in Thunder lore. If it wasn't the most memorable shot in franchise history, it certainly was the most excruciating. With Thunder fans hunting for hope that their team could slay the defending champions in a seven-game series, here came the league's reigning MVP, in the middle of his most magical stretch of an even more magical season, during the highest-rated regular season game since 2013, snatching hope away. And after Curry canned his cold-blooded dagger over the late-arriving arm of Andre Roberson, he danced. He shimmied. He C-Walked. He strutted all over the Thunder's home floor. The 121–118 overtime victory was the Warriors' 15th win in 16 games and improved them to 53–5, the best record in NBA history through 58 games. That night, the Warriors also became the first team since the 1987–88 Los Angeles Lakers to clinch a playoff berth in February.

NBA.com's initial box score listed Curry's kill shot as a 32-footer. It was later revised to 37'. ESPN's "Sports Science" segment measured it at a mind-boggling 38.4'. "He's got the greatest range I've ever seen," Thompson said. "He makes it look so effortless." And remember, this wasn't a heave. This was a natural shot. The basketball world was in awe and began buzzing immediately. "He's ridiculous, man," LeBron James posted on Twitter. "Never before seen someone like him in the history of ball!"

Curry entered the game averaging 35.7 points, 5.9 rebounds, and 7.4 assists in his previous nine games. He was shooting 54.5 percent from the field, 50.5 percent from three-point range (making 6-of-12 attempts on average), and 90 percent from the foul line over that span. Prior to that nine-game stretch, he had a 50-point game, six 40-point games, and eight other games in which he scored at least 35 points. "Stephen Curry has a chance to be the greatest player we've ever seen if he plays at this level for the next 4-5 years," Hall of Famer Magic Johnson said.

Here were the world-champion Warriors, having already skipped over the Thunder, hungrier than ever and in the middle of making regular-season history, with an MVP who had come back better and bolder. Even before the sensational shot, a small segment of the basketball community had inched Curry past not just Kevin Durant in the pecking order of best player in the world, but also James as king. Curry's final stat line that Saturday night: 46 points, 14-for-24 shooting, and 12-for-16 three-point shooting. His 12 three-pointers tied Kobe Bryant and Donyell Marshall for the most three-pointers made in a game. And tack on this to the legend: Curry did much of his damage after missing five minutes in the third quarter after Westbrook inadvertently landed on Curry's left heel after he drove to the basket, a major scare given Curry's history of ankle injuries.

So, yeah, hope had left the building.

For as much as fans worried about the Warriors having a perceived unstoppable juggernaut, as much or more hope dissipated due to the Thunder's self-inflicted troubles. Oklahoma City led by 12 points in the fourth quarter. The Thunder led by 11 inside the final five minutes of regulation and by four with 14.5 seconds showing. The final sequence of regulation then encompassed everything that made fans distrusting of this being the Thunder's year.

Thompson took an inbounds pass and got a quick layup with 11.8 seconds remaining in regulation. Durant got trapped in the corner in front of the Thunder's bench, panicked, and threw the ball high in the air toward a teammate at halfcourt. Thompson deflected it. Green saved it from going out of bounds, throwing it just past the fingertips of a charging Ibaka and right into Thompson's hands. Thompson looked up, spotted Iguodala, and fired the ball ahead with two seconds remaining. Iguodala used a pump fake to get Durant into the air. Durant came down on Iguodala as he was shooting. Iguodala made two clutch free throws to tie it at 103-all with 0.7 seconds showing.

In the game's most pivotal 15 seconds, the Thunder had a defensive breakdown, a horrid turnover, and a huge mental lapse. The sequence foreshadowed the manner in which the Thunder would fall to these same Warriors, inside the same building, in Game 6 of the Western Conference finals three months later. But back on that February night, it merely led to the eighth of the Thunder's league-leading 14 losses that season when owning a fourth-quarter lead.

Only this one was capped by one of the most memorable shots in NBA history.

74 Sonics History

Poor Mike Breen.

All the NBA's lead play-by-play man tried to do was put Serge Ibaka's perfect shooting night into perspective when partner Jeff Van Gundy interrupted and started down an impassioned rant. Ibaka was 12-for-12 late in the third quarter at Brooklyn on January 31, 2014. Breen noted it was the franchise's best shooting night since Gary Payton went 14-for-14 in 1995.

That's when all hell about broke loose.

Van Gundy: "Stop. Stop putting Seattle and the SuperSonics with the Oklahoma City Thunder. It's different teams. I don't want to hear about this anymore. They got their team taken away and now you're going to bring it up and put salt on the wound?"

Breen: "Will you stop yelling at me?"

Van Gundy: "No. Stop with this franchise. It's not the franchise."

Breen: [laughing] "He's got the Thunder record. The Thunder record is 9-for-9. Now do you feel better?"

Van Gundy: "I feel better now."

While the Thunder were busy blowing out the Nets, the broadcast tandem busied itself bantering for the next two minutes about why the Seattle SuperSonics' records were being tied to the Thunder. "That's what they've decided, to keep the franchise records a part of it," Breen explained.

"Does that make any sense to you?" Van Gundy asked, incredulously.

"No, I agree," Breen said. "And, actually, it bothers me that I say this, but I see what you're saying."

On live television, during a Friday night national ESPN broadcast, Breen and Van Gundy had entered into a topic fans in Oklahoma City and Seattle had been fuming over for years.

As part of the $45 million settlement between the Oklahoma City–based Sonics ownership and the city of Seattle in 2008, the franchise's entire history was transferred to OKC and would belong to the Thunder. That meant Sonics stats, records, retired jersey numbers, logos, the 1979 championship trophy and banner, the mascot, and the team name itself were all property of the Thunder. Team chairman Clay Bennett classified the material "a part of what we believe is the history that we purchased as part of this transaction."

"We will reserve the name Sonics and SuperSonics and the marks and the colors and will not use them," Bennett explained upon relocating in 2008. "But we will return them to Seattle if a team does indeed return to Seattle."

The Sonics' 1978–79 championship trophy remained in Seattle, where it is on display at the Museum of History and Industry. When he announced the parameters of the settlement,

Bennett said the Thunder's ownership group would create a replica trophy and banner, the likes of which have never been seen by the media or the general public of Oklahoma City.

The arrangement elicited all kinds of angst, from the Midwest to the Pacific Northwest and seemingly everywhere in between. Sonics fans didn't want to hear their history attached to Oklahoma City. Thunder fans didn't want any part of Sonics history. After two years of the franchise blowing in the wind, an ugly legal battle between city and ball club and, finally, a bitter relocation, the continued connection only caused confusion and further frustration.

"It's important to this organization and fans that we keep separate Oklahoma City records that are set here," said Brian Facchini, the Thunder public relations director in the team's inaugural 2008–09 season. "As for the future, there are legal issues."

In the 2011 NBA playoffs, the Thunder faced Denver in a first-round matchup. During a preview of that night's Game 2, NBA TV displayed a graphic saying the Thunder owned a 7–2 all-time postseason record at home against the Nuggets. Charles Barkley, one of three analysts on set inside the network's studios, couldn't help but question the stat.

"Hold on a second," Barkley demanded. "What do you mean 7–2 all-time at home against the Nuggets? That don't count. That doesn't count. You can't take another city's stats. Am I right or wrong guys?"

Chris Webber and Greg Anthony nodded in agreement.

"You know, me and Michael Jordan scored like 50,000 points," Barkley added. "You going to let Oklahoma City count Seattle stuff, I'm going to count Michael Jordan's points with mine. We from the same era. We were in the same draft."

Really, the shared historical records and stats became more of a hassle than anything. When Kevin Durant made 24 free throws in a January 2009 road loss at the Los Angeles Clippers, it was a "Thunder/Sonics" record. When Durant posted his sixth straight

30-plus-point game in January 2010, he was said to have "tied a franchise record set by Spencer Haywood in January 1972." Without fail, fans from both Seattle and Oklahoma City would grow incensed at all similar mentions. Soon, many reporters following the team went with "Oklahoma City–era record."

"It's just another punch to the gut to hear Oklahoma talking about Sonics retired jerseys and the history and all that, which we feel doesn't belong to anybody but us," said longtime Seattle sports talk radio host Dave "Softy" Mahler.

The Sonics won six division titles, three conference titles, and one league title. They retired six player jersey numbers and honored longtime broadcaster Bob Blackburn with a banner. None of those tribute banners hang from the rafters in Oklahoma City. Still, Kendrick Perkins was unable to wear No. 43 when he arrived from Boston via trade in 2011, and Cameron Payne couldn't continue wearing his preferred No. 1 when the Thunder drafted him in 2015. Jack Sikma wore No. 43 with the Sonics, and Gus Williams wore No. 1. Both numbers were retired in Seattle.

"The historical record, I mean, it is the same franchise that won the NBA title. It is the same franchise as Sikma and Gus Williams and Fred Brown and all those guys. So you can't rewrite history," *The Oklahoman* columnist Berry Tramel said during an appearance on Mahler's show. "But when you honor a legacy and honor a history and honor a tradition, there's no reason to think that those kinds of things travel 2,000 miles. Because, frankly, very few people—only old people like me—remember who Jack Sikma was. And the people who do remember don't really care."

75 Seattle Acrimony

Maybe they thought it could never happen, the Sonics leaving. Maybe they thought 41 years of tradition would trump all—the billionaire looking to make a buck, the out-of-state owners answering the knock, knock, knock of opportunity, the asleep-at-the-wheel city leaders oblivious to the gravity of their apathy.

For whatever reason, Seattle-area residents were in disbelief when the Sonics relocated, when two years of speculation morphed into reality. Denial quickly turned to anger, and the people of Seattle still haven't reached acceptance. They needed something, someone, to be their punching bag. Oklahoma received the brunt of their rage.

An unfortunate and at times ugly byproduct of Seattle losing the Sonics to Oklahoma City was bad blood that brewed between fan bases of both cities. A war of words ensued between the two. Seattle attacked. OKC went on the defensive. Both resorted to petty name-calling and pointing out every stereotype in the book about the other. It seemed nothing was out of bounds. The beef played out on blogs and message boards, websites and social media.

There was lots of emotion flying, and from Seattle's standpoint only so much of the fury could be hurled at Howard Schultz, the owner who struck the deal with the Oklahoma City–based investment group, or local government, which twice denied Schultz in his pursuit of a largely taxpayer-funded arena renovation. Clay Bennett, the new team chairman from OKC who oversaw the operation, was saddled with much of the scorn. Oklahoma City, its fans, and the team that eventually was renamed the Thunder also drew contempt. Mention the Thunder to a Seattle native even today and chances are you'll be met with the stink eye. When the Thunder landed in Oklahoma City, old Sonics fans swore Kevin Durant and Russell Westbrook would be on the first thing smoking out of town. When the Thunder journeyed to the 2012 NBA Finals, they openly rooted against them. And when Kevin Durant jilted Oklahoma, they didn't hesitate to rub it in.

"The team was here for 41 years," said Seattle resident Adam Brown in 2012. "People have no idea how that feels, to have something ripped away from you. Talk to me in another 37 years. Maybe I will start to get over it."

Brown and four Seattle friends were the brains behind *Sonicsgate: Requiem for a Team,* a 2009 documentary chronicling the history of the Sonics. One press release for the original 120-minute online version proudly proclaimed it was produced by Seattle-based filmmaker Jason Reid and "a crew of angry Sonics fans." CNBC acquired the broadcast rights in April 2012 and produced a re-cut version to fit a regular TV hour. "The team was sewn into the fabric of the community more than any of our other sports franchises," Brown said.

In the first few years following the franchise's relocation, die-hard Sonics supporters made the 2½-hour drive south to Portland for Thunder-Blazers games. Their sole purpose was to show they hadn't forgotten about their beloved franchise. They wore Sonics hats, T-shirts, jerseys, and jackets—anything in the team's classic green and gold colors. Most sat behind the Thunder's bench and ferociously booed their former franchise. One pocket of Sonics supporters even booed a teenager as he made his way to his seats because he was sporting a Kevin Durant Oklahoma City jersey.

"I understand both ways," said Nick Collison, who played his first five seasons in Seattle. "They're angry about the team moving. If they do boo, I don't feel like they're booing us personally. It's more what happened overall. I'd feel worse if there was nothing and people were just indifferent and didn't care."

The people of Seattle cared deeply.

Thunder fans should know most still do.

76 "Little Brother"

Jason Terry always was a talker. He couldn't help himself. He spoke his mind and called things as he saw them. It made the longtime Hawks and Mavs guard a media darling, someone reporters relied on as a go-to source when seeking something more substantial than stale quotes.

Terry once again delivered when the conversation shifted to the Thunder early in the 2011–12 season.

One day after helping the Mavs secure a 13-point home win over the Thunder on January 2, 2012, only six games into the lockout-shortened season that began on Christmas Day 2011, Terry turned his attention to the Suns and Spurs, the next two opponents on Dallas' schedule. Terry dubbed the two-game stretch "rivalry week." He excluded the Thunder, which prompted a reporter to ask about Oklahoma City.

"It's a big brother–little brother scenario," Terry explained of the Mavs and Thunder. "It is what it is. They're good. They're up and coming, and they're dangerous. When you got guys like Westbrook and Durant on your ball club, it's tough any time."

Terry was then asked whether the Thunder needed to beat the Mavs before the matchup could be considered a rivalry. "They've beaten us a number of times," Terry countered. "Now, if you want to say in a series, that would make some intensity come to the rivalry."

Back then, the Thunder were just finding their way. While doing so, Dallas dominated OKC, winning 11 of the first 17 regular season and postseason meetings. In the 2011 Western Conference finals, the Mavs eliminated the Thunder with a 4–1 series win. One of the Thunder's six wins in that stretch came with Mavs star Dirk Nowitzki sidelined. Still, Thunder coach Scott Brooks refuted Terry's claim and stuck up for his team prior to the next meeting in that 2011–12 season.

"I don't feel that way at all. I think we're a good team just like they are," Brooks said. "They had a great year last year. But they had a lot of tough years prior to that. But one year—you have to keep doing it every year, hammer away at it and they've done a great job."

Brooks, of course, was taking the high road, praising Dallas for how it had sustained success—at least in the regular season—with 11 consecutive 50-win seasons from 2000–01 to 2010–11. "I think the strength of their team is their stability," Brooks continued. "They've been together a while. They did not break it up when things didn't go well.... But I don't look at it as they're a big brother. I look at it as they're a very good team and we are, too. And we're going to keep fighting each other."

The Thunder had no answer for Dirk Nowitzki in those early days. He averaged 30.7 points, 7.5 rebounds, and shot 54.7 percent in his first 11 games against the Thunder. In five postseason games in 2011, Nowitzki averaged 32.2 points, 5.8 rebounds, and shot 55.7 percent. Asked what the Thunder couldn't overcome when the Mavs were in command of the matchup, Kendrick Perkins was blunt. "A younger Dirk," he said. "That's what the difference was."

But Dirk and Dallas got old, and the Thunder came of age. The Thunder beat the Mavs nine out of 10 times during the 2011–12 season, including two preseason games and four postseason games.

Dallas' lone win was that 13-point January triumph that got Terry talking. From there, Oklahoma City peeled off 11 straight wins against Dallas, including a first-round playoff sweep in 2012 and a four-game regular season series sweep in 2012–13.

Dallas did the Thunder—and the rest of the league—a favor when it dismantled its 2011 championship team. The Mavs were never the same after parting with Jason Kidd, Tyson Chandler, Caron Butler, J.J. Barea, and DeShawn Stevenson. But it didn't matter. The Thunder were now the big brother.

"The thing that impresses me the most about them is that they have a certain look in their eye right now," Dallas coach Rick Carlisle said after the Thunder's four-game sweep in the opening round of the 2012 playoffs. "Not just that they belong, but that this could be their time."

It wasn't quite Isiah Thomas and the Detroit Pistons overcoming Larry Bird and the Boston Celtics or Michael Jordan and the Chicago Bulls finally figuring out Thomas and his Bad Boy Pistons. But for Oklahoma City, the Dallas Mavericks during that four-year stretch were the closest thing the Thunder had to a conference opponent standing between them and the Promised Land.

"They took a huge step," Nowitzki conceded following the Thunder's 21-point drubbing of Dallas in February 2013. "They went to the Finals last year and, to me, they were actually the favorites to win it the way they ran through the whole Western Conference. Obviously, now they're more experienced. Going through tough times, you learn from losing tough games. They got a really tough team."

77 Attend a Mavs Road Game

The Thunder held a 3–0 series lead and were looking to polish off their first postseason sweep after a 16-point road win over Dallas in Game 3 of the opening round of the 2012 playoffs. Mavs fans weren't blind. They could see what was coming. So they jumped ship, selling off their tickets to Saturday night's potential season-ending Game 4 inside American Airlines Center.

And Thunder fans took full advantage.

An army of the team's orange-clad faithful, at least 1,000 strong, showed up and showed out. Many had made the three-hour trek down I–35 to invade the Mavs' arena. They were loud. They were proud. Every OKC basket produced boisterous cheers that pervaded the building. When the Mavericks' public address announcer urged the home crowd to join in on a "Let's go Mavs" chant, the Thunder army drowned out the Dallas die-hards with an obstinate "O-K-C" chant.

It was a surreal scene, one of the most impressive of any on the laundry list of examples that illustrate the passion of Thunder fans. Here was a franchise, in only its fourth year of existence, flaunting a following that straight took over an opponent's building. In a playoff game. Against the defending champs. This wasn't normal. This was behavior seen from fans of only the most storied franchises. Think Boston Celtics. Los Angeles Lakers. Chicago Bulls. But here were Thunder fans, owning their counterparts in the stands as their team owned the Mavs on the court.

It was one of the most memorable moments in Thunder history, and it's why Thunder fans must make it a priority to attend a Mavs road game.

Top Five Arenas

As a full-time traveling media member during my time covering the Thunder and New Orleans/Oklahoma City Hornets for *The Oklahoman,* I was fortunate to attend a game at every NBA arena between 2005 and 2015. Here are my top five arenas, with priority placed on atmosphere.

1. Madison Square Garden

The New York Knicks' on-court product hasn't been much to see since Patrick Ewing patrolled the paint. But it remains a legendary building—even after several rounds of renovations—that has a palpable aura from the moment you step foot inside the arena. A bucket-list destination for any hoops head.

2. Moda Center

Home to the Portland Trail Blazers and some of the best fans in basketball, Moda Center is a rocking arena when the home team is rolling. You'll be amazed at how in tune Blazers fans are with the action. Their organic chants and cheers prove they know exactly how to provide a boost to their team at just the right time.

3. Oracle Arena

Even when the Golden State Warriors were an afterthought nationally, their crowds were incredible. Those fans were as passionate as they come and would scream their lungs out for their Warriors. Oracle Arena set quite the standard for the team's new digs across the bay in San Francisco.

4. United Center

From the classic pregame introduction video to Michael Jordan's No. 23 jersey hanging from the rafters, the Chicago Bulls' home will give you goosebumps. An underrated aspect here is the still of the arena (it doesn't blast music all night), which highlights the intensity of the fans.

5. Staples Center

It's *the* place to see and be seen, and generally that's as entertaining as the game itself. From Angela Bassett to Zac Efron, you never know who you might see during Lakers games. Also at Lakers games, you'll likely find yourself fixated on the jerseys of some of the game's all-time greats that hang from the rafters.

Honorable mention: TD Garden (Celtics), Bankers Life Fieldhouse (Pacers), AT&T Center (Spurs), Air Canada Centre (Raptors), and Vivint Smart Home Arena (Jazz).

As the Thunder rose in popularity, fans in blue Oklahoma City jerseys began filling opposing venues. You'd see them everywhere, from Denver to Detroit, Phoenix to Philly. No place on the NBA circuit, however, could top the turnout the Thunder received in Dallas. And when Thunder fans raided the Mavs' arena, it was a sight to see. Much of the mayhem, of course, could be attributed to Dallas being the closest NBA city to Oklahoma City. Many Oklahomans also annually relocate to the Dallas–Fort Worth area. Kevin Durant supporters from his University of Texas days no doubt made a ripple as well during the team's glory days.

After a game at Dallas on January 6, 2011, a 99–95 Thunder win, a horde of fans waited for Durant over the tunnel leading to the team's locker room as he was being interviewed by the late Craig Sager. When Durant finished and strode to the locker room, the crowd roared. The moment was a prelude to the scene that played out in the following season's series-clinching Game 4.

But there is another benefit in high-tailing it to Dallas to take in a game. Even if the Thunder isn't one of the league's wildly popular franchises, the Mavericks are good for a show. The team's game-night entertainment is top notch. The Mavs have a great atmosphere that is loose, interactive, and fan-friendly. If you've never been to Dallas for a Mavs game, do yourself a favor and plan a trip. You won't be disappointed.

Especially not if you catch a night the Thunder army is in attendance.

78 "Where He Gonna Go?"

Serge Ibaka sounded so sure.

He was hardly the only one.

But when the Thunder forward sat at his exit interview immediately following the team's heartbreaking end to the 2015–16 season and stridently shared his belief that Kevin Durant would return the next season, he became the first teammate to publicly say what so many had reasoned.

Durant's highly anticipated free agency had loomed large over that Thunder season. July 1, 2016, the day Durant would be an unrestricted free agent for the first time in his career, became the date that drew everyone's attention. GMs spent years planning for it. Fans hitched their hopes to it. Media were mesmerized by it. But when the games began, Durant and his teammates mostly were spared from the non-stop narrative. Save a few cities—New York, Los Angeles, and Washington, D.C.—free agency chatter never developed into a daily irritant. Players weren't asked about Durant's impending decision at every stop. When they were, they mostly downplayed the gravity of what waited at year's end or deflected the focus back to the team.

Ibaka broke rank and veered off message just hours before packing bags and heading abroad, where he annually spent the majority of his off-seasons. With Durant exactly one month from hitting the open market on the day of exit interviews, Ibaka insisted he wasn't nervous about Durant potentially leaving. When a reporter's follow-up question inquired whether he was confident Durant would remain in Oklahoma City, Ibaka doubled down.

"I'm confident, yeah, of course," Ibaka said in his Congolese accent. "Where he gonna go? Tell me. After what we did this year in the playoffs?"

Ibaka snickered.

"Where?" he again asked, rhetorically. "If he goes somewhere, I don't know, tell me where. I don't know."

The sound bite echoed the sentiments of scores of Thunder fans and epitomized the overwhelming belief, not just among Oklahoma City's fan base but also around the country, that Durant would almost certainly re-sign with the Thunder for at least one more season.

Outside of prayerful opposing fans, it seemed, pessimists, and cynics were the only ones who considered Durant bolting a possibility. None of the obvious destinations made complete sense: Washington and New York were laughingstocks, while the Los Angeles Lakers were on the verge of joining them as such. Miami and Boston had a handful of nice pieces, but neither would be championship ready even with Durant—not to mention he'd be forced to deal with LeBron James before the NBA Finals. San Antonio and the Los Angeles Clippers had their respective long-established cores in place and the Thunder's core owned a combined 3–1 postseason series advantage over those two West rivals.

It just didn't add up. Signing elsewhere meant Durant would have to walk away from superstar sidekick Russell Westbrook and Ibaka, their sensational two-way glue guy. He also would be leaving a carefully constructed cast of promising young players: Steven Adams, Enes Kanter, Andre Roberson, Cameron Payne, and Dion Waiters, each of whom fell between the ages of 21 and 24 and could flank Durant, Westbrook, and Ibaka as they entered their primes. When you add the fact the Thunder appeared headed for an encouraging new direction following an impressive debut season by Coach Billy Donovan and top it off with how league rules permitted OKC to pay Durant more than all other suitors, a move made no sense. The Thunder were his team, in what had quickly become his town.

As if that wasn't enough to make you believe Durant would stay, you thought, surely, the Thunder's stunning ousting from the Western Conference finals after leading 3–1 would compel Durant to give it one more go.

"There's unfinished business here, and he wants to get it done," said Randy Foye, who played 27 games with the Thunder that season following a deadline-deal that brought him over from Denver.

Foye's comment also came at that June 1 batch of exit interviews. It was delivered from the same table at which Ibaka sat and the same one at which Durant gave one of his last interviews as a member of the Thunder. The answer he supplied to the eighth of 18 questions he fielded in that day's 18-minute session might still sting when you read them today. The potentially telling response came when Durant was asked whether Westbrook would be among the select few he would include in his decision-making process.

"It's kind of hard to talk to one of my teammates," Durant said. "Obviously, we've been through a lot. We know each other very, very well, but it's one of these things where I just—I got to just hear from me and hear what I want and talk to myself about what I need and how I can make this thing work for myself and just try to be a little selfish a bit. Obviously, I want to ask for advice, but I also want to make a decision that's best for me."

79 Tyson Chandler

In Tyson Chandler's mind, it was about the money.

One day he was headed to Oklahoma City to join Russell Westbrook, Jeff Green, and Kevin Durant. The next day—literally—he wasn't.

After agreeing to acquire Chandler from the New Orleans Hornets on February 17, 2009, the Thunder reversed course roughly 24 hours later. Oklahoma City rescinded the trade because of concerns over Chandler's health. The 7'1", 245-pound shotblocking center who was taken second overall out of high school in 2001 had a bum toe. Chandler failed his physical with the Thunder and was sent back to New Orleans.

One day before the trading deadline, the 13–41 Thunder backed out of an unforeseen blockbuster that everyone agreed made them significantly better.

"I honestly feel it had more to do with the salary," said Chandler, who was making $11.3 million that season and was due nearly $25 million over the next two. "Because when I looked at it, it just didn't make sense. I just didn't see that being that big of an issue. It all seemed fishy, to be honest with you."

Depending on your perspective, Thunder General Manager Sam Presti, 32 years old at the time, either dodged a bullet or cost OKC a championship. Scores of Thunder fans saw it as the latter. That's how good they felt about the prospects of adding Chandler. That's how much it stung seeing him slip away.

"Yesterday, we were excited to add Tyson, but at the same time we have to make tough decisions," Presti tried to explain. "There were some things in the medical process and outside consultants that gave us some concern.

"We have to listen to the people [conducting] our medicals. We feel the right decision for us was to move in another direction. We're disappointed it did not work out."

Much of Chandler's appeal to Thunder fans stemmed from memories of his time in OKC as a member of the displaced Hornets only two seasons earlier. Running with Chris Paul and David West, Chandler found his way in Oklahoma City after five turbulent seasons in Chicago. He averaged 9.5 points, 12.4 rebounds, and 1.8 blocks in 2007 before helping the Hornets come one win short of the West finals in 2008.

Thunder fans also knew their team had a gaping hole at center. Nenad Krstic had arrived one month earlier, but he was still coming off the bench while Nick Collison served as the starter. Fans could see, too, that the Thunder were giving up peanuts to get Chandler: Joe Smith, Chris Wilcox, and the draft rights of DeVon Hardin. John Hollinger, writing for ESPN.com at the time, graded the trade an 'A' for the Thunder and a 'C' for the Hornets.

"He's really growing into one of the best centers in the league," Desmond Mason, a wing on that 2009 Thunder team who teamed with Chandler in 2006–07 with the displaced Hornets, said after the trade.

Chandler became too expensive for the Hornets. They stared at a $76 million payroll the following season and became sellers. Presti was being his opportunistic self. In the process, he nearly came away with one of the league's most athletic big men in exchange for spare parts with expiring contracts.

That's where Carlan Yates comes in.

Yates was the Thunder's orthopedic surgeon. He was the same orthopedic surgeon the Hornets used during their two-year stay. When Chandler missed the final seven games of the 2006–07 season because of a toe injury, Yates knew all the particulars. And when Chandler underwent surgery on the toe two days after the Hornets' season finale, Yates performed the operation.

"There was a lot more in there that they had to clean up than they thought," Hornets coach Byron Scott said following Chandler's toe surgery.

Yates was now making the call on the Chandler deal. He believed the risk of re-injury was too great.

"He said he doesn't know how long I'll last," Chandler said. "He told me, 'I have no doubt you can play on it. I'm just saying it could take a turn for the worse if you come down on somebody's foot or hyperextend it or something.'"

The rescinded trade gave critics of the Thunder ammunition that fit the narrative that the franchise was cheap. But Chandler had a well-documented history of injuries. The toe injury alone bothered Chandler during the 2008 playoffs, and he withdrew from Team USA that summer because of the discomfort. Often overlooked as well was how Chandler missed 67 of a possible 164 games due to injuries from 2008–09 to 2009–10. A staggering 62 of those missed games came after the Thunder pulled the plug on the trade.

But Chandler got healthy, and by the 2011 postseason his contributions to the eventual champion Dallas Mavericks had Thunder fans certain Presti blew it. Chandler played in 74 games in 2010–11 and averaged 10.1 points, 9.4 rebounds, and 1.1 blocks, earning NBA All-Defensive Second Team honors. New York signed him to a four-year, $55 million contract, and Chandler became the 2012 Defensive Player of the Year, a 2012 All-Star, and a 2013 All-NBA Third Team selection with the Knicks.

The Thunder ended up with Kendrick Perkins.

Years later, Chandler was asked if he ever thought about what could have been with the Thunder.

"The only time I thought about that was in the summertime, playing with Kevin Durant and Russell Westbrook, two good friends of mine," Chandler said. "I really enjoyed playing with them.

"Sometimes life throws you lemons, and you've got to make lemonade. It was one of those cases where I was a little baffled about the situation. I didn't understand it, but everything happens for a reason."

Maybe it all worked out.

Consider this. With Chandler, the Thunder might have left Serge Ibaka overseas rather than bringing him over from Spain, where Ibaka was stashed for one season following the 2008 draft. Eric Maynor and Thabo Sefolosha were both later acquired via trade—Sefolosha and Nick Collison later re-signed cap-friendly deals—only because of the salary cap space the Thunder had after backing out of the Chandler deal. And if Chandler was healthy enough to usher in just a few additional wins in 2008–09, the Thunder could have seen its luck change in the NBA Draft Lottery and lost out on the 2009 No. 3 overall pick, James Harden.

Or maybe the Thunder blew a future championship.

Mayor Mick Cornett

The footage is legendary.

Fat chance Mick Cornett ever lives it down.

In 1992, while working as a sportscaster at KOCO-TV, the ABC affiliate in Oklahoma City, Cornett went absolutely bonkers while calling the game-winning play of a Triple A Oklahoma City 89ers playoff game.

Cornett emerges into the picture—decked in khaki pants, a sport coat, and tie—along the third-base line while continuing to provide play-by-play of Keith Miller's walk-off home run. As Miller rounds third, Cornett extends one hand while holding the microphone in the other. Cornett audibly asks for a high-five and receives it as Miller takes his final strides toward home plate. He then follows Miller, and while standing outside the scrum at home plate sticks the mic above the players' huddle, capturing live audio of the celebration. Within seconds, Cornett corrals Miller, holding him with one hand around his shoulder as he petitions the player for instant reaction. "The power of YouTube," Cornett cracked years later.

In that moment, Cornett's enthusiasm for sports was on full display. Twelve years later, that same spirited sportscaster became Oklahoma City's mayor. But all of Oklahoma should be happy he did.

Elected as the successor to Kirk Humphreys on February 24, 2004, Cornett became Oklahoma City's longest-serving mayor, the first to serve four terms. During his near 14-year stint in the mayor's office, Cornett made it his mission to improve both the quality of life and the reputation of his city and state. While he went to great lengths to do so, history will remember Cornett most as the mayor whose passion for sports positioned him perfectly to play a central role in bringing the NBA to Oklahoma City.

A graduate of Putnam City High School and the University of Oklahoma, where he earned a degree in journalism, Michael Earl Cornett began his professional career as a sportscaster in the 1980s. He spent 20 years in television, transitioning to news later in his career and covering City Hall. While still a sportscaster, he contributed to the creation of the Oklahoma Sports Hall of Fame, and in 2014 Cornett was inducted into the Hall he helped create. Cornett was elected as a councilman in 2001 before winning the mayor race three years later.

Cornett was a personable mayor. He was eloquent, charismatic, and gracious. Above all, he possessed an extremely positive, can-do attitude and a passion for moving Oklahoma City forward. Cornett drew national attention for putting Oklahoma City on a diet.

The city habitually appeared on humiliating lists that ranked the country's unhealthiest communities for diets, health, and fitness. Cornett challenged OKC residents to lose 1 million pounds, and he walked the walk by losing more than 40 pounds.

But in Cornett's mind, nothing could alter the national perception of Oklahoma City like a major league sports franchise. The city had been branded by tragedy ever since the 1995 bombing of the Alfred P. Murrah Federal Building. And even though the community poured its heart and soul into rebuilding in the bombing's aftermath, little was done in the way of casting aside what had become the city's claim to fame. Cornett didn't care for his city to be thought of simply as the city where tragedy struck. And he refused to settle for that stereotype.

He began laying the foundation for Oklahoma City to lure a major league franchise shortly after taking office. He commissioned a sports council comprised of business leaders and long-standing event promoters. He embraced major league exhibition games to show OKC could draw crowds. But his most significant step was securing sit-down meetings with Gary Bettman and David Stern, the respective commissioners of the NHL and NBA. In those, Cornett sold his city to the most powerful men running two of North America's four major leagues.

Cornett met with Bettman in August 2004 while in New York for the Republican National Convention. The NHL, however, had just entered into a work stoppage after a breakdown in labor negotiations. The timing wasn't right. But in January 2005, Cornett scored a meeting with Stern in his New York City office. He delivered the same sales pitch: Oklahoma City stands ready in the event of NBA relocation or expansion. Stern countered with the idea of OKC acquiring a WNBA or D-League franchise. Cornett respectfully but boldly declined. Upon a return trip to New York in April 2005 for the 10th anniversary of the bombing, Cornett again met with Stern. This time, the Commissioner playfully classified

Cornett as "the Mayor that won't go away." Cornett again tried to sell Stern on Oklahoma City as an NBA destination. Stern again was unmoved, ending the meeting by famously saying, "I'm sure there is an NHL team in your future."

Four months later, on August 29, 2005, Hurricane Katrina wreaked havoc on New Orleans and the Gulf South. When it became clear the NFL's New Orleans Saints and NBA's Hornets would be unable to play their upcoming seasons in their host city, Cornett called Stern to inquire about the Hornets. They needed a temporary home, and Oklahoma City, thanks to Cornett's best efforts, was on Stern's radar.

On September 21, 2005, the NBA announced Oklahoma City would be the Hornets' temporary home. Cornett negotiated to have the team name be the New Orleans/Oklahoma City Hornets. The team's jerseys also featured a hexagonal patch on the right shoulder that read "OKC." The Hornets enjoyed two wildly successful seasons in Oklahoma City and paved the way for the arrival of the Seattle SuperSonics.

Cornett again was instrumental in the city's pursuit of the Sonics, this time leading an initiative to renovate the Ford Center through a 1-cent sales tax on Oklahoma City residents.

When the Thunder touched down in 2008, it was Cornett who stood at center court on opening night alongside Commissioner Stern and welcomed Oklahoma City to the NBA.

"It's time to get rowdy," Cornett told the crowd. "It's time to cheer for our team."

81 Mr. Unreliable

Here's the story of the headline heard 'round the world.

It appeared in *The Oklahoman* newspaper on the morning of May 1, 2014, a Thursday.

Mr. Unreliable, it screamed.

Its target: Kevin Durant.

Through five games of the opening round of the 2014 play-offs, the Thunder star had largely been ineffective. On the surface, you couldn't tell. He was averaging 28 points, 9.8 rebounds, four assists, one steal, and 1.8 blocked shots against the "Grit n Grind" Grizzlies. But his 28-point average through five games came on 25 shots per game. His field goal percentage dipped from 50.3 in the regular season to 40 percent. His three-point percentage fell from 39.1 percent in the regular season to 28.6 percent. And his four assists per game were offset by four turnovers per game. Worst of all, his subpar play had the Thunder staring at a 3–2 series deficit and an elimination Game 6 at Memphis. His short-comings simply couldn't be ignored with the Thunder's season on the brink.

And so *The Oklahoman's* sports department produced a plan.

Berry Tramel, the paper's lead columnist, tackled Durant's uncharacteristic play, specifically how Memphis, led by notorious defensive goon Tony Allen, had gotten inside Durant's head and taken him out of his game. Accompanying Tramel's column on the cover of the sports section was my story on how Durant needed a signature performance in Game 6. He faced the brutal reality of becoming the fourth player in NBA history to win the league's Most Valuable Player Award and be bounced in the first round of the playoffs, joining Wes Unseld, Karl Malone, and Dirk Nowitzki.

Neither of the articles was scathing. But buried 268 words into Tramel's column was the innocuous line that became the source of the headline.

"For six years, Durant has shot foul shots on a string. Mister Automatic. Now he's unreliable," Tramel wrote.

Durant, a career 88 percent foul shooter, was connecting on only 71.8 percent of his free throws through those first five games. Tramel's words were accurate, and he intended them only for Durant's free throw shooting. A member of our copy desk, however, took those words out of context and ran with them.

As Tramel, four coworkers, and I made the seven-hour trek in a Ford Excursion from Oklahoma City to Memphis for that pivotal Game 6, we worked to finish our stories for the next day's paper. Tramel is a machine so, per usual, he finished first. As we approached Memphis, his column was sent out via Twitter. It contained the headline. Tramel thought nothing of it, assuming it was just Twitter and someone was being silly. Surely it wouldn't appear in print.

The next day I was scheduled to do a radio interview with a local Memphis station to preview Game 6. The call came before 8:00 AM. It was my wake-up call. The voice on the other end said, "Your paper has stirred the pot." Having no idea what the host was referring to, I tried to fake it until he provided details. Then I pulled up Twitter, turned on the television, and fired up my laptop. "Mr. Unreliable" had become the story of the sports world.

What no one knew, or cared to take the time to hear, was this wasn't some witch hunt. It was one man's doing, and it slipped through the cracks because our checks and balances system was flawed. No one outside of maybe five people on the copy desk saw that headline before it went to print. And none of those five stopped and said, "Are we sure?"

Then sports editor Mike Sherman issued a rare newspaper apology, saying the headline "missed the mark" and declaring "the words were overstated and unduly harsh."

Kevin Durant's subpar performance in the opening round of the 2014 playoffs led to a controversial headline that admittedly missed the mark when it labeled him "Mr. Unreliable." (AP Photo/Eric Gay)

Durant handled the slight with the utmost class and professionalism.

"It's all good. I don't really care," he said when asked about the slight on the morning of Game 6. "Coming from my paper back at home, that's what they're supposed to write. I didn't come through for the team. So they got to write that type of stuff."

Twelve hours later, Durant walked out of Memphis after dominating the Grizzlies with a game-high 36 points and 10 rebounds. He made 11-of-23 shots, 14-of-15 free throws, and sent the Thunder back to Oklahoma City, where they would host a Game 7 after taking a 104–84 victory. Durant stood tall and delivered a signature performance.

82 Enes Kanter

For six-and-a-half seasons, Thunder fans shouted for a low-post scorer.

But the Thunder had the toughest time landing one. They came to town with Johan Petro, Mouhamed Sene, and Robert Swift. They soon added Serge Ibaka, Nenad Krstic, Etan Thomas, and Byron Mullens. They then cycled through Cole Aldrich, Nazr Mohammed, Kendrick Perkins, Daniel Orton, Hasheem Thabeet, and Steven Adams.

But on February 19, 2015, mere minutes before the 2:00 PM trade deadline, the Thunder finally found a low-post scorer. In a three-team trade with Utah and Detroit, the Thunder acquired Enes Kanter from the Jazz. Oklahoma City shipped Reggie Jackson to the Pistons and Kendrick Perkins, Grant Jerrett, Tibor Pleiss, and a first-round pick to the Jazz. The Thunder also got Steve Novak from Utah and D.J. Augustin, Kyle Singler, and a second-round pick from Detroit. But the real prize was Kanter, the third overall pick in the 2011 draft.

A 6'11" center from Turkey, Kanter was a throwback. He was a banger, a bruiser, a prototypical back-to-the-basket scorer who did his best work from the low blocks. He had textbook footwork, terrific timing, and impeccable patience. He was a load on the offensive glass, a fantastic finisher around the rim, and could step out and knock down jump shots. With the Jazz, however, Kanter stepped onto a team that already had an abundance of what he brought. Al Jefferson and Paul Millsap were starters. Derrick Favors, the 2010 No. 3 overall pick, came off the bench. Playing time was sporadic in Kanter's first two seasons. When Jefferson and Millsap moved on in 2013–14, Kanter became a spot starter, averaging 12.3 points and 7.5 rebounds in 26.7 minutes. But the Jazz went 25–57, and Kanter was growing disgruntled. By the 2014–15 season, he was publicly requesting a trade, and with second-year center Rudy Gobert waiting in the wings, the Jazz gladly granted Kanter's wish.

The Thunder pounced, shedding only a similarly disgruntled young player in Jackson, a proud but declining center in Perkins, and a pick. It was pennies on the dollar. "Enes gives us a player and an option that we haven't had before," Thunder GM Sam Presti said. "He creates some lineup opportunities that we think will be very beneficial for us going forward. We think his best basketball is in front of him. At 22 years old and to have four years' experience in the league, that's a rare thing, and he's improved each season."

Kanter arrived with questions, though. In Utah, he developed a reputation as a one-trick pony. Regardless of how many different ways he could put the ball in the basket, that's all he was known for—scoring. Meanwhile, he had yet to show a high level of awareness passing out of the post. He was turnover prone. And his defense was considered abysmal. The Thunder also had its center of the future in Adams as well as an entrenched starting power forward in Ibaka. Kanter seemingly was stepping into the same sort of logjam and headed for the same frustrations he experienced in Utah.

Only the opposite happened. Kanter couldn't have been happier. He dropped double doubles in his first two Thunder games, first a 10-point, 13-rebound effort at Charlotte, and then a 20-point, 12-rebound explosion against Denver. Kanter benefited from late-season injuries to Adams and Ibaka and started all 26 games he appeared in following the trade. He averaged 18.7 points, 11 rebounds, and one assist in 31.1 minutes. After seemingly every game, he gushed about Russell Westbrook and how much he loved playing with his new point guard. Kanter also developed a fun-loving bond with Adams. The two Thunder giants grew mustaches and became known as the "Stache Bros."

In the summer of 2015, Portland threw a four-year, $70 million contract at Kanter, the maximum allowable under league rules. The Thunder had the right to match and ultimately did despite much criticism. But with the salary cap soon skyrocketing, Kevin Durant soon coming up for an extension, and the Thunder lacking the means to land a comparable replacement, OKC couldn't let Kanter walk. The decision was a no-brainer. "We traded for Enes last season with the intention of keeping him as a member of the Thunder for several years to come, and we are excited that he will continue with us," Presti said in a statement announcing the deal.

When the Thunder returned to full strength in 2015–16, Kanter accepted his bench role and averaged 12.7 points and 8.1 rebounds in only 21 minutes per game. He blossomed into one of the league's most efficient big men and began changing his reputation for the better. By 2016–17, Kanter had emerged as a Sixth Man of the Year candidate.

83 Sunset Jerseys

The third alternate jersey in Thunder history was the team's most polarizing.

It was unveiled on September 25, 2015. And it was orange.

The uniforms had "OKC" emblazoned across the front of the jersey in large blue block letters, outlined in white. They had blue trim, and on the back the players' last names sat under the jersey number as opposed to the traditional placement above the number.

Each of the previous four uniforms in the team's regular rotation were much safer color schemes. There were the traditional home whites and road sky blues. There was the first alternate, a navy set with the team name inscribed vertically down the right side of the jersey. Then there was the second alternate, a white-sleeved rendition featuring the team's logo on the chest.

Some fans expressed displeasure with both the sleeved jersey—an NBA mandate for all 30 teams—and the navy blues. But none of the threads drew as much mixed reaction as that fifth set.

"This is a state, after all, where orange has long been associated with Oklahoma State," *The Oklahoman* columnist Jenni Carlson wrote. "It's a color of Bedlam. It's a symbol of rivalry. Half the state loves it. Half the state loathes it."

Much of what made the Thunder such a smashing success early on was the franchise's ability to bring Oklahomans together like never before, making friends out of OU fans and OSU fans, Oklahoma City residents and Tulsa residents. Folks who had long been foes finally had something in common, something they could collectively cheer. The Thunder were aware of that luxury and were careful never to jeopardize it by catering to one fan base at the expense of the other.

Thunder chairman Clay Bennett holds strong ties to the University of Oklahoma, where he attended college and was appointed to the school's board of regents in 2011. He also married into the family whose name adorns OU's football stadium, Gaylord Family Oklahoma Memorial Stadium. Still, Bennett walked that tightrope at a 2008 press conference unveiling the team name, logo, and colors.

"Our primary color blue is the color of our state flag. This is very much an Oklahoma organization," Bennett said before delivering a preemptive punchline to cool any potential Bedlam bad blood.

"The sunset is red and orange," he added. "Not too red and not too orange."

The Thunder were so sensitive to the Bedlam rivalry that the team never referred to the fifth alternate as orange. Instead, the Thunder labeled it "sunset." In a 315-word press release announcing the new uniform, the word "orange" never appeared. The word "sunset" was written eight times.

"We've been very careful to stay in the middle," said Brian Byrnes, the Thunder Senior Vice President of Sales and Marketing.

Despite the team's best efforts, the uniform was just orange to everyone else. That included Oklahoma State, which immediately took to social media and seized an opportunity to welcome the Thunder to the orange-clad family.

"Nice color," the athletic department's official Twitter account tweeted to the Thunder, with an accompanying "Orange Power" hashtag.

An online poll conducted by *The Oklahoman* in September 2015 found that 51 percent of people liked the jerseys, while 38 percent said they disliked them. Ten percent of respondents said they were indifferent.

The timing of the sunset jersey certainly was strategic. Fans had seven years to catch Thunder fever before the team dared roll out an orange jersey. Had the Thunder unveiled the color scheme upon relocating to OKC, far harsher criticism would have been likely.

That's not to say there wasn't resentment.

"I love the Thunder, and I would be very disappointed if they wore puke orange," said Romie Mason, a Sooners fan from Cedar Valley, Oklahoma. "I would find it difficult to watch them play in that color."

Oklahoma might be the only NBA market where a franchise would go to such great lengths to be considerate of the local universities. But it speaks to the passion Oklahomans reserve for their schools. The Thunder, of course, was wise for being sympathetic. Prior to their arrival, Oklahoma and Oklahoma State athletics were the only games in town, and the two fan bases made up the bulk of the sports community.

But it was just a jersey.

"It's hard to imagine in New York that anybody would get worked up over a cross-sport conflict like that," said Paul Lukas, founder of Uni-watch.com. "That's something I can't quite wrap my head around."

The sunset alternate debuted on November 1, 2015, a Sunday night. The Thunder beat Denver 117–93 inside Chesapeake Energy Arena that night. Oklahoma City wore the sunset alternates 18 times in the uniform's debut season, including all Sunday home games.

Most importantly, OKC went 11–7 in 2015–16 when wearing the sunset jerseys. The Thunder had gone 6–5 in the debut season of the navy alternate, giving fans more reason to dislike those threads.

But just like the navy alternate, which the Thunder last wore in the 2016 postseason before doing away with them, the sunset alternate is expected to have a limited shelf life.

"When it's an alternate uniform like that, it's only going to be around a couple of years, then they'll get rid of it and put another one in there," Lukas said. "That's the way alternate uniforms work in the NBA. Like it or hate it, you won't have to look at it very long."

84 Kevin Martin

He wasn't James Harden.

Regardless of how good Kevin Martin was, he never was going to replace the Thunder's former sensational sixth man. Not on the court with his production and not in the hearts and minds of fans.

Martin was the stopgap the Thunder acquired when they traded Harden to Houston on October 27, 2012. Then a 29-year-old sharpshooter who carried an 18.4-point career scoring average, Martin was the lone proven player OKC received in the deal. The rest of the package was made up of future assets—rookie guard Jeremy Lamb and draft picks. After journeying to the NBA Finals the previous postseason, the Thunder's plan was to use Martin as a one-year rental to remain in championship contention while the other assets bloomed around the team's core. Martin was making $12.9 million in the final year of his contract, but, like Harden, he was third banana at best behind Kevin Durant and Russell Westbrook.

But Martin didn't seem to mind. Publicly, he embraced his new role, which called for him to come off the bench for the first time in 6½ seasons as Thunder coach Scott Brooks stuck with his tried and true starting lineup. Much of Martin's willingness stemmed from years spent as the featured player who posted superb scoring averages on bad-to-mediocre teams. He hadn't made the playoffs since 2006, and that trip, the only one of his career to that point, ended after just six first-round games against San Antonio. He was toiling in relative obscurity.

The only 50-win team Martin had been part of was the 2004–05 Sacramento Kings. He was just 21, a rookie who averaged only 10.1 minutes. From his second to eighth seasons, Martin's teams compiled a 241–318 record even though he averaged 20 points or more in five of those seasons. Before trading places with Harden, Martin's best two teammates were Ron Artest and Brad Miller.

Individual success got old. Losing took a toll.

"You want to sacrifice things for wins," Martin said. "I've been wanting to be in a situation like this for a long time instead of putting up numbers and being done playing in April.... So I'm ready to sacrifice whatever they want me to."

Martin carried a well-established reputation as one of the game's elite scoring guards. In his best season, he averaged 24.6 points for the Kings in 2008–09. "Kevin can fill it up pretty quickly," Durant said. Martin had an unorthodox shooting form that Brooks once described as "not the prettiest shot, but it goes in and that's all you worry about." Martin was also quite efficient. He drew free throws at a high rate—sometimes as a result of flopping; he became the first Thunder player to violate the league's new anti-flopping rule that season, drawing a $5,000 fine for two offenses—and prided himself on scoring in bunches while playing in a system and not forcing the issue. Taking quality shots was one of his biggest strengths. He once scored 50 points in a road game against Golden State. He needed only 22 shots, becoming just the second player since the 1983–84 season to score 50 on 22 shots or less.

"There's a lot of high-scoring guys in this league that score 28 points, but they'll shoot 25 times to do it," Martin said. "I never wanted to be that guy. I always wanted to be a shooting guard that a point guard loves to play with, that helps them get assists and not just jacking up shots."

Added Brooks: "If you [study] 15 shots of his, you might get one or two that's a tough, contested shot."

With the Thunder, Martin had to do even more with less. In 77 games, he averaged 14 points on 10.1 shots per game, the fewest attempts since his second season. It was 2.8 points less than Harden averaged on the same number of shots the previous season. While crafty, Martin was far from the wizard Harden was with the ball in his hands. More than ever, Martin's scoring opportunities resulted from moving without the ball and spotting up beyond the arc. Roughly 74 percent of Martin's field goals were assisted, and as the season went on he developed great chemistry with Nick Collison, who replicated the same read and react two-man game he and Harden had mastered.

But the marriage was imperfect. After getting off to a hot start—averaging 17.1 points on 48/51/94.5 shooting splits through his first 10 games—Martin saw his scoring average dip in each successive month, from 15.9 points in November to 10.8 points in April. He became marginalized to a spot-up shooter, drifting around the perimeter, waiting on passes that never came. His biggest scoring nights also came in blowouts. His highest scoring output, 16.1 points, came in 14 games in which the Thunder won by 11 to 15 points.

"I cannot demand the ball," Martin said, "because I'm not going to be a guy where I'm taking horrible shots and killing our offense."

The Thunder won plenty that season despite it all. Oklahoma City finished first in the West that season with a franchise record 60 wins. The Thunder also led the league in scoring differential at 9.2 points per game.

But in the postseason, Martin's shooting percentage plummeted, going from 45 percent to 38 percent from the field and from 42.6 percent to 37 percent from three-point range. It was the year Westbrook suffered a knee injury against Houston in Game 2 of the opening round and missed the remainder of the postseason.

In July, Martin agreed to a four-year, $28 million deal with Minnesota. The Thunder, teetering on the brink of the luxury tax and content with turning over the second unit to Reggie Jackson and Lamb, let Martin walk, but not before agreeing to a sign-and-trade deal that landed them a $6.6 million trade exception.

In his third game with Minnesota, a 30-point performance in a nine-point win at New York, Martin delivered what sounded like a shot at Thunder players.

"This is such a fun team to play on," Martin said. "Nobody is trying to lead the league in scoring here. Everybody has the big picture of getting to the playoffs."

But while he was in Oklahoma City, the soft-spoken Martin kept a low profile and did his best to replace the player who would prove to be irreplaceable.

"I knew exactly what my role was going to be," Martin said in his last interview as a member of the Thunder. "I knew I was going to go from being the first option to being the third option. I was going to have to embrace it, and that's what I did. I came in here just trying to be a positive influence with what they had already started to create around here and just help the team in any form I can."

85 Meet Rumble the Bison

Well, they had to come up with something.

All the good names, characters, and costumes already were taken. Still, the new NBA team in the new NBA city needed a new mascot.

The fictional backstory of Rumble the Bison, though, was about as ridiculous as it gets.

Introduced on February 17, 2009, Rumble the Bison was a legendary beast whose story had been told around Native American campfires for hundreds of years. As legend has it, Rumble led his herd to safety during a ferocious storm only to be trapped alone atop the Arbuckle Mountains. There, Rumble was struck by lightning. The four-legged beast, by the power of the god of Thunder, suddenly walked on two legs like a man and possessed amazing strength and agility to jump higher, run faster, and think more clearly than any creature. But because he was no longer a bison, and not yet a man, he was alone. Not until a group of men with similar powers came to Oklahoma City did Rumble find somewhere he belonged. So he joined their team.

That really is the story the Thunder sold.

Brian Byrnes, the Thunder's Senior Vice President of Ticket Sales and Marketing, said the mascot's name was chosen because it is both the sound of thunder and the sound of bison, which is Oklahoma's state animal.

"The bison is powerful, surprisingly fast, close-knit, and travels as a herd, and represents the Thunder in an appropriate way," Byrnes said.

Thunder officials spent five months weighing dozens of options and dedicating countless hours to choosing everything from the right character and name to the right touch for a costume.

"Even though it's fictional, it takes the tone of a bison, the history of this community," Byrnes said. "The bison itself is going through a renaissance, having once been near extinction, now coming back in great numbers. We feel that's a parallel story to what this city, this state is going through. We're hoping our team is part of this renaissance, this growth, a 'Yes We Can' optimism. The story takes on that tone, that Rumble didn't just drop in out of thin air Tuesday night."

His story was silly, but it didn't matter. Rumble the Bison now belonged to Oklahoma City fans. He was all theirs, and he was a hit.

Rumble made his grand entrance on a Tuesday night against the New Orleans Hornets, the first game back from 2009 All-Star Weekend. And he nailed it.

He descended from the rafters playing the drums. He danced with the Thunder Girls. He performed with the trampoline dunk team. He climbed atop a 16' ladder and raised a sign that read "GET LOUD." He posed for pictures, gave hugs, and dished high-fives.

The Thunder had played the first 53 games of that inaugural season without a mascot. Prior to that, the temporarily displaced New Orleans Hornets had just spent two seasons using their lovable mascot, Hugo the Hornet, to make everyone in attendance happy. An expectation for certain entertainment had been created. But the Thunder left all things SuperSonics in Seattle, including the wildly popular mascot Sasquatch. In lieu of mascot mayhem, the Thunder filled timeouts with their drum team, acrobatic dunkers, and Thunder Girls.

But when Rumble the Bison emerged from the wilderness, he gave Thunder fans a new treat.

He continues to do so and now ranks as one of the best mascots in the NBA.

"Having a mascot as talented as Rumble is an important part of our game-night experience," Byrnes said. "Rumble is very versatile and will appeal to fans of all ages on and off the court. Thunder fans are in for a real treat as they are entertained by Rumble, and we have no doubt it will be a fan favorite for years to come."

86 Victor Oladipo

Hours before the start of the 2013 NBA Draft, rumors started flying on social media. The juiciest of all involved the Thunder, a rare occurrence given how close to the vest the franchise kept even the most trivial news.

The report: Oklahoma City was pushing hard to trade up to get Orlando's No. 2 overall pick. The target: electrifying shooting guard Victor Oladipo. Armed with three of the top 32 draft picks—Nos. 12, 29, and 32—the Thunder had ample assets to enter serious negotiations. The Minnesota Timberwolves reportedly were in the running as well, allegedly offering a package centered on forward Derrick Williams and picks No. 9 and No. 26.

In the end, Orlando stood pat, keeping its pick and plucking Oladipo. The Thunder drafted Steven Adams at No. 12, traded up three spots from No. 29 to snag Andre Roberson at No. 26, and selected Alex Abrines at No. 32.

Three years later, almost to the day, all four prospects would become teammates. It's funny how things turn out. To get their man, the Thunder didn't need to relinquish draft picks or a combination of picks and young prospects. On draft night 2016, Oklahoma City instead traded evolving yet increasingly erratic forward Serge Ibaka to the Magic for Oladipo, veteran forward Ersan Ilyasova, and the draft rights to Domantas Sabonis, the No. 11 overall pick.

"There's certain guys in every draft that we look at and really feel strongly about that really would be great fits in our organization," Thunder GM Sam Presti said following the trade when asked how bad he wanted Oladipo in 2013. "Very rarely can you get them because everyone's looking for high-character, competitive, team-first guys that are also really good players. He's on a short list. And when those guys come around to you, it's a rare opportunity."

A three-star recruit coming out of DeMatha Catholic High in suburban Washington, D.C., Oladipo turned himself into a can't-miss prospect at Indiana after choosing the Hoosiers over Notre Dame, Maryland, Marquette, and Xavier among others. Despite teaming with Cody Zeller, a McDonald's All-American, in his final two seasons at Indiana, Oladipo often stood out with his toughness, intensity, and fearlessness. His athleticism, versatility, and defensive tenacity also jumped out. Oladipo began shooting up draft boards late in his third and final year at Indiana, rising from a late first/

The Thunder long coveted Victor Oladipo, but it took three years for OKC to get its man. After the Thunder did, Oladipo lasted in OKC for only one year. The front office flipped him for Paul George in June 2017. (AP Photo/Sue Ogrocki)

early second round selection to a potential lottery pick to a consensus top five choice. At the 2013 NBA Draft Combine, Oladipo unveiled a 42" vertical.

But it was Oladipo's make-up the Thunder loved most. His tough-mindedness. His competitiveness. His selflessness. "He is a guy that we really feel like not only brings things on the floor for us," Presti said, "but I think he's going to be a real add to our environment, our culture on an everyday basis. So we're thrilled about having him." The Thunder, it seemed, finally had landed the two-way wing player fans coveted. No more defensive specialists. No more limited sharpshooters.

Oladipo was equally excited. He spent his first three seasons in a floundering Magic organization. He played for three coaches in three years. He toiled through one losing season after another, going 83–163 and never finishing in the top 10 in the East standings. When asked by anyone in his inner circle his reaction to the trade, Oladipo texted emojis of rings. "Because that's what my goal is," he explained. "To help this team win a championship. It's like going from one extreme to another."

Eleven days later, Kevin Durant skipped town. When he left for Golden State, he took the Thunder's championship hopes with him. Oladipo and the Oklahoma City organization had to quickly move on. On October 31, 2016, the Thunder signed Oladipo to a four-year, $84 million contract extension.

It took three years, but the Thunder finally got their man.

87 The OKC National Memorial

The date will live forever as the worst day in Oklahoma City history.

April 19, 1995.

9:02 AM to be exact.

That's when 168 Oklahomans lost their lives at the hands of a domestic terrorist attack, a gutless truck bombing that destroyed one-third of the Alfred P. Murrah Federal Building in downtown Oklahoma City. The event, which paralyzed a community, has become known in Oklahoma simply as "the bombing."

But on the fifth anniversary of the bombing, an outdoor memorial was dedicated where the Murrah Building once stood. Nearly a year later, an adjacent memorial museum was dedicated. The Oklahoma City National Memorial has since welcomed more than 4 million visitors and sees an average of 350,000 visitors per year. Among them each year will be a handful of Thunder players.

Nearly every player the Thunder acquires must journey to the intersection of Harvey Avenue and NW 5th Street. There, new additions receive their first lesson on the community they'll be representing. Thunder General Manager Sam Presti sees to it that acquisitions familiarize themselves with what took place there. "When we first arrived in 2008, we felt it was really important that we understood where we were," Presti said. "If you're going to represent a community...it was imperative that we spent time understanding the history. Obviously, the memorial is a gateway."

At the memorial, players take in a powerful tour that illustrates the heartache Oklahoma City has experienced and the resiliency and courageousness it displayed in the face of tragedy. Like all visitors, the players are met by The Gates of Time, two bronze gates that frame the moment of destruction: with 9:01 carved into the interior of the eastern gate to represent the city's innocence before the attack, and 9:03 carved into the interior of the western gate, signifying the moment the city was forever changed. On the exterior of the gates is an inscribed message, a mission statement of sorts.

"We come here to remember those who were killed, those who survived and those changed forever. May all who leave here know the impact of violence. May this memorial offer comfort, strength, peace, hope and serenity."

In the middle of the gates rests a rectangular Reflecting Pool. Its thin layer of water shows visitors their reflection, indicating "someone changed forever by their visit to the Memorial." Sitting on the slightly sloped hill to the immediate south of the Reflecting Pool is the Field of Empty Chairs, 168 in all, each one hand-crafted from glass, bronze, and stone. There is one for each person who lost their life. They're arranged in nine rows to represent each floor of the building. Each chair has the name of someone killed on that floor etched into its glass base. Nineteen smaller chairs stand for the children who lost their lives.

The outdoor memorial includes many more symbolic elements, including a Survivors' Wall, The Survivor Tree, The Memorial Fence, a Children's Area, and Rescuers' Orchard. Inside the museum are powerful reminders of that tragic day. There's a recording of the bombing, harrowing news footage of the ravaged building, a moving Gallery of Honor, a room lined with personal photographs and artifacts of those lost, and so much more.

"I was stunned," said Royal Ivey, who spent three seasons with the Thunder as a reserve guard before rejoining the franchise in a coaching role. "That's why every time I get to show somebody else, I take them there."

Ivey has taken his parents, a girlfriend, and several friends. He's been more than a half dozen times. "Every time I go, I get a different experience," he said. "What went down on that day was devastating to this community and to the state of Oklahoma."

It's not just Thunder players who must make the trek to the Memorial. Most every new Thunder employee has to schedule a visit. Presti stresses the importance. He first took in the Memorial and Museum in 2004, when he was in Oklahoma City for the McDonald's All-American Game as director of player personnel for the San Antonio Spurs. He was so moved by his visit he made it a required stop after becoming the Thunder's general manager. He later became a member of the Memorial's Board of Trustees.

"Because I am not a native Oklahoman, I want to constantly enhance my understanding of the city," Presti said. "I strive to always be listening and asking questions about the community, its evolution, the people that it impacted, its growth, and really trying to understand what makes this city and this state what it is. If you want to contribute, I think you have to seek to understand."

88 Trade Exceptions Galore

Sam Presti never liked losing an asset without getting a return on his investment.

So the Thunder general manager, one of the league's most opportunistic GMs, often orchestrated trades to net something for players who were on the verge of leaving for nothing. Generally, those deals turned into trade exceptions.

Unfamiliar?

In essence, a trade exception is a one-year credit that allows teams to acquire replacement players in future deals. Because of the one-year window, the league labels such deals non-simultaneous. They're triggered when one team sends out more salary than it takes back. Each trade exception is worth the original traded player's salary, plus $100,000. A team can then use that credit when trading with a different team rather than having to match salaries to complete the non-simultaneous trade.

The exception cannot be used to sign free agents, although the exception can be used to acquire another team's free agent in a sign-and-trade deal. Trade exceptions also cannot be combined with any other exceptions to trade for a more expensive player. But a team with a trade exception can split the exception on multiple players so long as they are within the value of the exception.

For Presti and the Thunder, trade exceptions became a valued roster-building tool. And while transforming the Thunder into a perennial power, Presti stockpiled a heap of trade exceptions.

Byron Mullens, Eric Maynor, Hasheem Thabeet, Ryan Gomes, Thabo Sefolosha, Perry Jones, Reggie Jackson, Ish Smith, Kevin Martin, and Luke Ridnour were all players who netted the Thunder trade exceptions. The value of those trade exceptions ranged between $861,000 and $6.6 million.

"The trade exception essentially gives us flexibility in terms of roster building to try to make additions to our core group without infringing on that group," Presti explained.

Not every deal that landed the Thunder a trade exception was made purely to net something for a player whose days in OKC were numbered. At times, Presti simply sought to cut cost or clear up a roster spot. But he always looked to maximize the team's assets while doing so. Operating in one of the league's smallest markets also called for creativity. For Presti, that meant using the strategy so the team could be well positioned to avoid potential bidding wars for complementary pieces in free agency.

The best example of Presti putting the strategy to work with the Thunder came in July 2014. Sefolosha was an unrestricted free agent that summer and was set to sign a three-year, $12 million deal with Atlanta. Instead of watching him walk for nothing, Presti convinced the Hawks to do a sign-and-trade deal that netted the Thunder a $4.1 million trade exception. With that credit, Presti then acquired Dion Waiters from Cleveland in a three-team deal six months later. Thanks to the trade exception, all the Thunder had to relinquish was a late first-round pick (No. 26 overall) and Lance Thomas.

An ancillary benefit to trade exceptions was the one-year window itself. For all intents and purposes, that one-year window allowed the Thunder to extend the lifespan of assets. Even if players were traded, the Thunder gained a calendar year to use their outgoing salary to improve the roster.

Presti, however, sparked frustration, if not all-out outrage, among some in the Thunder's fan base for annually allowing the trade exceptions to go unused, which league rules also allow. The trade exception acquired in Sefolosha's sign-and-trade to Atlanta was the only one Presti used to acquire a replacement player.

"It's part of our job to do our due diligence. But sometimes when you're looking at opportunities and evaluating them, you've got to show some discipline," Presti explained. "And what we want to try to do is be very methodical, very thoughtful in each decision we make. Just because we have an asset doesn't necessarily mean that we're going to use it unless it really makes sense for us and what we're trying to establish."

One of the most amusing aspects of Presti's nearly annual hunt for trade exceptions was the obscure international players that were included. Because league rules mandate both teams attach an asset to every trade, names like Giorgos Printezis, Szymon Szewczyk, Sofoklis Schortsanitis, and Tomislov Zubcic typically became throw-in pieces. They were players who had been drafted years prior but never played in the league because they didn't pan out or at some point in their journey they said no thanks to the NBA.

89 Dion Waiters

Dion Waiters was traded to the Thunder from Cleveland on January 5, 2015.

It was a three-team trade that saw Oklahoma City send a protected first-round draft pick to the Cavs and Lance Thomas to New York. The Cavs sent Lou Amundson, Alex Kirk, and a future second-round pick to the Knicks, and New York sent Iman Shumpert and J.R. Smith to Cleveland. It was a sweetheart deal for the Thunder, who used the $4.1 million trade exception acquired in the sign-and-trade deal it had done with Atlanta for Thabo Sefolosha the previous summer.

Despite being selected with the fourth overall pick out of Syracuse just three years earlier, Waiters had worn out his welcome with the Cavs. He played for three coaches in his two-plus seasons in Cleveland, bounced in and out of the starting lineup, had a rumored feud with star point guard Kyrie Irving, and fizzled into an afterthought when LeBron James returned.

"We're gonna make him feel wanted," Kevin Durant vowed. "I don't think he felt that the last couple of years. He's gonna fit in well. He's gonna get comfortable real quick."

After going into the tax for the first time to acquire Waiters, the Thunder went to great lengths to make sure he was happy. Thunder coach Scott Brooks immediately shifted sixth-man duty to Waiters from Reggie Jackson, and in his first month with the team Waiters averaged 28.2 minutes. Waiters also quickly established bonds with Durant and Westbrook. After only four games, the Thunder even transitioned Waiters' stall from one end of the locker room to the other so he could be closer to the star duo, and perhaps farther away from Jackson, who had grown disgruntled. "They brought me in since Day 1 with love," Waiters said. "It seems like I've been here forever. It seems like I've been playing with them forever, too. When I came here, we clicked right away."

Waiters arrived in Oklahoma City with the reputation of a perplexing player. He was a ball-dominant, shot-happy guard who believed in himself more than anybody else ever could. He had an affinity for taking high-degree, low-efficiency shots such as stepback jumpers and long two-pointers. He often took one unnecessary dribble after catching passes with no defender near him before hoisting corner threes. And more than anyone, maybe ever, he loved screaming "and one" after shot attempts, his way of expressing his belief that he had been fouled on a play. His antics turned him into an Internet sensation, with numerous clips spliced together showing Waiters, whether in Cleveland or Oklahoma City, standing on the perimeter fervently clapping for the ball despite it being in the hands of more reliable options like James or Durant. "Listen," Waiters said after only five games in a Thunder uniform, "they give me the ball. Like, I touch the ball. Like, I actually, like, you know, touch the ball."

Waiters finished 2014–15 averaging 12.7 points—on 12.9 shots per game—2.9 rebounds, 1.9 assists, and one steal in 30.3 minutes per game. He made just 39.2 percent of his shots and only 31.9 percent from three-point range. Despite his offensive inefficiency, he added toughness to the Thunder's lineup and showed unexpected defensive tenacity while starting 20-of-47 games in the team's injury-plagued season. "I'm just trying to show them I'm a two-way player," Waiters said.

The 2015–16 season wasn't much different for Waiters. He averaged 9.8 points—on 9.1 shots and 39.9 percent shooting—but again showed flashes of breaking his bad habits and transforming into a smarter, more efficient player. No stretch showed Waiters potential like the run to the 2016 Western Conference finals. He became a ball-mover, a quality shot-taker, an improved finisher, and a dogged defender. Still only 24, Waiters suddenly seemed like a long-term fit.

But the Thunder renounced Waiters' rights when he hit restricted free agency in July 2016. The move allowed the team to re-negotiate Russell Westbrook's contract. Although he assembled a solid debut postseason, Waiters couldn't cash in during free agency. He ultimately signed a two-year, $6 million deal with Miami.

90 Loud City

The upper deck of Chesapeake Energy Arena is affectionately referred to as Loud City. The nickname, a title given to the boisterous fans who filled the 300-level, originated with the New Orleans Hornets, the building's primary tenants while displaced from 2005–07 following the devastation of Hurricane Katrina.

The Hornets had a simple but wildly successful marketing strategy: embrace the economical fan.

"Instead of higher prices and the place being half full, I'd rather have it full at a lower price," then Hornets owner George Shinn explained.

The Hornets had just 40 days to transition their entire franchise from New Orleans to Oklahoma City. So much needed to be done, and chief on the checklist was selling tickets to a community that had never experienced live NBA basketball. But rather than focusing on high rollers, the Hornets concentrated on filling the cheap seats. The idea was to lure casual customers in, show them a great time, and make sure they didn't leave until they were hooked.

That first season, the Hornets sold 4,000 upper deck tickets to each game for just $10. The league mandated each team make a minimum of only 500 tickets available at that price point. The Hornets offered another 3,500 tickets for $20 or less. Upstairs season tickets also started as low as $379.

"Yes, it's about the short time frame," said Tim McDougall, the Thunder's Chief Marketing Officer at the time. "But it's also the philosophy of getting people in. If we can do that, they'll come back. We're a believer in, 'Let's just get them in.'"

On the first day the team began selling season tickets, the Hornets received more than 5,000 deposits. They sold 10,000 season tickets within 10 days. The final tally that first season was approximately 11,500 season tickets, which ranked the Hornets sixth among all teams.

When the fans showed up, the Hornets showed out.

Rather than allowing fans to grow negative attitudes with what is commonly referred to as "nosebleed seats" because they're so high, the Hornets transformed their upper deck into a season-long party. The rowdier the better. Soon, the upstairs seats became part of the show. Fans screamed at the top of their lungs. Loud City Patrol members ran and jumped from section to section, hyping up the crowd. Chants rained down on the court. Yellow thunderstix drove up the decibel level.

It all made the folks up top feel special. It gave them an identity. A two-year standard was set. When the Sonics relocated in 2008 and became the Thunder, the new tenants carried on the tradition.

"We think the fans established that, not necessarily the Hornets," said John Leach, Thunder director of events and entertainment. "So we want to make sure the fans still have that Loud City because it sets the tone really for that upper level."

With the Thunder fans pulling off what seemed impossible and matching if not surpassing the roar of the old Hornets crowds, the nickname Loud City later doubled as a nickname for the entire arena. But it started with the screamers upstairs.

Former Hornets coach Byron Scott once said his team wouldn't have lost a game to Phoenix had the contest been played inside the Ford Center rather than in front of a dismal Baton Rouge, Louisiana, crowd. With New Orleans Arena undergoing renovations following Hurricane Katrina and the people of the region still rebounding, the game was played inside Louisiana State University's Pete Maravich Assembly Center before an announced crowd of 7,302. The Hornets started the fourth quarter with a 14-point lead and got outscored 37–10 in the final 12 minutes.

"In the back of my mind, when I went into the locker room, I said, 'If this game would have been in Oklahoma City, it wouldn't have been this close,'" Scott said. "If we would have had a 14-point lead going into the fourth quarter, we'd have won the game."

Before the Thunder played their first game, players knew what to expect from their new home fans.

"We know it's going to be sold out," Kevin Durant said before the start of the inaugural 2008–09 season. "It's going to be loud through the whole game. This is going to be my first time playing in something like this since college. I'm excited. I can't wait to start."

91 Nenad Krstic

When the Thunder were toiling through a horrific 3–29 start and in need of a major upgrade in talent during their inaugural season, help arrived in the form of a sharpshooting 7' Serbian center.

Nenad Krstic was signed on December 30, 2008, and his arrival coincided with the Thunder turning the corner and blossoming into a perennial playoff contender.

Oklahoma City was leaning on Nick Collison, Johan Petro, Joe Smith, Chris Wilcox, and Robert Swift to man the middle. Collison and Smith were limited, Petro and Wilcox were wildly inconsistent, and Swift was injury prone.

Enter Krstic, a skilled 25-year-old who was the 24th overall pick in 2002. He was nimble for a man his size but far from an elite athlete. What he lacked in athleticism he made up for with smarts and sound, fundamental play. He had good hands, a smooth shooting stroke, a soft touch, and the ability to find the open man. He had a way of slipping into open areas and positioning himself for a putback or an easy score off a teammate's pass.

Few Thunder fans were familiar with Krstic prior to his arrival. But in his third NBA season, the 2006–07 campaign, Krstic was approaching All-Star status before a torn ACL derailed his career. He was averaging 16.4 points and 6.8 rebounds in 26 games with New Jersey when he sustained the injury. Krstic saw his production plummet the following season, a contract year, and in the off-season signed in Russia rather than accepting a deal he deemed below his market value as a restricted free agent.

Two months into the 2008–09 season, the Thunder signed Krstic to a three-year offer sheet worth nearly $16 million. It was a deal no one saw coming—the mid-season acquisition of a player competing internationally is believed to be the first signing of its kind—yet one everyone considered shrewd. The Nets had seven days to match. But they wanted to maintain maximum salary cap flexibility to pursue a franchise player in the star-studded 2010 free agent class, which was highlighted by LeBron James. So New Jersey declined.

"He's going to help us a lot," Thunder coach Scott Brooks said.

Thunder fans had to wait three games for Krstic to make his debut thanks to a delay in getting his work visa approved. But he quickly proved he was worth the wait. From the start, Krstic established great chemistry with Russell Westbrook. Together, they played a beautiful two-man game in which Krstic would set a screen near the free throw line and Westbrook would run off it before flipping a pass back for Krstic, who seemed to swish nine of every 10 shots out of those sets. The play instantly became a staple in the Thunder's otherwise erratic halfcourt offense.

Krstic played a reserve role behind Collison for his first 18 games. But he was inserted into the starting lineup two games after the 2009 All-Star break. He soon became a stabilizing presence. Soft-spoken and easygoing, Krstic stepped into the locker room and exhibited a lead-by-example approach that endeared him to his teammates and coaches.

"He just does his business and he does it well," Brooks said.

The Thunder went 17–29 with Krstic in the lineup. He averaged 9.7 points, 5.5 rebounds, and 1.1 blocked shots in 24.8 minutes per game that first season. The next year, Krstic started 76 games and helped the Thunder enjoy a 27-win improvement and a first ever postseason berth.

Krstic had his share of flaws. He was a below-average rebounder and an average-at-best defender, and he was injury prone. Though he never missed significant time, Krstic always nursed some sort of nagging injury: a dislocated pinkie, a sprained thumb, a jammed ring finger, a fractured index finger, a sore Achilles, a bruised knee bone, tendonitis, back spasms. But he never complained and never made excuses.

Krstic's 2010–11 season, his last in a Thunder uniform, began with him apologizing at media day. One month earlier, Krstic hurled a chair at an opponent during an on-court brawl in an international game between Serbia and Greece. The chair landed on the player's head and drew blood. Krstic spent a night in jail for his actions.

"The good thing is the guy who I hit with the chair, he didn't press charges on me," Krstic later said. "If he did, I probably would have had to stay longer."

Before the regular season began, it had become clear Krstic had younger teammates, namely second-year forward Serge Ibaka, beating down his door for minutes. Meanwhile, the Thunder had gotten all it could from starting the undersized Jeff Green at power forward. Green and the Thunder at that time also were in a stalemate in negotiations on his rookie extension.

On February 24, 2011, the Thunder traded Krstic and Green to Boston. It was the first major trade in Thunder history, and it closed the book on the Thunder as a playoff contender and opened their window as a championship contender.

92 The Broadcasters

Brian Davis leads the Thunder's television broadcast team as the play-by-play voice. Prior to the start of the 2014–15 season, Davis was joined by color commentator Michael Cage.

Davis, a Baltimore native, called games for the Seattle Seahawks, Chicago Blackhawks, and the Chicago Fire. He also covered the

Chicago Bulls during the Michael Jordan era as a game host for NBA Radio and a sideline reporter for the network during the 1991 playoffs and NBA Finals. He later hosted Bulls broadcasts on FSN Chicago. Before being named the Thunder television play-by-play announcer, Davis hosted Seattle SuperSonics broadcasts on FSN Northwest.

Davis got a late start as a sportscaster. He didn't enter the profession with an athletic background—"I was the short, fat kid, so I never played. But I always loved going to games," he said—and didn't call his first game until he was 35. A high school teacher who was a former newspaper reporter inspired him to pursue a career in print journalism. "I wanted to write for the *New York Times*," said Davis, a Northwestern graduate. "I wanted to write for one of the great American newspapers." Davis' first taste of television work was the Illinois high school state swimming and diving championships. He has since covered the Olympics, NBA Finals, and Stanley Cup Finals.

On Thunder broadcasts, Davis is known for his storytelling and animated expressions such as, "He put it on his head," "Thunder by a stickman," "Rattlesnake jam," and "Chicken salad out of chicken something else." Davis also incorporates a team's region into his calls whenever a player hoists shots from well beyond the three-point line. "That was from Vancouver, Washington, on the other side of the Columbia River," Davis says on deep three-balls taken during games at Portland. "People who are watching our shows, I want them to turn the TV off a little bit smarter about something," Davis said.

Cage, a West Memphis, Arkansas, native, played 15 seasons in the NBA with the Los Angeles Clippers, Seattle SuperSonics, Cleveland Cavaliers, Philadelphia 76ers, and New Jersey Nets from 1984–2000. As a 6'9" post player, Cage appeared in 1,140 career games and averaged 7.3 points and 7.6 rebounds. He led the league in rebounding in the 1987–88 season, pulling down 13 per game that season and capturing the crown by snagging 30 rebounds on the final day of the regular season. Cage's signature lines include, "That's nasty," and "I'm lovin' it." He also frequently disagrees with fouls called against the Thunder by saying, "That's a tough call."

In September 2014, Cage replaced Grant Long as the team's color commentator. Long had held the position since the team's inaugural season, but he resigned amid controversy stemming from a dispute with an Oklahoma City jewelry store owner. Long owed the man more than $5,000. The businessman claimed Long promised to introduce him and his high-end jewelry to Thunder players, a claim Long denied. Long left the Thunder and joined the Detroit Pistons broadcast crew as an analyst and sideline reporter.

The radio voice of the Thunder is Matt Pinto, who has more than 25 years as an NBA broadcaster. Born and raised in Boston, Pinto grew an affinity for sports at an early age. "I knew at age 6 that I either wanted to play or broadcast," he said. Pinto's signature call, "Cha-ching, that's a Thunder money ball," comes after each made three-pointer by Thunder players.

Pinto made his NBA debut with the original Charlotte Hornets during the franchise's second season. He broadcasted Hornets games for eight seasons before moving on to the Dallas Mavericks, the Los Angeles Clippers, and the Seattle SuperSonics. Pinto lists legendary NBA announcers Johnny Most and Chick Hearn as his idols. As a standout prep baseball player—he was a middle infielder and pitcher whose fastball reached the mid-80s—Pinto was recruited to play major college baseball. He calls the sport his first love and believed he would someday be a Major League Baseball announcer before his career took a different path.

Pinto works radio broadcasts without an analyst by his side but provides crisp and clear play-by-play that keeps the audience abreast of fast-paced action with a descriptive and detailed announcing style. Pinto has said there are advantages to both working alongside an analyst, as well as calling games solo. "If you get a game where both teams are wanting to run and it's a 115 to 110 type of game, an analyst can get in the way a little bit," he said. "When you have a game where the officials are whistle-happy and there are 50 free throws, an analyst comes in real handy." Pinto also hosts a weekly radio show, *Thunder Full Court Press*, on the team's flagship radio network. At home games, Pinto's oldest son, Darryl, has provided stats for him. Pinto named his youngest son, Nash, after point guard Steve Nash.

Lesley McCaslin was named the team's sideline reporter prior to the start of the 2012–13 season. As part of her role, McCaslin hosted *Thunder Live*, the team's pregame show, and was a frequent video contributor to the team's website. Occasionally, McCaslin also served as a studio host. McCaslin joined the Thunder after serving as an anchor and reporter on Fox Sports Southwest, covering the Dallas Mavericks and Texas Rangers as well as Big 12 Conference and Conference USA football games. McCaslin replaced Kelly Crull, who had a two-year stint as the team's sideline reporter. Prior to Crull, Elissa Walker-Campbell, a former basketball player at the University of Oklahoma, and Tom Werme split the sideline duties during the 2009–10 season.

Thunder broadcasts typically toe the company line. All broadcasters are team employees who keep reports and analysis simple and mostly focus on the team's positives. Rarely do the broadcasts criticize Thunder players, the coach, or the team's play.

"Our entire crew works hard to put on what we think is one of the best shows in the NBA," said Davis. "We're very proud of what we do—that's bring the excitement of Thunder basketball to our fans."

93 P.J. Carlesimo

P.J. Carlesimo was best known by casual NBA fans as the coach who Latrell Sprewell viciously attacked during a Golden State Warriors practice in 1997.

More than a decade later, the unfortunate incident still hung over Carlesimo like a Midwestern storm cloud when he arrived in Oklahoma City as the first coach of the Thunder.

"It had a big impact on both of our careers," Carlesimo said. "But I think people in the league think of me as an NBA coach. I think people who are not in our league go, 'Oh, that's the guy that…' That's always going to be the same."

Lost on most casual observers was this: Carlesimo had come to Oklahoma City with nearly four decades of coaching experience. He earned his first college head coaching job at 26, guiding Southern New Hampshire to the 1975–76 Mayflower Conference championship. He led Wagoner College to two NIT appearances. He twice won Big East Coach of the Year while at Seton Hall, a program he steered to six NCAA Tournament berths, including a run to the Final Four in 1989. And as an assistant with the Spurs, he won three NBA championships in the 2000s.

But outside of San Antonio, Carlesimo's NBA coaching resume was largely pedestrian. In 5½ seasons as the lead man with Portland and Golden State, Carlesimo compiled a 183–222 record. In the final season of the Seattle SuperSonics, Carlesimo suffered through a franchise-worst 20–62 campaign with a baby-faced rookie named Kevin Durant. He totaled three postseason appearances as an NBA head coach, losing in the first round in each trip.

By the time Carlesimo landed in Oklahoma City, he not only was branded by the Sprewell incident, but he was also considered a coaching retread.

When he hired Carlesimo prior to that final Seattle season, then 30-year-old General Manager Sam Presti explained the decision by trumpeting Carlesimo's teaching skills. Presti and team chairman Clay Bennett opted for Carlesimo over Dwane Casey, who had been fired by Minnesota midway through the 2006–07 season.

"One of the reasons P.J. is the guy is his ability to teach," Presti said. "And I think we have a number of players on this team who want to get better and want to be coached and have come from programs where they have been coached. Ultimately, at the end of the day, it's about improving your ball club."

Development was dubious. Improvement was at best incremental. The Sonics limped to a 5–23 finish in their franchise-worst final season. Months later, the Thunder started their inaugural season 1–12 under Carlesimo, including 10 straight defeats. Oklahoma City lost those first 12 contests by 13.3 points per game. Three of the Thunder's last four defeats in that span were each by 20 points or more.

The last two losses were particularly disturbing. On November 19, 2008, the Los Angeles Clippers thumped the Thunder by 20 in OKC, prompting a first by the city's rabid fan base. When the Clippers used a 42–12 run over a 12-minute span to turn a 15-point second-quarter Thunder lead into a 15-point third-quarter Thunder deficit, frustrated fans booed the home team for the first time in the city's NBA history, which included two years hosting the temporarily displaced New Orleans Hornets. The final straw for Carlesimo then came two nights later. The Thunder suffered an embarrassing 25-point home loss to New Orleans, a game in which they turned the ball over a season-high 25 times.

Carlesimo was fired between the final buzzer and the team boarding a plane to New Orleans for a rematch the next night.

Presti promoted Scott Brooks to interim coach. Things had gotten so bad Brooks and Thunder players immediately vowed to put out a better product, promising to play with more desire and determination, energy and enthusiasm, passion and purpose—all this from a professional basketball club.

"It's embarrassing. It's disheartening," guard Damien Wilkins said. "If you would have told me at the start of the season that we would come out and start like this, I would have laughed at you."

94 The Skirvin

A Chicago Bulls player said she slammed shut his bathroom door. A Phoenix Suns player said she filled his bathtub with water. A Los Angeles Lakers player claimed she molested him.

It seems everyone in the NBA has a story about Effie, the rumored ghost haunting The Skirvin Hotel in downtown Oklahoma City. "There are too many stories. Something is going on in there," said former New York center Eddy Curry, who before a game against the Thunder in 2010 complained of being so spooked he spent most of his evening in teammate Nate Robinson's room and ultimately got only two hours of sleep.

There have been ghost stories from other stops on the NBA circuit, most notably The Pfister Hotel in downtown Milwaukee and the Claremont Resort, the swanky Oakland hotel that sits in the Berkeley Hills. But none have garnered more national attention than the Skirvin, the 14-story, triple-tower brick building that sits at the corner of Broadway and Park Avenue, one block west of the city's Bricktown district. The tales have been chronicled in the *New York Times*, the *New York Daily News*, and ESPN.com among other media outlets. The late Craig Sager spent a night at the Skirvin for an amusing story for TNT's award-winning show *Inside the NBA*. Bill Simmons once wrote about his encounter with Effie. Reggie Miller also recounted a story of a water bottle mysteriously being moved from one nightstand to another while he was asleep.

As legend has it, Effie was a housekeeper who became pregnant after an affair with the hotel's founder, William Balser "Bill" Skirvin. To avoid being shamed, Skirvin locked Effie on the 10th floor. When the baby was born, she grew so depressed she jumped out of the window with her baby in hand, ending both their lives. The hotel, which opened in 1911, sat vacant for nearly 20 years before undergoing renovations and reopening as a Hilton property in 2007, a year before the Thunder arrived. Effie has since come to be known as a prankster, knocking on doors, opening drawers, and causing commotion in the hallway. Guests have reported being awoken to the sound of a baby crying.

While with the Lakers during the 2016–17 season, Lou Williams and Larry Nance Jr. avoided the Skirvin altogether, choosing instead to check themselves into a different hotel to avoid a possible encounter with Effie. "I'm not going to play with that," Williams said about the supposedly haunted hotel. "I'd rather pay for my peace of mind. If they say it's haunted, that's enough for me. I'm not going to roll the dice."

Meanwhile, their Lakers teammate, Metta World Peace, the colorful character born Ron Artest, claimed he was molested by ghosts during the same visit. "The ghosts were all over me," he said, insisting he was serious. "They touched me all over the place. I'm taking one of the ghosts to court for touching me in the wrong places."

During the 2015–16 season, Justise Winslow and Tyler Johnson, teammates on the Miami Heat, were so spooked from all the stories they shared a room after one of the players alleged he heard the bathroom faucet turn on by itself in the middle of the night. The next season, Winslow claimed the door to his bathroom began moving on its own as he showered one morning. "That really happened," Winslow insisted. "I'm just trying to get through this trip as quickly as possible. I try and spend the least amount of time in my room. I go down, sit at the bar, get me something good to eat, watch TV, watch football, but I don't spend a lot of time in that room." Udonis Haslem, their veteran teammate and one of the league's genuine tough guys, however, said he wasn't afraid of ghosts. "A ghost will have a helluva time," Haslem warned. "He might as well go to another room because he'll have the fight of his life if he comes to my room. It will cost him so much trouble he'll just say, 'I'm just going to the next room.' He'll say, 'Not tonight. This ain't the room I need to be in.'"

Steve Lackmeyer, a real estate reporter for *The Oklahoman* who co-authored *Skirvin*, a book chronicling the hotel's history, is skeptical of all the stories. "I don't think Effie exists," Lackmeyer once said. "If you had a maid suffer a bloody ending, it would not have been kept quiet. This was a small town."

Others, like former Thunder guard Thabo Sefolosha, think the ghost stories are simply an excuse opposing teams use for trips to Oklahoma City that generally end in defeat. When asked about the Skirvin during a press conference, Thunder GM Sam Presti once joked the hotel could become the Thunder's secret weapon.

"Some locker rooms are really small and really hot," Presti said. "I guess that'll be our thing."

95 The Ray Allen & Rashard Lewis Trades

Sonics fans wanted Sam Presti's head on a spike.

And frankly, many probably still do.

They'll never forget the night Presti, in his first move as the Seattle SuperSonics' general manager, traded Ray Allen, then the face of the franchise, to the Boston Celtics. It was a stunning draft-night deal on June 28, 2007. Presti was three weeks into the job. He was 30 years old.

Two weeks later, Presti cut ties with the team's second-best player, forward Rashard Lewis.

Both moves were met with overwhelming backlash. Sonics fans were enraged. They charged Presti and team chairman Clay Bennett with purposely gutting the team, cutting costs, and creating fan apathy as part of a grand plan to split for Oklahoma City. But those two controversial decisions marked the start of Presti's rebuilding plan and set the stage for the glory days of the franchise that became known as the Oklahoma City Thunder.

"You don't wake up one day and look to move a player like a Ray Allen," Presti assured.

Allen and Lewis had only one winning season and just one postseason appearance in their 4½ seasons together. The Sonics went 172–185 in that span. Seattle wasn't going anywhere with the duo. So Presti and his staff shipped them out and started anew.

"One of the worst things you can do in this league is be a middle-of-the-road team, in the playoffs one year, out the next," said Rich Cho, a former assistant general manager for the Sonics and Thunder. "One of the tough things about a middle-of-the-road team is you never get really good draft picks. That makes it hard to have sustained success. Sometimes you have to take a step back to take two steps forward."

So that's what Presti did. He tore down before he built up.

In exchange for Allen, Boston sent Seattle guard Delonte West, forward Wally Szczerbiak, and that year's No. 5 overall pick, which Presti used to select Jeff Green. Sonics fans even accused Presti of choosing a less talented player than the prospect they really coveted, supposed Chinese sensation Yi Jianlian.

Ray Allen and Rashard Lewis needed to be traded in 2007 in order for GM Sam Presti to start his rebuilding plan. (AP Photo/Elaine Thompson)

At the time of the trade, Allen was weeks away from his 32nd birthday. Despite averaging 24.6 points during his time with the Sonics, Allen was entering his post-prime years. He was also coming off ankle injuries that limited him to 55 games in the 2006–07 season, and he was due $52 million over the next three years. Still, the widespread belief was Allen, a seven-time All-Star, could team with Lewis and prized rookie Kevin Durant to get the Sonics back to the playoffs. But just before NBA Commissioner David Stern announced Durant as the No. 2 overall pick, news of the Allen trade was reported on ESPN. It was met by a chorus of boos at the team's draft party at Fisher Pavilion in Seattle.

"All along, I felt like it made sense," said Nick Collison, who teamed with Allen and Lewis for three seasons in Seattle. "It wasn't like we were breaking up a team that had a ton of success. It was just one of those things that had to be done. I think it was the right decision."

Allen admitted the same. "The team has been floundering in the Northwest [Division] the last couple of seasons," he said then. "It almost seemed appropriate for change at this point."

Thirteen days later, Presti parted with Lewis, agreeing to a sign-and-trade deal with Orlando. The Magic committed $118 million over six seasons to Lewis. It was widely believed to be one of the worst contracts in NBA history. Lewis averaged 13.6 points over the life of the deal.

The moves freed the franchise of future financial burden and opened opportunities for Durant and Green to develop at a more rapid pace due to increased playing time as featured players.

"I'm glad they did it that way," Durant said years later. "I like the route they took with helping me grow as a player and also Jeff. I guess it was a blessing in disguise."

The Sonics took a step back, going 20–62 in 2007–08, but those two decisions became the foundation for all the success the Thunder ultimately enjoyed over their first eight seasons.

"It was tough losing like that, but it turned me into the player I am," Durant said. "It put a lot of onus on me growing up fast and helping me become a better leader. Because if those guys would have been there, none of the responsibility would have been on me. I would have just been another rookie learning."

The Lewis deal carried more significance that helped shape the Thunder. By agreeing to a sign-and-trade deal, Presti netted a $9.3 million trade exception and a second-round pick. He then used those assets to acquire Kurt Thomas from the Phoenix Suns, who were in cost-cutting mode and needed to unload his $8.1 million contract. The Suns threw in two first-round picks in 2008 and 2010, which turned into Serge Ibaka and, after a later trade, Cole Aldrich. Presti then flipped Thomas to San Antonio for Francisco Elson, Brent Barry, and a 2009 first-round pick that ultimately became Byron Mullens.

Allen went on to help Boston win a championship in 2008. Lewis helped the Magic reach the Finals in 2009. And both of their trades triggered a rebuild that put the Sonics/Thunder in position to draft Russell Westbrook with the fourth overall pick in 2008 and James Harden with the third overall selection in 2009.

Presti didn't sabotage a franchise. He rescued it.

Seattle fans just never saw it come to fruition.

96 *Thunderstruck*

In the summer of 2012, Warner Bros. Pictures released *Thunderstruck*, the kid-friendly feature-length film starring Kevin Durant.

Prideful Oklahomans and innocent pre-teens loved Durant's first major motion picture. Everyone else seemed to lump it with *Kazaam*, the notoriously awful kid flick in which Shaquille O'Neal played a genie.

"The movie has good intentions, but overall is not very good," Jason Black wrote in *The Washington Times*. "It is a low-budget movie looking to hit the DVD shelves soon trying to capitalize on Durant's popularity. It's a little too much *Kazaam* and not enough *Space Jam*."

Durant, who plays himself in the movie, magically yet unintentionally swaps skill levels with a hapless high school kid. Durant suddenly can't make a shot while the kid goes on to become the star of his high school team. The two must make things right before the swap costs the Thunder the season.

The plot wasn't original in any way, and the acting was tolerable at best, but in Durant the film had the perfect player for a cheesy motivational kid movie. At the time, Durant was one of the league's fastest-rising superstars, a clean-cut, bible-carrying, backpack-wearing baller who could roll out of bed and drop 30. He was also one of the league's most fan-friendly players, having established a reputation for going out of his way to interact with fans, by taking pictures and signing autographs at home and on the road, or by showing up at community parks to play pickup games and intramural flag football.

"If you're a kid and you're an NBA fan trying to emulate the plays of players, he's one of the guys that you're trying to emulate," *Thunderstruck* producer Mike Karz said in 2011. "And then just in the last year that we've developed the project, he had the big playoff run and was the scoring champion. So we feel our [timing] is really fortunate."

Durant filmed the movie during the NBA lockout in the fall of 2011. Most of it was shot in Baton Rouge, Louisiana, because of more favorable tax breaks. The scene that establishes the movie's plot—the high school kid attempting a $20,000 halfcourt shot at halftime before a chance run-in with Durant led to their talent swap—was filmed inside the Thunder's home, Chesapeake Energy Arena.

The movie originally was slated to be titled *Switch*, and unbeknownst to most it once had a screenplay turned down by LeBron James. After some initial reservations, Durant accepted the part and decided he'd have fun with the project, even taking the eventual digs in stride when his work quickly became a punchline.

"My agent at the time brought it to me, and I said no at first. I didn't want to be a part of something like that because it takes so long," Durant explained. "But then I thought about it and said, 'It will be cool, and it will be something for the kids to watch.' I've got a lot of little cousins, so I thought it'd be nice for them to see their big cousin in a movie. So I thought, 'Let's do it.'"

97 Cole Aldrich

Cole Aldrich made his NBA debut on his 22nd birthday.

It was a Sunday night, a Halloween home game against Utah. Aldrich checked in with 90 seconds remaining in the first quarter.

On his first offensive possession, the rookie center out of Kansas set a screen for James Harden on the left wing. When Harden went right and pulled up for a jumper, Aldrich attacked the paint. The ball bounced off the back of the rim as Aldrich took flight. With one hand, Aldrich corralled the ricochet and ferociously slammed back the miss. In his first 30 NBA seconds, Aldrich brought the crowd to its feet.

It was the highlight of Aldrich's two-year stint with the Thunder—and Oklahoma City went on to lose by 21 that night, perhaps a fitting end for a game that became a microcosm of Aldrich's short stay in OKC.

Aldrich was supposed to be the long-term solution at center. He instead became the Thunder's biggest bust.

Armed with three first-round picks in the 2010 draft—the 18th, 21st, and 26th selections—the team was in great position to add to the stable of young talent that had just pushed the defending champion Lakers to six games. On draft night, Thunder General Manager Sam Presti pulled the trigger on moving up. He packaged picks 21 and 26 to New Orleans for the draft rights to Aldrich, who was taken at No. 11. The Thunder also had to take Morris Peterson's expiring $6.6 million contract.

"I don't think Cole could have gone to a better place than Oklahoma City," Kansas coach Bill Self said. "He'll be so much more comfortable with the environment that exists there. That organization has done a fabulous job, not just at winning games but creating a family-type environment I think Cole will thrive in."

Aldrich averaged 11.3 points, 9.8 rebounds, and 3.5 blocked shots during his junior season. He never was hyped as a future star. But he was expected to provide the Thunder with the same rugged rebounding and defense he supplied for the Jayhawks.

"Cole brings a blue-collar approach to the defensive end of the floor that complements our current core," Presti said.

"I'm not going to try to go in and do spectacular things," Aldrich said. "I'm going to stick with the things I'm good at. I'm very good at shot-blocking, defending, and rebounding, and I think that's how I'm going to make my presence [felt] on the court early is by doing those things."

Aldrich rarely saw the court. In two seasons with the Thunder he appeared in only 44 games. Thirty-three of those were decided by double-digits, illustrating how much garbage time Aldrich played.

In separate transactions at the 2011 trade deadline, the Thunder added Kendrick Perkins and Nazr Mohammed. Together, they held down the center minutes for two seasons. The moves helped transform the Thunder into Western Conference champions. But they also stunted Aldrich's growth.

Aldrich had a handful of putback dunks similar to his first NBA bucket. The others always came when the game's outcome had long been decided, but each one showed Aldrich's nose for the ball and knack for rebounding. In sporadic minutes, Aldrich played with tremendous energy on defense and found ways to impact the game through sheer effort. He wasn't a great athlete or a gifted offensive player, and his pick-and-roll defense needed a ton of work, but he always played hard when given the chance.

Aldrich averaged 1.7 points, 1.9 rebounds, and 0.5 blocks in 7.2 minutes per night with the Thunder. He was traded to

Houston in the deal that sent James Harden to the Rockets days before the start of the 2012–13 season.

Though Aldrich will be remembered as Presti's worst draft pick, two important facts lower the volume on talk of Aldrich being a huge bust—the 2010 draft class lacked depth and left the Thunder with slim pickings when they were in dire need of a big man, and Aldrich went on to enjoy a productive career as a journeyman role player.

98 Kyle Singler

Kyle Singler walked into Time Warner Cable Arena in Charlotte, North Carolina, on the morning of February 21, 2015, and walked into a new world. It was the first time he took the court with his new Thunder teammates as they went through a shootaround session in preparation for that night's game against the Hornets.

Scott Brooks, the Thunder coach at that time, pulled Singler aside and informed him he'd be starting in place of the injured Kevin Durant. Singler hadn't had a single practice. Hadn't even met all his new teammates. But he was being charged with the unenviable task of filling in for the reigning MVP his first day on the job.

"It was challenging," Singler remembered.

It was the start of the most confounding chapter of Singler's career and the dawn of the most disappointing acquisition in Thunder history.

Singler came to the Thunder from Detroit two days earlier in the three-team trade that sent Reggie Jackson to the Pistons and Kendrick Perkins to Utah. The 6'8" small forward had been a serviceable role player with the Pistons and had long been a target of Thunder General Manager Sam Presti. Several mock drafts projected the Thunder to select Singler, a former McDonald's All-American and a four-year standout at Duke, with the 24th overall selection in the 2011 draft. Singler himself thought he'd be a member of the Thunder. Instead, the Thunder went with Jackson out of Boston College.

"Yeah, there was a moment when I thought it was going to happen," Singler said. "I worked out for Oklahoma City and felt like I had a decent workout for them. But I've always felt that they liked me and they thought I had what it was to be a Thunder basketball player. In the back of my head I always knew that it would be a possibility that I would end up playing here at some time."

The Singler who showed up wasn't the Singler that Presti coveted. He came with career averages of 8.7 points, 3.5 rebounds, and one assist in 218 games. He was a 37.9 percent career three-point shooter and was converting a career-best 40.6 percent from long range for the Pistons at the time of the trade. He was billed as a blue-collar glue guy, a player who did some of everything and prided himself on doing anything to help his team win.

"Whenever I play, I play hard and I play to win," Singler said. "I just try to help the team out as much as possible, whatever that is. I'm just a utility guy. I want to play hard. I want to do the right things. I want to help as much as possible. I would guess that's what they're expecting here."

Singler played the game the right way. He just wasn't always effective. In fact, he rarely was effective, but you never could question his effort, his motives, or his instincts. He didn't take bad shots. He made the extra pass. He understood proper spacing, positioning, and timing on both ends. There were large stretches, however, where most of those "little things" he was said to be so good at barely made a ripple. Despite all the "winning plays" he supposedly provided, he didn't impact winning. Too often you couldn't even tell he was on the court.

Singler started the first 10 games following the trade and averaged 3.8 points on 29.3 percent shooting while logging 19 minutes a night. By his 11th game, Brooks was forced to replace Singler in the starting lineup with Dion Waiters. It wasn't until Andre Roberson went down with a sprained ankle in late March that Singler returned to a starting role and recouped some of his minutes. He started in eight of the final 12 games and finally played like the player the Thunder thought it had acquired from the Pistons. After missing 20 of his first 30 three-pointers, he finished the season making 14-of-24 from deep. But he scored in double figures just once in 26 games with the Thunder in 2014–15.

"I feel during the year I could have been more effective," Singler said. "I was ready regardless, but I thought I could have been a much better player for this team than I was."

On the opening day of free agency in the 2015 off-season, the Thunder swiftly agreed to re-sign Singler, a restricted free agent, to a five-year, $25 million deal. The deal included a team option for the fifth season that could have kept Singler in Oklahoma City through the 2019–20 season. With the Thunder being over the salary cap and luxury tax, Presti considered the deal a no-brainer given the team's limited ability to land a comparable player in free agency. The league's impending salary cap spike also would soon make Singler's contract look like a sweetheart deal comparatively.

But Singler never lived up to expectations in a Thunder uniform. By the 2016–17 season, his worst season as a pro, he was completely out of the team's rotation.

"Just like any player, it's hard when you're coming from a different situation and being thrown into the fire with a team that's already together," said D.J. Augustin, a reserve point guard who arrived with Singler from Detroit. "I think Kyle did his best."

99 Nate Robinson

Everyone knew the Thunder targeted only certain types of players.

The franchise offered no apologies for that.

"We do try to look for people who are reliable and consistent," GM Sam Presti once said. "Teammates with enough self-awareness to recognize and overcome their own agendas and in turn are capable of embracing sacrifice and accountability."

Doesn't exactly evoke the name Nate Robinson.

Robinson was a throw-in to the 2011 deadline deal that swapped Kendrick Perkins for Jeff Green. And Robinson was far from the Thunder's type. To many, Robinson was a poor-defending, shot-happy, look-at-me, combustible sideshow. Brash, vibrant, and outspoken, Robinson was a free-spirit on and off the court, the kind who wouldn't ask for permission and couldn't care less about your forgiveness. He arrived with a checkered past. He had been whistled for 34 technical fouls in his first 5½ seasons and was at the center of the ugly 2006 Madison Square Garden brawl featuring his Knicks and the Carmelo Anthony–led Denver Nuggets.

"Tons of talent, little understanding of what it means to be a successful NBA player on a successful NBA team," NBA analyst Zach Lowe once wrote of Robinson.

But fans loved him.

He was small, which was fun but may have been his first obstacle in Oklahoma City. The Thunder didn't do small. The brain trust long believed that undersized players wouldn't prosper the same in the playoffs. Despite standing just 5'9", Robinson was one of the league's most athletic players—he attended the University of Washington on a football scholarship before concentrating on basketball and was a three-time Slam Dunk Contest champion. He was also a fierce competitor who was tough as nails and had the heart of a lion.

Robinson landed in Oklahoma City with an established reputation of an X-factor, a spark plug off the bench who could score and score in bunches. He had dazzled Knicks crowds with four 30-point games and three 40-point games, including a career-high 45-point explosion only two seasons prior to joining the Thunder.

Thunder fans, however, never got the full Nate Robinson experience.

Robinson stepped into a backcourt that included Russell Westbrook, Eric Maynor, Royal Ivey, Thabo Sefolosha, James Harden, and Daequan Cook. Robinson then missed three weeks after undergoing arthroscopic surgery on his right knee. By the time he returned, whatever opinions the Thunder might have held about Robinson's playing style hardly mattered. The team was 13–2 in March and rolling to a 55-win season. Robinson was out of the rotation.

That's when he became a sideshow, acting as the excessively animated leader of the Thunder's excessively enthusiastic bench. There was no limit to the number of reactions Robinson ad libbed to celebrate a teammate's made three-pointer, blocked shot, or highlight dunk. But it was Robinson who established Oklahoma City's bench party tradition.

"We're just trying to do whatever we can to keep positive energy flowing," Robinson explained.

It was a commendable show of professionalism by Robinson, who could have helped on the court but was reduced to a cheerleader.

"Nate was an unbelievable teammate, really helped me out, helped a lot of guys out," Kevin Durant said. "He brought us so much energy. He always gave us confidence no matter what."

With Robinson entering the final year of his contract, the Thunder drafted Reggie Jackson with the 24th pick in the 2011 draft.

Two weeks before the start of the lockout-shortened 2011–12 season, the Thunder announced Robinson would remain in his native Seattle rather than report to training camp.

"Nate is an accomplished player, but with the current composition of our roster, it will be unlikely he will have an opportunity to contribute on a nightly basis," Presti said. "Given the compressed period of time that we have been given to work through the current situation, it has been decided that Nate will not attend training camp while we work with his representatives to resolve the situation. We will not be commenting on this subject further but will provide notification when a resolution is reached."

On the eve of the regular season, Christmas Eve, the Thunder waived Robinson.

He appeared in seven games with the Thunder. Five were decided by 15 points or more.

Robinson went on to play 221 more NBA games from 2012 to 2016 with the Warriors, Bulls, Nuggets, Clippers, and Pelicans. He averaged 10.6 points, 1.9 rebounds, and 3.6 assists in 21.9 minutes. He then bounced between professional basketball overseas and the NBA Development League. In June 2016, Robinson, at 32, tried out for his hometown Seattle Seahawks of the National Football League.

100 The Others

With the 29th pick in the 2014 NBA Draft, the Thunder tried to get creative. They selected Josh Huestis, a 6'7" small forward from Stanford. He was a little-known prospect who was projected as a second-round selection. But OKC had a pre-arranged deal in place.

If the Thunder selected Huestis in the first round, then he would spend his first season in the NBA Development League. The arrangement allowed the Thunder to save salary cap space in 2014–15 and develop Huestis in the minor league on the cheap, while giving Huestis a guaranteed rookie scale deal—two guaranteed years and two years at the team's option—he likely wouldn't have otherwise received. The agreement made Huestis the first domestic "draft-and-stash" player to be selected in the first round. It was forward-thinking at its finest.

Only the Thunder selected the wrong player.

Huestis, who averaged 11.2 points, 8.2 rebounds, 1.2 steals, and 1.9 blocks as a college senior, was heralded as one of the best athletes in the 2014 draft, a player capable of defending multiple positions. But he proved to be a fringe NBA player at best. The Thunder ultimately made good on their end of the deal, signing Huestis to his rookie scale contract prior to the 2015–16 season. But in his first two years, Huestis appeared in only seven games with the Thunder. He played more than eight times as many games with the D-League's Oklahoma City Blue and rarely showed much promise at that level.

For all the criticism lobbed at Thunder GM Sam Presti, for the James Harden trade and for not luring top-flight free agents, for losing Kevin Durant and for never winning a championship, an overlooked critique was the number of players who simply didn't pan out. Make no mistake, on Presti's watch the Thunder had several players turn into stars, including Durant, Harden, Russell Westbrook, and Serge Ibaka. Several other players, namely Jeff Green, Thabo Sefolosha, Reggie Jackson, Andre Roberson, and Steven Adams, transformed into serviceable if not sensational role players.

But the projects were mostly failed experiments.

Huestis was perhaps the most prominent given his pre-draft arrangement. But the others included Robert Vaden, DeVon Hardin, Grant Jerrett, Tibor Pleiss, Kyle Weaver, D.J. White, Byron Mullens, Perry Jones III, Jeremy Lamb, Shaun Livingston, Daniel Orton, Lazar Hayward, DeAndre Liggins, Latavious Williams, Ryan Reid, Mitch McGary, J.P. Tokoto, and Hasheem Thabeet. None turned into impact players in Oklahoma City, and that proved costly given the franchise's conservative approach to free agency.

Despite all the comparisons to San Antonio, the Thunder never could replicate the Spurs' knack for netting under-the-radar talent. San Antonio fortified a dynasty by cultivating one late-first-round pick after another, while annually supplementing its roster by sprinkling in sneaky second-round selections or undrafted and underappreciated prospects who blossomed into rotation players—Malik Rose, Tony Parker, Bruce Bowen, Manu Ginobili, Beno Udrih, Matt Bonner, George Hill, DeJuan Blair, Gary Neal, Tiago Splitter, Danny Green, Cory Joseph, and Jonathan Simmons.

Outside of Ibaka, Jackson, and, to a lesser degree, Roberson, that was never the Thunder's reality. Of course, not all of the blame is to be pinned on Presti. Some rests with the coaching staffs. Some is on the scouting department. Some is on the players.

But whatever the reason, the Thunder has a long history of struggling to consistently locate and land diamonds in the rough.